Notes on Contributors

Sandra Curtis Comstock is currently a Fellow at the Charles Warren Center for Studies in American History at Harvard University. She completed her PhD thesis at Cornell University (entitled 'Imperial Denim: the place of blue jeans in the consolidation and transformation of American power in the 20th century'), and has worked previously as Adjunct Research Professor at the Department of Sociology, University of Western Ontario.

Moritz Ege is a PhD candidate at the Department of European Ethnology at Humboldt University in Berlin, Germany, and a fellow of the German Academic National Foundation. Ege is the author of a book on "Afroamericanophilia", race and new subjectivities in 1960s and 1970s Germany (*Schwarz werden. "Afroamerikanophilie" in den 1960er und 1970er Jahren*, 2007). His research interests include popular culture and subcultural theory, particularly processes of appropriation and institutionalisation; anthropological and sociological theories of culture, particularly as they intersect with aesthetics and urban life; and methods in ethnography and cultural analysis.

Daniel Miller is Professor of Material Culture at the Department of Anthropology, University College London. Recent publications include *The Comfort of Things* (Polity, 2008), *Stuff* (Polity, 2010) and *Au Pair* (Polity, 2010, with Zuzana Burikova), and the edited collection *Anthropology and the Individual* (Berg, 2009). Forthcoming publications include *Tales from Facebook, Technologies of Love* (with Mirca Madianou) and *Denim: The Art of Ordinary* (with Sophie Woodward). Along with Sophie Woodward, he established the Global Denim Project, and also runs (with Haidy Geismar) the blog: www.materialworldblog.com.

Mylene Mizrahi received her PhD in Cultural Anthropology from the Federal University of Rio de Janeiro in June 2010. Since 2002, she has carried out extensive fieldwork in Rio de Janeiro, Brazil, among creators and spectators of Funk Carioca, a local musical movement. Her theoretical interests include aesthetics, creativity, connectivity and the role played by objects and images on those topics. She is the author of articles on material culture, consumption, fashion and clothing, religion and irony, alterity and mimesis. She is currently preparing a monograph, provisionally entitled *Rio Funk Aesthetics: Creation and Connectivity with Mr. Catra*.

Bodil Birkebæk Olesen is post-doctoral fellow at the Department of Anthropology at Aarhus University in Denmark, and a Research Associate at the Sainsbury Research Unit for the Arts of Africa, Oceania and the Americas at University of East Anglia. Her main regional focus is West Africa where she carried out her doctoral research on *bogolan* cloth from Mali. She has also conducted ethnographic fieldwork in North America. Her research and publications focus on art and material culture, museum anthropology, economic anthropology and cloth, textile and dress.

Rosana Pinheiro-Machado is a Lecturer in Anthropology at the College of Advertising and Marketing (ESPM/RS), Brazil, with a PhD in Social Anthropology from the Federal University of Rio Grande do Sul, Brazil. She specialises in the ethnography of Chinese and Latin American societies and she has been carrying out multi-site fieldwork in both of these regions over the last ten years. Previous topics on which she has published include social inequalities, capitalism in emergent economies, guanxi, informal economies, kinship and migration, legality and illegality, human rights, globalization, fakes and brands.

Roberta Sassatelli is Associate Professor of Cultural Sociology at the Department of Social and Political Studies at the Università degli Studi di Milano. She has previously taught at the University of East Anglia, UK, and the University of Bologna, Italy. She has published widely on consumer culture, the sociology of the body, gender and sexuality and cultural theory. Her English-language books include *Consumer Culture: History, Theory, Politic*s (Sage, 2007) and *Fitness Culture: The Gym and the Commercialization of Discipline and Fun* (Palgrave, 2010).

Clare M. Wilkinson-Weber was educated at Durham University and received her PhD (anthropology) at the University of Pennsylvania. Her research interests include material culture, gender and media production. Her work has centred in India and has focused on local conceptions of creativity and skill in artistic practice, and shifting aesthetic and social patterns in the Hindi film industry. Her articles have appeared in *Visual Anthropology Review, Anthropological Quarterly* and *Journal of Material Culture*. Her book *Embroidering Lives: Women's Work and Skill in the Lucknow Embroidery Industry* was published by SUNY press in 1999. She is currently working on another book titled *Fashioning Bollywood: The Making and Meaning of Hindi Film Costume*.

Sophie Woodward is a Lecturer in Sociology at the University of Manchester. She researches into material culture, consumption and clothing and has a continued interest in feminist theory and innovative methodologies. She is developing further research into personal life and closeness. She is the author of *Why Women Wear What They Wear* (Berg, 2007) and *Why Feminism Matters* (Palgrave, 2009, with Kath Woodward). Forthcoming publications include *Denim: The Art of Ordinary* (with Daniel Miller) and an edited special edition of the journal *Textile*. Along with Prof. Daniel Miller she established the Global Denim Project.

Introduction

Daniel Miller and Sophie Woodward

To state that denim jeans are a global presence is, in itself, not a radical claim – the production, design and trade in denim evidently spans the globe, as does wearing jeans. But as we started to develop the Global Denim Project, we became increasingly aware of the sheer extent of denim's global reach. Every time he went abroad for a conference Miller began to count 100 random people who passed him on the street to see how many were wearing blue jeans. This included a good range of sites from Seoul and Beijing to Istanbul and Rio. On the basis of these observations, along with some global denim surveys (Synovate 2008), we suggest that (discounting the major populations of rural South Asia and China) perhaps the majority of the people in the majority of the countries of the world are wearing blue jeans on any given day. Yet despite their global ubiquity, a lack of academic attention is given to denim jeans. After twelve years in publication there is not a single paper devoted to the topic in the journal *Fashion Theory* and, with the exception of historical works, any writing from a social science perspective is minimal.

Existing research into denim falls within the domains of textile technology, marketing and consumer perceptions, the global denim market, and historical research. Firstly, research within textile chemistry and technology analyses aspects of the material performance of the fabric (Tarhan and Sarsiisik 2009) as this relates to quality (Chowdhary 2002), including dyeing (Card et al. 2005), and the fate of reclaimed denim products (Hawley 2006). Secondly, running in tandem with this is literature within the arena of marketing and branding, which considers consumers perceptions of jeans and brands, as this relates to specific regions (Wu and Delong 2006). Thirdly, the existing literature includes papers on jeans production and labour conditions (Bair and Gereffi 2001; Bair and Peters 2006; Crewe 2004; Tokatli 2007; Tokatli and Kızılgün 2004).

The final area of writing on the topic of denim is also perhaps the largest, and includes books on the historical iconography of denim jeans (Finlayson 1990; Marsh and Trynka 2002; Sullivan 2006) and the way blue jeans became an American icon, linked to particular generations and values (Reichs 1970) and a part of popular culture. It is this historical narrative that, in turn, is generally accepted and adopted as the explanation for why blue jeans became ubiquitous, as though this was some kind of common sense. In the existing literature there is very little social science work that is not historical, and in particular very little qualitative or ethnographic work. Fiske (1989) discussed how the meanings and wearing of jeans are contested, as a medium through which people live the contradictions of popular culture, yet this is in specific relation to American-ness. The approach of this book, instead, is ethnographic but we are also simultaneously attempting to understand the global. When we say 'global' it should be noted that our book does not refer to every country in the world, which would anyhow be beyond the scope of one collected volume – as there are, for example no papers in this volume on African or Middle Eastern countries (although work by, for example Hansen 2005, indicates the importance of jeans in Zambia).

The paucity of social science research into denim is notable when compared to the seemingly endless books and papers that are devoted to the clothing by major designers that exists primarily on the catwalk, and is subsequently worn by very few people. This suggests a paradox at the heart of studies of clothing and fashion: the significance attributed to clothing in such studies is probably in inverse proportion to the importance that items of fashion and clothing have to the population as a whole. This book is part of an attempt to shift attention from the spectacular to the mainstream and the everyday. In the paper that launched the Global Denim Project (Miller and Woodward 2007) we suggested that denim is the subject of that felicitous phrase, 'the blindingly obvious'. That is, certain things have become so deeply taken for granted and omnipresent that we have become blind to their presence and importance. This book is, then, the first ever published specifically devoted to the topic of blue jeans as a global phenomena that effectively dominates contemporary clothing and fashion.

Of course, it is not a particularly attractive proposition to suggest that academics should study something just because it is there, and in this introduction we are really asserting something quite different. We argue, instead, that the study of denim, and more specifically blue jeans, matters as it can provide us with insights, understandings and advances in fashion and clothing studies beyond that of almost any topic that we might otherwise have focused upon. Coming from anthropology we tend to see the ubiquitous not as boring and taken for granted but as the critical point of departure for understanding our relationship to the world more generally.

Furthermore, this book is not just about denim – it is specifically about global denim because, once again, there are advantages to taking this particular perspective from which to expand our view of denim as a whole – to show how we can simultaneously understand the existence of denim as a global phenomenon and that which is specific and unique. We argued in the manifesto paper, that as social scientists, and especially as anthropologists, our explanations depend on the nuances of local context – that is, on knowledge about what people in South Korea do as opposed to Argentineans, or upper class as against lower class, shop workers as against factory workers. The problem is that none of these more parochial studies helps us to explain the existence of a global phenomenon such as denim. The explanation for the global has to be more than the aggregate of all the local explanations for why something is present in each place.

It is this problem that gives birth to the Global Denim Project. It was an appreciation that, to actually come to terms with global denim, the kinds of studies and approaches that exist in academia at present are insufficient. We need something radically different. The project has sought, since its inception, to find new ways to conceive and carry out academic research appropriate to the scale of the phenomenon we are trying to explain. We argued that to hope for the kind of profound insights that we believed an investigation of denim was capable of, we need to bring together people from many different places and disciplines and have them converge around this particular issue. We created a structure aimed at achieving this goal, loosely based on a kind of 'open source' model for academic contributions. Admittedly this was partly because, apart from a small research grant for our joint ethnography to help with transcription costs, neither of us has raised any money for an overarching global denim project. But in this case, necessity was the mother of invention. We used the Internet effectively to create the Global Denim Project as a self-proclaimed entity, inviting anyone who is seriously interested in furthering the understanding of this phenomenon to join in. There would be no actual formal organization – rather we agreed to foster and organize collaboration and debate. We expect this to continue for several years, but already there are clear results from this collaboration, which this volume is intended to disseminate. If the manifesto laid a foundation for starting the project, this volume will consolidate our infrastructure and prepare us for building the next stage.

Putting out a kind of random call to the world at large is something of an adventure. Ideally we hoped to have people involved in this project from different disciplines, working in a wide range of regions on a vast spectrum of issues. Somewhat astonishingly, this is exactly what happened. All the papers in this book come from academics who embraced this call, but they by no means exhaust this list, which at present amounts to over twenty independent studies committed to denim (www.ucl.ac.uk/global-denim-project, accessed 11 June 2010). Some of these existed prior to the project and others have been devised in the light of the challenge posed by the project itself. They include historians, sociologists, geographers and anthropologists and, apart from those in this volume, cover areas such as Turkey, Japan and Sweden. As well as this volume, which focuses on issues that help us bring together the simultaneity of both a highly localized and global phenomenon, we are also working on a further special issue for the journal *Textile* (2011) that focuses more on the textile itself and its implications. For the future we are also discussing still more radical ways of undertaking such work including writing from a truly open source perspective in the style of a wiki rather than with named authors.

Yet, however original the approaches, intentions and perspectives that are brought to bear on the topic, the value of this collection lies ultimately in the original insights it can contribute to our understanding of global denim. To appreciate this we propose to review briefly some of the underlying theoretical issues raised in the original manifesto paper and then see how these are developed in the light of the actual findings reported in the individual chapters of this volume. Firstly, the manifesto includes the question of how we relate global and local explanations of clothing and how we both account for and overcome this issue of the blindingly obvious. Secondly, we consider what, if anything, global denim says about global homogenization. Extrapolating from the work of Woodward (2007), in particular, the third question we pose is whether there are specific aspects of modernity that create common responses. For example, is the growing consciousness of the immensity of the global world linked to a kind of anxiety that people feel when selecting clothing? Does this in turn lead them to use denim as a kind of default clothing worn because they fear anything more conspicuous or specific (Clarke and Miller 2002; Woodward 2005; Woodward 2007)?

The fourth question that we posed derived from observations about denim as something unique, because the reason to focus on denim is not dependent entirely upon its global presence. It is unique in several other ways. One of the most evident of which is its relationship to distressing. We noted that distressing developed from a period in the 1970s when jeans became the most personalized and intimate apparel as they essentially disintegrated on the flesh through being worn to death by the nomadic and relatively impoverished hippies of the time. During this period jeans also became softer and more individual to the person. The paradox was that at the very time when blue jeans were becoming the global ecumene of clothing, they were simultaneously becoming the most developed expression of specific individuality. Finally we asked whether in response to these questions there was some 'value added' in the collaboration between projects that came from different disciplines and different regions to constitute a self-conscious global denim project and how this might help us confront these larger questions.

If we were to sum up the implications of these questions and this initial analysis of denim as a clothing phenomenon, the evidence is that jeans seem to have taken on the role of expressing something about the changing world that no other clothing could achieve. It was almost as though jeans were expanding even as the world itself was expanding. The more global the world then the more global the jeans but also the more the world created a sphere for the personal and the intimate the more this applied also to jeans. The more people tried to find ways to bring these two extremes of the intimate and the global from flying apart in their lives the more they wore jeans as the instrument for keeping this simultaneity of local and global experiences. At one level, jeans may be merely a pair of trousers, but they exhibit three extraordinary characteristics: jeans are amongst the most global clothing in the world, they express their capacity to become the most intimate clothing in the world, and they have become the default mode for people uncertain as to which clothes to wear. To understand them we have to start from the relationship between these three points. That, for example, distressing, as an expression of the ability of jeans to become worn to our body and thus intimate and personal exists as a phenomenon precisely because it is also jeans that are global.

These may sound like sweeping statements. One could say that shirt wearing is equally global but it is relative to their specific colour and fabric that blue jeans are so remarkable in their ubiquity. One could say that lingerie is necessarily more intimate than denim. But our point is that while lingerie occupies a more intimate relation to the body, it is distressing that makes a garment gradually personalized to the specific body that wears it, which gives denim a capacity for intimacy that lingerie does not possess. Finally, our observations on denim as default wear is based on fieldwork by Woodward in London, we cannot know at this point whether it applies, for example, to elderly people in Mexico. But what we do know is that these are three extraordinary traits that denim does clearly exhibit for people in some places, and at least for London in direct relation to each other. So there are grounds for asserting that to understand denim we simply have to ask ourselves why these traits would ever be found in respect to the same garment

As anthropologists we turned to jeans the way the anthropologist Claude Levi-Strauss (1966) (no relation to the jeans designer) turned to myth. Jeans are not an explicit statement of philosophy but, in practice, they may achieve something of that which philosophy is also aiming to achieve. Instead of expressing such dilemmas abstractly and intellectually they are the practical means to partially resolve them. By simultaneously being both global and intimate in this sense of personal represented by distressing, blue jeans demonstrate the degree to which we the wearers can be simultaneously the most global and most intimate. Instead of seeing these as a contradiction, wearing jeans makes them feel compatible. The word 'feel' is important here because most people are not looking for abstract philosophy – they are simply looking for a way to literally *feel* better about themselves and about the world. An item of clothing is ideal for this purpose. In order for jeans to accomplish such a task, they need to act as a material culture (Kuchler and Miller 2005; Miller 2010) directly analogous to those philosophical engagements, and their ability to do so is attested by their very ubiquity.

If these claims are already present or implied in the arguments of the manifesto paper then what is the purpose of this volume relative to those claims? The answer comes in the central dialectic of academic enquiry that constantly moves us backward and forward from the particular to the general. We can now state at a very general level something of the meaning that blue jeans have to the modern world. This may satisfy some academic interest in making such highly generalized statements analogous to philosophy. But we are not philosophers – we are students of clothing and fashion, social scientists and historians and we have a deep concern with the specific populations that we study. None of us would be satisfied merely to leave these claims at such an abstract level. For us the point of the enquiry is only realized when we address the kind of question a sceptic might pose to this philosophical rendition, the question of 'so what'? How, from the general, do we then return to our specific fields of enquiry and populations with a new appreciation of their lives and experiences? While we may use jeans to express our relationship to the global, we are always simultaneously local and our primary concerns will always be with these far more specific engagements.

Having established the quite extraordinary significance of jeans to express and perhaps to some degree resolve the growing antinomies of our contemporary world – the simultaneous growth of the world as increasingly global and personal – we now use this volume to directly address the 'so what?' question. We aim to show, for example, what for particular populations it means to be intimate, or what it means to be global, and how this impacts upon their particular experiences. At this point global denim becomes far more than just a neglected field of clothing studies: it is the quintessential case of a global object posed as an issue of academic comprehension and thereby a challenge to contemporary academia itself. It implies the potential of denim to become a catalyst in the emergence of new forms of studies and new perspectives.

Given the scale of the project and of global denim itself, we will not be able to offer a comprehensive answer to the questions we have posed. Instead, this initial volume aims to start a dialogue, an imagination of this new terrain and a commitment to future work and collaborations on denim. What we hope this volume will achieve is an impact on the wider study of clothing and fashion that persuades its practitioners of the importance of this quest. That it can demonstrate how the study of denim contributes not only to the understanding the clothing that dominates what people wear everyday but also to many critical questions about who we are in the contemporary world.

The Current State of Global Denim[1]

One of the arguments for the importance of understanding denim in a global context is that denim is not only present in all countries in the world, but, as global denim surveys on the wearing of jeans demonstrate,[2] it has also become a widely worn garment within these places. The global average (more accurately the average for the selection of countries included in this particular survey) in 2008 was for people to wear jeans 3.5 days a week (*Global Lifestyle Monitor* 2008) with the highest amount being in Germany where jeans are worn 5.2 days of the week (and ownership is on average 8.6 pairs per person). In the same sample of countries, more than six out of 10 (62 per cent) of consumers say they love or enjoy wearing denim, with the highest responses coming in, for example, Brazil (72 per cent) and in Colombia. By contrast, in India a mere 27 per cent stated they loved wearing jeans. According to another recent survey of selected countries (Synovate 2008), 31 per cent of those surveyed own three or four pairs of jeans, 29 per cent own five to ten pairs of jeans. In Brazil, 14 per cent of respondents own ten or more pairs of jeans and 40 per cent owned five to ten pairs. By contrast, the numbers of people who do not own jeans is relatively low, with, for example, 13 per cent of Russians not owning jeans, although the figure for Malaysia reaches 29 per cent.

Notwithstanding the broad trends in all these countries towards the wearing of jeans by the majority of the population, there are clearly national differences. This is especially evident in how much people are willing to spend on a pair of jeans; most people will not spend more than US$80 for their jeans (seven out of ten of all those surveyed). Interestingly, American citizens are the lowest spenders on denim, as the survey finds that 76 per cent would only be prepared to pay up to US$40 on a pair of jeans. At the other end of the scale, in Russia, 26 per cent would spend US$120 or more on a pair of jeans, with 10 per cent prepared to spend more than US$200 and 5 per cent US$280 or more. In both Taiwan (where 3 per cent would pay US$280+) and Serbia (where 25 per cent would pay US$120+) there was also an evident will-ingness amongst at least some of the population to spend more. The issue of price is particularly marked in a UK context; in a 2007 survey (Mintel 2007), 63 per cent of people stated that they has spent less than £30 ($47) on their last pair of jeans, and only 3 per cent had spent more than £70 ($109) This spectrum of jeans buying is enabled by the wide price range of jeans, which span from supermarket and value stores such as Primark, up to the top range designer jeans, which sell in excess of £250 ($389). As such, there is both an increased democratization of denim, where even those on the lowest incomes can afford a pair of jeans yet, at the same time, this wide price spectrum means that denim simultaneously retains a considerable capacity to mark social and class differentiation.

One of the key arguments we made in the manifesto paper was that denim is as much a refutation as an acceptance of capitalist pressures such as fashion. The core style of a pair of denim jeans is much the same today as the first ever pairs of Levi's in the late nineteenth century. When asked, in the Synovate (2008) survey, why people chose jeans, the strongest response was the quality of denim (39 per cent), and secondly the cost (22 per cent). The response, 'they are fashionable' was not a significant overall response, although in a couple of countries (11 per cent of Russians and 10 per cent of French) it was cited as a feature. Although in fashion and clothing studies there has been an emphasis upon the growth of designer jeans, in practice the significant development that has effected much larger populations has been the growth of supermarket jeans, or jeans at discount stores such as Primark. Even within the designer jeans market there is a clear complexity, as seen in the expansion of Turkish denim manufacture and the complex network of contract-ing and subcontracting for denim brands, including the emergence of several local brands from these producing countries (Tokatli and Kızılgün 2004). The point being that the main expansion has come in the market segment that is least profitable and least related to fashion.

The continuity in the basic style of a pair of jeans therefore occurs hand-in-hand with changes within the denim sector, such as in the global trade in denim, and sites of production. For example in the UK, between 2003 and 2007 there was a rapid growth in imports as jean production in the UK continued to fall. In 2006, 41 million pairs of men's jeans and 43 million pairs of women's jeans were imported (Mintel 2007). The origin of supply to the UK has also changed. In 2003 only 53 per cent of men's jeans and 64 per cent of women's jeans were imported from Asia, that figure in 2006 was recorded as 70 per cent for men's jeans and 81 per cent for women's. The increasing dominance of China (Li, Yao and Young 2003) as a source of production seems as evident in this market as many others.

A key feature in shifts in the denim market is changes in trade agreements. To take, as an example, the case of Syria – the Greater Arab Free Trade Area (GAFTA) in 2005, allowed garments manufactured in and imported from other Arab countries to enter Syria's formerly protected retail sector (International News Service 2008). As a result many international brands, such as Benetton or Miss Sixty (which are manufactured in the Middle East) could enter the country. Despite this, due to low income levels of many, there is still a dominance of locally produced brands. In the case of the US, as a result of NAFTA (a North American trade agreement), Europe's supply of denim to the US declined from 83 per cent of US denim to a mere 7 per cent after a massive shift to Mexico (Li, Yao and Yeung 2003: 20) and blue jeans are consequently Mexico's most important export (Bair and Peters 2006: 210). Equally, there has been a very rapid expansion of Chinese denim production, with over 1,000 firms now involved (Li, Yao,and Yeung 2003) and with Hong Kong developing as a major point of brokerage. In the midst of these shifts in the denim market, Turkey has emerged as a key player, with significant export markets in Europe, Russia and the Middle East (International News Service 2008).

Changes in production, and the importing and exporting of jeans are also evident in the relative popularity of jeans, which may not remain constant (as evidenced by the plunge in denim sales in the 1990s in the UK). Yet most significant for our purposes is the fact that, in recent years, denim jeans have increased in their dominance as the choice of everyday wear. During 2007, three pairs of jeans were sold every second of every day in Britain alone (Mintel 2007) – the approximately 86 million pairs of jeans bought constituted a 40 per cent increase over the previous five years. In short in major markets denim was not just ubiquitous – its dominant position as everyday wear seems to be ever increasing.

The Origins and Consequences of Global Denim

It is clearly not the case that all populations in all places are saturated with denim, nor is denim the only garment to have achieved global prominence. But these statistics all point in the direction of affirming our starting point and the reason for the Global Denim Project, which is that for such as specific garment in terms of textile and colour denim has achieved a quite astounding global presence. As this is evidently the case, the danger is that this then becomes merely taken for granted, a given quality in the world, as though this was somehow inevitable. It becomes a kind of common sense, and usually in such cases this is accompanied by a simple narrative that explains why this should be – if people can even be bothered to ask or answer the question why jeans are ubiquitous. In the case of jeans, the common sense story arises from the popular histories of jeans as the rise of an American icon that makes the global spread of jeans come to appear inexorable (Sullivan 2006).

When we asked the basic question 'why are blue jeans blue?' in our London ethnography, almost no one could even start to give an answer. Yet this would surely be the obvious place to start such a narrative. As it happens, there may have been periods in prehistory or early historical times when this very same blue was just as ubiquitous to the world as it is today (Balfour-Paul 1998). Indigo was unique in being the only commonly available natural dye that did not require some kind of mordent or fixing quality to work on fabrics. Its usage was not simple because not being soluble in water is one of its attractions as a dye, but it was easier to use than alternatives. Since indigo and the closely related woad were found in most areas of the world it is likely that it dominated early clothing in most areas of the world. But it does not follow that our contemporary ubiquity represents this historical ubiquity. Looking at paintings and portraits during various historical periods in various re-gions of the world it is clear that there have been intervening times when indigo was not so prominent and not especially favoured.

Even if we narrow the story back to the popular idea of jeans as part of US ico-nography, this volume gives us reason to challenge at least the colloquial versions. Most popular accounts (such as Marsh and Trynka 2002) go straight from jeans as working men's garments to the actions of alienated youth as portrayed by James Dean and Marlon Brando, which makes jeans the key to a 1950s youth movement that establishes them as the US icon. But the chapter by Comstock reveals an early substratum to this story that had already established jeans as a symbol of egalitarian-ism and shared suffering that could appeal to middle as well as working classes following the Depression.

Indeed, if we follow Comstock, it seems that the very first indication of what was to become this global presence, the establishment of denim as a dominant US icon, was in fact a quite fragile and almost fortuitous coming together of a wide variety of forces. Not necessarily production. as defined by the interests of commerce, not nec-essarily consumption defined as the desire of consumers. It was just as much the in-fluence of the state on production and of popular culture on consumption. Central to Comstock's argument is that it was the disruption of commerce, particularly through the Depression, rather than its expansion, which gave rise to this response, whether through changes in labour and constraints on imports or through the empathetic en-gagement with suffering found in popular culture such as Steinbeck's *The Grapes of Wrath*. Comstock's chapter radically changes the popular and accepted story of the history of denim. Furthermore Comstock shows that crucial to its success was the new ambiguity and flexibility of jeans that made them an instrument of diversity as well as stability – a factor that takes centre stage in many of the subsequent chapters.

So already this opening chapter of our volume puts us in a different league from previous studies of denim. The constantly repeated 'myth' or more precisely 'just-so story' of how denim came to dominate the modern world turns out to be somewhat distorted. Things no longer appear so inevitable and taken for granted. In a volume that is devoted to scholarship we are very fortunate to have as our starting point this elegant demolition of one glib story and its replacement by something much more nuanced. There are then some fascinating parallels between Comstock and the following chapter by Wilkinson-Weber in that if the former looks at how denim became mainstream in the 1930s, Wilkinson-Weber is examining a parallel situation with regard to India today. Furthermore, in both papers we have a similar attempt to refuse simple adjudications as to whether it is consumption desires or production needs that facilitate the success of denim. In both cases the role of popular culture and film is seen as critical, which is a field with its own autonomy and concerns. This is perhaps particularly true in the India case, where there are many specific implications and constraints which make Bollywood a kind of microculture in its own right, with its own supply chains, its own arbiters of taste.

A difference lies in the much more overt relationship between commerce and the film industry in India. This may be seen in the prevalence of direct product placement but also in the central role that key film heroes and heroines have in the advertising and marketing of jeans. In Kerala, for example, advertising for denim was seen as more-or-less synonymous with the presence of key film stars. It is important, therefore, to position Wilkinson-Weber's arguments in relation to the discussion of Kannur in Miller's chapter because it is precisely the presence of stars such as Akshay Kumar with their highly sexualized campaigns, that make clear to people in areas remote from the Indian metropolitan regions what is at stake in the spread of jeans and why therefore it is essential to resist them in various ways. This volume is clearly not intended to provide a comprehensive historical account of how blue jeans took over the world. But this combination of Comstock's revision of the key moment in the development of jeans within the US along with Wilkinson-Weber's appreciation of how these garments are being developed in the contemporary Indian market demonstrates how such a comprehensive and scholarly account could be achieved. It also shows us how such an account might link these more specific regional stories with a central stream that flows towards the sea of denim in which our world is now situated.

For this volume, even a rewriting of the history of denim becomes merely one instrument of a rather grander ambition, stimulated by this ever present sceptical 'so what?' Our point is that if the ubiquity of denim has its cause it also has its consequence, and we are better off understanding the one directly alongside the other. What this volume does, is to pitch chapters such as Comstock and Wilkinson-Weber directly against papers such as Olesen. Olesen's argument could not make sense without the outcomes of the trajectory laid out by Comstock, since the starting point is precisely the ubiquity of jeans within the US context. Even if we resist the assumption that, for other places, jeans signify Americanization, we can still concede that jeans within the US have achieved a significant status as a kind of metasymbol that stands for the collectivity. This is exactly what Olesen demonstrates when she shows that it is jeans in particular that are used to make the bridge between the collectivity of the workplace and the desire to express that larger social whole in acts of philanthropy or in a concern for the environment found in the recycling of used denim. As such she shows how the position that denim has achieved as a transcendent icon is here leveraged to act as the medium by which people enact their commitment to the planet as a whole.

As Olesen's chapter shows, one of the factors that makes jeans American is that they play on a quite specifically US concept of individualism. A relationship between the individual and the ethical and spiritual dimension that is clearly expressed in, for example, US Pentecostalism. We tend to assume jeans would express US capitalism, but actually it is hard to imagine a more perfect example than Olesen's chapter, of the relationship between the individual and civil society in the US as recorded by the French writer Alexis de Tocqueville in the 1830s prior to the development of modern capitalism. So while Olesen shows just how effectively modern corporations exploit this relation, its source is much wider than simply the intentions of commerce. This ethical dimension in the recycling of jeans has, then, a much deeper ideological inflection.

If we are trying to match cause with consequence then we might well expect that ubiquity also stimulates rejection. Once jeans become sufficiently associated with the spread of cosmopolitanism, whether this is Indian or American, this makes them ideal for the objectification of conservatism. This is where Miller's chapter is intended to balance the previous focus on the rise and spread of jeans. Taking a small town in the state of Kerala, Miller shows how jeans have become implicated in a wide range of social dimensions. There is a clear gradation from gaudy jeans associated with toddlers through to the unacceptability of jeans for executive wear for older men. There is the sequence from jeans wearing for young girls to its unacceptability for married women. There is the growing opposition between the associations of more elaborate jeans with Muslims to the more drab styles associated with Hindus. All of these in turn contribute to the way in which the town of Kannur itself creates a new conservatism in which the outer world, which is now associated with jeans wearing, is matched by what emerges as the relative stability and value of the town. The point is that to understand global denim it is not sufficient to see jeans simply as signs of modernity, or cosmopolitanism that are welcome everywhere. Rather, jeans become a parameter of many differences and distinctions that allows us to create both a bridge and a stretch between tradition and modernity, parochialism and cosmopolitanism. What this chapter demonstrates is that we can learn as much from the refusal of jeans as from their acceptance.

The general ideas sketched out in the introduction to this book are now starting to be given flesh. We can already see how our dialectical approach should operate. We start by establishing a claim that global denim can be conceptualized as analogous to philosophy, as that which can bridge the growing antinomy of the local and the global. This is, however, only the first stage in our global denim project. The next stage needs to negate this universalism, by showing the consequences of this general analysis for our more specific encounters with jeans – how a general analysis gives greater meaning and depth to the parochial encounter and vice-versa. It is only in the light of our more advanced understanding of how jeans become a US icon that we can understand the very possibility of the contemporary use of jeans documented by Olesen. By the same token it is only in the light of Olesen that we can see the contemporary consequences of the historical work done by Comstock. It is only in the light of quite deliberate and systematic attempt to spread jeans in India documented by Wilkinson-Weber that we can understand why jeans, of all things, have become central to the way people in Kannur protect their conservatism and regionalism. It is only in the light of Miller's insistence that we look at places where jeans have been prevented from becoming ubiquitous that we can understand the implications for when jeans do succeed in becoming ubiquitous. We now have our answer to the sceptical 'so what?' We can show why it really does make a difference having a global denim project that directly matches history and anthropology, the direct impact of globalization on new forms of localization and not just the other way around.

Intimacy and Antinomy in Jeans

The implication of the last section is that this volume is intended to take the analytical findings of our more philosophical reading of jeans and turn this back into the heat of lived experience and consequence. Nowhere is this achieved more literally than through Mizrahi. In reading her chapter we can almost feel how a theoretical or analytical point can simultaneously be something that is essentially sensual. By the time we have allowed ourselves as readers to be drawn into the heat, sweat and movement of a funk ball, it is as though we see, for the first time, denim emerging through the haze of movement and music. These jeans are not some abstract closed-off entity but appear to our vision as an integral part of that dance; its eroticism and its integrity with the surrounding music, atmosphere and play between the male and female aesthetic. Here the precise materiality of the jeans, their elasticity and form has a lithe dynamic that cleaves not just to the body of the wearer but refuses to be separated off by the violence of any analytical gaze that will not acknowledge its integrity with this context of performance. In her other publications, Mizrahi (2002, 2006) has analysed the development of 'Brazilian jeans' as a particular kind of stretch fabric that has become associated with the export of a general sense of the erotic associated with Brazil. This chapter takes this to the source, which lies not just in the technical quality of the denim but in this almost idealized anthropological illustration of a holistic environment in which the jeans are given life. Jeans here appear seamless as part of the mobile, suggestive appeal of clothing that dances before our eyes.

If Mizrahi's paper stands as emblematic of this erotic presence and potential of contemporary jeans, this begs a question as to how this may be related to the other aspects of jeans appeal. A question that fortunately receives a very clear and systematic answer in the chapter by Sassatellli. By the end point of Sassatelli's paper we reach something akin to that of Mizrahi. Jeans for young Italians also have an erotic potential that has become central to the way they view the power and idealized possibilities of their own bodies. This comes as almost the end point of a process in which a person who wants to look *fit*, in the current colloquial meaning of that term, has first to consider the implications of fit in a more mundane and literal translation of that word. The sexiness of the public performance emerges out of the private acts of considering the body in the bedroom. The argument builds upon Woodward's (2005, 2007) previous work on watching women getting dressed, where the act of trying on clothing in front of the mirror is an act of establishing what is 'me', yet always through the imagined and remembered opinions of others. What emerge are three closely connected arenas of fit: to the body, to fashion and the need to look *fit* in the eyes of the opposite sex. The sexualization of the body depends upon the core dynamics between the individual and conformity. The starting point is the often problematic construction of the body as confident in a pair of jeans and finding just the right pair that is seen to fit. Basically in order feel sexy, a woman has to first feel confident about how her body looks to others. How does one take a garment that excels as the unseen and ordinary and use it to make visible the sexualized body? As in Mizrahi's wider study of the commercial foundation of stretch fabric jeans in Brazil, the issue of the erotic is no longer an entirely autonomous field of performance. It depends upon quite similar resolving of contradictions in the fashion industry and the wider dialectics of singularity and conformity as it pertains to the perception of the body.

In Mizrahi's and Sassatelli's chapters we remain within a realm that at least seems relatively familiar. Women wear jeans that attract men and men wear jeans that attract women. Jeans serve then to enact sexuality and especially the heightened sexualization in the sweat and motion of clubbing. The ways in which they do this may sometimes be extraordinary but not the fact that they do this. By contrast, Woodward's chapter starts from something rather less predictable: not a woman wearing a woman's jeans to entice a man. Instead these are women who have already found their man and now have taken to wearing his jeans. As such this chapter takes one of the central issues of denim studies, the centrality of distressing, a stage further. Jeans are the one garment that we regularly buy already looking at though they were pre-worn. We know that the development of distressing came after the hippie period, when jeans were worn to destruction, a time that focused very clearly upon the individual. Here this entire sequence is now replayed as gender and as relationships to others, as women wear the jeans that men have already worn before them. Commerce has quickly appropriated the phenomenon to create a commercial category of *boyfriend* jeans that turn this intimacy into a commodity in much the same way that commerce previously took the hippie experience and turned it into distressed jeans. This gives us a narrative but does not explain its causes.

As Woodward notes, the ambiguity of commercialized *boyfriend* jeans is prefigured even in the non-commercial version. Do these jeans stand in relation to an actual boyfriend, an imagined boyfriend or a sequence of boyfriends? Is it already abstracted as a cultural genre even prior to being commercialized as one? Georgia is not merely wearing a relationship; she is wearing her relationship to relationships more generally. At the very same time when commerce renders this a purely abstract concept of *boyfriend*, the three figures that appear in Woodward's chapter in three different ways develop their resonances through actual relationships. As such they reflect the parameters of this book as a whole. Denim jeans in Woodward's chapter are a medium to express a core contradiction and ambivalence. This theme can be seen in many versions in this book: from people who use jeans to merely extend an actual relationship to an individual, through to the relationship people have to the US in Comstock's and Olesen's papers, right through to a prefiguration of the arguments that come at the end of this introduction, when through a consideration of Ege and Pinheiro-Machado, we see jeans mostly in relation to issues of alienation and ambiguity, something evidently prefigured in Woodward. It is hardly news to suggest that many women feel that they really don't know where they stand in relation to either a particular man or men in general. But what we have found, yet again, is that it is jeans of all things that speak directly to this dilemma. Jeans are a medium through which women come to literally feel their feelings.

Jeans and Alienation

What we have written so far could be read as though jeans have an endless capacity to express globality at its extreme, locality at its extreme and the ability to resolve these. However, that would be naïve and a rather romantic reading of jeans today. Although, we are claiming in all of these chapters that jeans have this unrivalled capacity to express globality and simultaneously intimacy, the problem comes when we turn to the issue of resolving the antinomies between these two extremes. We clearly do have cases where this would be a reasonable proposition, where distressing somehow makes people feel more able to live in and through such extremes than would otherwise be the case. But jeans are of this world, and this is a world where the given condition of humanity is as much one of alienation as inalienability. It is far more accurate to suggest that jeans represent a struggle towards resolution than to suggest they actually succeed in this task. We therefore have to pay equal attention to the way jeans express that alienation, frustration and struggle.

While not yet forefronted, this has in fact been evident in the previous chapters. It is clearly there in the situation Miller describes for Kannur a situation where the resistance to denim reveals a town feeling increasingly under siege from the forces of cosmopolitanism and modernity. The conservatism being expressed there runs parallel to new religiosities in many contemporary societies from Pentecostal to radical Islam. Mizrahi's context also lies at the fringes of society coming from the impoverished and often violent *favelas* of Rio. At a more personal level we have just seen this ambiguity expressed in the case of Georgia, as presented by Woodward's chapter, where the jeans are expressive of her own ambivalence about her relationships. Although based in the intimacy of *boyfriend* jeans, there is an obvious link through the concept of alienation with much more general and collective issues.

The point is explored extensively in the paper by Ege, where we have a classic instance of exclusion and alienation leading through anxiety to assertiveness and ambiguity. The population he describes within Germany – 'boys and young men with Turkish, Arab, and other immigrant backgrounds, most of whom come from working-class, relatively low-income families' – are pretty much exactly those where we might anticipate such feelings of an uncomfortable presence with regard to the mainstream. The cultural genre that these youths claim allegiance to, that of gangsta rap, is about as close as we have come to an international emblem of adherence to alienated youth culture. Ege's contribution is that he sees how this is channelled into a much more specific sartorial expression of their underclass status in the form of these Picaldi 'carrot-cut' jeans.

Ege shows that this situation cannot be simplified as either merely an expression of agency amongst those otherwise lacking in empowerment or, at the other extreme, seeing them as merely the structural expression of their position relative to dominant or hegemonic power. Above all these jeans are redolent of ambiguity. Alienation does not give rise to just one position; it creates anxiety and thereby uncertainty and contradiction. Most people do not actually desire to embody some kind of unremittingly bad, negative or confrontational position against cultural norms. They have their own powerful moral and positive understandings of themselves, much of which is tied to wider networks of families and peer-group moralities. Picaldi is not the same as gangsta rap but it is an emergent form within this particular milieu that acts as an external form through which they can find out who they are. The style elicits a response; people love it or hate it, identify with it or despise it, but they seem less likely to ignore it. For this group, being the centre of concern is one way to become of significance. Running the risk of retrospective ridicule or embarrassment, they here have a mirror through which they can better see themselves. The implication of Ege's chapter is that making ambiguity visible marks a step, if not in resolving it, then at least in coming to make it visible and to understand it.

Through this focus upon ambiguity Ege seems to conclude our argument. But actually he does so only with respect to the wearing of jeans. To bring us full circle we clearly need the final chapter by Pinheiro-Machado and the criticism she makes of the entire global denim project from the perspective of her ethnography. It is only too easy to start with the kinds of issues of production and distribution that are explored with Comstock and Wilkinson-Weber and assume that the consequences of production are to be found in consumption. What this ignores is the way in which consumption always, in turn, has consequences for production and more especially for peoples involved in the commerce of jeans. Here, at the end, we come to a position diametrically opposed to the idea of jeans as an expression of the agency of people. On the periphery, there are people who become the pawns of a much larger political economy in which jeans are hugely important simply as a commodity. The growing ubiquity of wearing jeans makes them increasingly important to global systems of production and sale.

As a result the people presented by Pinheiro-Machado seem powerless, even in comparison to Ege's disaffected youth. The very term Voluntários da Pátria with its semantic ambiguity of *volunta* (becoming engaged in prostitution) makes this pretty clear. These people are forced to sell things they don't particular want to sell, moved to a place of sale where they don't particularly want to be. As Pinheiro-Machado makes abundantly clear, even given their disadvantaged position these vendors naturally struggle to find some position of comparative advantage, to at least make some money out of this situation. They strive to find a 'business model' that will allow them to undercut others, to reposition themselves so that they can find a niche they can exploit. Yet this chapter does not flinch from concluding with their failure rather than their success, forcing us to acknowledge the degree to which they remain the pawns of wider forces. Even their own customers remain blind to the opportunities they try to open to them. For all their background in the wiles of trading, they still cannot find a way out of the position that, by the end of this paper, seems more like a trap than an opportunity

This is why Pinheiro-Machado's chapter is appropriate as the ending to this first collection of the global denim project: because in the end we need to be confronted with the consequences of our arguments. By the time we have worked out our explanations for why denim is so ubiquitous, and appreciated its power and its resonance, we are also ready also to face up to its effects. Throughout the world there will be people on the margins where the importance of denim is not that they can express themselves through it, but rather that they become subject to its immensity. Faced with the sheer scale and strength of denim, people in all sorts of places dotted around the world find themselves defined by it, pushed into selling something they may have no particular identity with or affection for. In many respects they are the victims, the detritus of this ever growing presence. We should not forget those who are distressed by denim.

Conclusion

The stance of this introduction, and indeed of the entire Global Denim Project, is dialectical: from the concrete to the abstract from the abstract to the concrete and now finally to the abstract again. We start with the most concrete, our observation of the ubiquity of denim as an empirical phenomenon that requires explanation. Why is it so ubiquitous? How does it seem to refute the logic of something as powerful as the fashion industry? These questions lead us to the kinds of abstractions that were the subject of the manifesto paper and the launch of the Global Denim Project. We can then see why denim is ubiquitous and how it has achieved a unique presence directly expressive of the extremes of the modern world. With the growth of modern media and constant exposure to the sheer size and diversity of the world we live in today, we all become desirous of embracing this vast global humanity and simultaneous recoil from it and become protective of our singular and personal humanity. Very few people are only concerned with one or other of these entirely opposed relationships to the world. The vast majority of us want both simultaneously.

Denim appears, then, as both the expression and the resolution of this contradiction. As expressed in distressing, it is the emblem of personalization and individuality, our most intimate garment that wears itself to the precise contours of our body as a mode of practice and engagement with the world. It is as if our lives are so full of life and labour that our jeans gradually disintegrate into a pattern expressive of that abundant life. Actually, in practice, we are so busy that we do not, it seems, have time to live our own full lives and so commerce provides us with this 'as if' scenario in pre-distressed jeans. So at the very moment that we are confirmed in our desire for singularity we are wearing a garment that we know full well is the single most homogenizing and ubiquitous presence in the entire world today. That we are indeed *Citizens of Humanity*, ironically one of the most expensive denim labels, members of an ecumenical, stateless, citizenship of the global.

At this level of abstraction denim becomes an ideal of anthropology: a form of philosophy that is not expressed in words or by esoteric and abstract thinkers. It is instead a philosophy found in everyday practice, as a thing that speaks what its wearer cannot say. When we feel dumb and inarticulate, our blue jeans speak for us and demonstrate that we too have this understanding of the need to resolve the contradictions of modern life. It no longer matters whether we are academics joining together in a global denim project committed to this mode of understanding through research and writing, or whether, when we have finished typing our denim research on the computer, we go out to have a drink with our friends actually wearing denim. Both are equally resonant of the capacity of denim to be expressive of our philosophical position relative to our understanding of the world we live in.

This is also the uniqueness of denim itself. The vast majority of entitles in the world cannot become a work of philosophy in this manner. A bottle of whisky, or game of football may be found in most countries but they remain relatively specific and limited. They don't reach down to anything like the same extent as a garment that is worn all the time and actually dominates the street scene in almost every place, everyday. More than that, they don't extend that ubiquity to the individual in their most private and personal representation of themselves as they get up in the morning and go to bed at night. Compare the potential rival symbols. We might visit a McDonald's and drink a Coke, but both retain much more of their point of origin in the US and both are specific and relatively occasional events. There is no equivalent to distressing or boyfriend jeans, to the eroticism of Milan and Rio. They are not what we see constantly and what we are constantly – to anything like the same extent.

So the point of global denim is that it is in many ways unique, extreme, and extraordinary. It thereby has capacities that nothing in the world can rival as it manages to be universal by losing all particularity. Many people wear jeans without any sense of which brand they are, where they purchased them, what type or style they are, any implication of Americanization, or any other specific quality. They are just the jeans they took out of the wardrobe that morning so they didn't need to think about anything at all except that they were getting dressed. In a study based on our own ethnography in north London, with the title *Denim: the Art of Ordinary,* we will expand to a book-length discussion this concept of the ordinary and unmarked. It is this that gives denim its universality, where it transcends its specificity as the idiom of ubiquity.

At this point we have reached our apogee of philosophical abstraction by discussing what jeans are as an entirely generalised concept, and explained jeans as though it was a single thing and we a single humanity – all people and all jeans. This is why the manifesto paper leads inexorably to the Global Denim Project and why the Global Denim Project leads inexorably to this particular volume of writings. As academics we must remain true to this dialectic. Having achieved our abstraction then the next stage is to return to the specifics to examine the consequences of the points we have just made for particular populations and for particular jeans. Only at the end of this book, when all the chapters are read, have we fulfilled the commitment of the project itself. Every one of these chapters shows in its specific way what happens as a result of this process: when jeans become philosophy and what this enables people to do or what this forces people to become.

Compare, for example, the essays by Mizrahi and Olesen. In Mizrahi's paper jeans repudiate entirely their impersonal relation to the world to become seamlessly integrated into the specific sensuality of the Funk Ball. At the other extreme, jeans for Olesen manifest a commitment by the particular to the universal in the form of a concern with the environment and the future health of the planet. It is only when jeans become the looming presence of the ubiquitous that the people of Kannur take up arms against jeans in particular and defend themselves against their assault. It is the way they straddle the extremes from ubiquity to singularity that explains how Picaldi jeans can become a sign of ambiguity; a source of resistance and also of embarrassment, an ambiguity also very evident as a form of both identity and distance in boyfriend jeans. Similarly contradictions are found in the relation between production and consumption discussed by Comstock and Wilkinson-Weber, then rewoven together by Sassatelli's ability to relate fit and *fit*. Finally we come to the places where these contradictions just remain as contradictions in the chapters by Ege and Machado, where street vendors find themselves defined by jeans in a process over which they have very little control.

The definition of contemporary material culture studies is that we need to be at least as concerned with how objects make people as with how people make objects. Jeans are a quintessential example of material culture. They transcend any simple opposition of subjects and objects. The idea that they are a simple expression of people's identity is clearly absurd. In many ways their ubiquity is the very negation of the project of identity; they are about the least identifying form of appearance available to us today. They are not objects that represent subjects. Equally they are only sometimes the oppressive object force that is experienced by Rio vendors. In the main they are doing, as a form of practice, more or less the same things that we are doing as a form of academia. They are an attempt to understand the basic antinomies of the contemporary world and through that understanding they are the very means by which we struggle in our attempts to live with and through those oppositions, in our individual resolution of collective expression.

Notes

1. Our thanks for Naomi Braithwaite for undertaking the task of gathering these statistics for the project and to Joanne Eicher for her critical comments and suggestions.
2. The two main ones being the *Global Lifestyle Monitor* report (2008), which surveyed people in Brazil, China, Colombia, Germany, Thailand, Turkey, India, Italy, Japan, and the UK, and the *Global Denim Survey* (Synovate 2008), which was carried out on people in the USA, Canada, Brazil, France, Taiwan, Korea, Malaysia, Serbia, Russia and South Africa.

References

Bair, J. and Gereffi, G. (2001), 'Local Clusters in Global Chains: The Causes and Consequences of Export Dynamism in Torreon's Blue Jeans Industry, *World Development*, 29(11): 1885–903.

Bair, J. and Peters, E. (2006), 'Global Commodity Chains and Endogamous Growth. Export Dynamism and Development in Honduras and Mexico', *World Development*, 34 (2): 203–21.

Balfour-Paul, J. (1998), *Indigo,* London: British Museum Press.

Card, A., Moore, M. and Ankeny, M. (2005), 'Garment Washed Jeans: Impact of Laundering on Physical Properties', *International Journal of Clothing and Science Technology,* 18(1): 43–52.

Chowdhary, U. (2002), 'Does Price Reflect Emotional, Structural or Performance Quality?' *International Journal of Consumer Studies,* 26(2): 128–33.

Clarke, A. and Miller. D. (2002), 'Fashion and Anxiety', *Fashion Theory,* 6: 191–213.

Cotton Incorporated (2005), 'Return of the Dragon: Post Quota Cotton Textile Trade', *Textile Consumer,* 36 (Summer): www.cottoninc.com/TextileConsumer/TextileConsumerVolume26/ (accessed 14 June 2010).

Crewe, L. (2004), 'A Thread Lost in an Endless Labyrinth: Unravelling Fashion's Commodity Chains', in A. Hughes and S. Reimer, *Geographies of Commodity Chains*, Harlow: Longman.

Downey, L. (1996), *This is a Pair of Levis Jeans: Official History of the Levis Brand,* San Francisco: Levi Strauss & Co Publishing.

Finlayson, I. (1990), *Denim: An American Legend,* Norwich: Parke Sutton.

Fiske, J. (1989), *On Understanding Popular Culture,* Boston: Unwin Hyman.

Global Lifestyle Monitor (2008), *Global Lifestyle Monitor Survey on Denim,* Cotton Council International, Cotton Incorporated and Synovate: www.cottoninc.com/supplychaininsights/europeanviewsonfiberanddenim/europeanviewsonfiberanddenim.pdf (accessed 14 June 2010).

Hansen, K.T. (2005), 'From Thrift to Fashion: Materiality and Aesthetics in Dress Practices in Zambia' in D. Miller and S. Kuechler (eds) *Clothing as Material Culture,* Oxford: Berg, pp 107–20.

Hawley, J.M. (2006), 'Digging for Diamonds: A Conceptual Framework for Understanding Reclaimed Textile Products', *Clothing and Textiles Research Journal,* 24(3): 262–75.

International News Service (2008), *Middle East Denim Market Review.* Bromsgrove: Aroq Limited.

Küchler, S. and Miller, D. (eds) (2005), *Clothing as Material Culture,* Oxford: Berg.

Levi-Strauss, C. (1966), *The Savage Mind,* London: Weidenfeld & Nicolson.

Li, Y., Yao, L. and Newton, E. (2003), *The World Trade Organisation and International Denim Trading,* Cambridge, Woodhead Publishing.

Li, Y., Yao, L. and Yeung, K.W. (2003), *The China and Hong Kong Denim Industry,* Cambridge: Woodhead Publishing.

Marsh, G. and Trynka, P. (2002), *Denim: From Cowboys to Catwalk.* London: Aurum Press Ltd.

Miller, D. (2010), *Stuff,* Cambridge: Polity.

Miller, D. and Woodward, S. (2007), A Manifesto for the Study of Denim, *Social Anthropology,* 15: 335–51.

Mintel Market Research (2005), *Essentials* – April 2005. Mintel International Group.

Mintel Market Research (2007), *Jeans* – April 2007. Mintel International Group.

Mizrahi, M. (2002), A influência dos subúrbios na moda da Zona Sul [The Influence of the Outskirts on the Southern Area]. Monograph. Universidade Estácio de Sá.

Mizrahi, M. (2006), "Figurino Funk: uma etnografia dos elementos estéticos de uma festa carioca", in D.K. Leião, D.N.O. Lima, R. Pinheiro-Machado (eds), *Antropologia e Consumo:diálogos entre Brasil e Argentina*. Porto Alegre: Age.

Reich, C. (1970), *The Greening of America: How the Youth Revolution is Trying to Make America Liveable,* New York: Random House.

Synovate (2008) *Fact Global Denim Survey,* http://www.synovate.com (accessed 14 June 2010).

Sullivan, J. (2006), *Jeans: A Cultural History of an American Icon,* New York: Gotham Press.

Tarhan, M. and Sarsiisik, M. (2009), 'Comparison among Performance Characteristics of Various Denim Fading Processes', *Textile Research Journal*, 79(4): 301–9.

Textile: The Journal of Cloth and Culture (2011), Denim Special Issue, *Textile* 9(1).

Tokatli, N. (2007), 'Networks, Firms and Upgrading within the Blue-jeans Industry: Evidence from Turkey, *Global Networks,* 7(1): 51–68.

Tokatli, N. and Ö. Kızılgün (2004), Upgrading in the Global Clothing Industry: Mavi Jeans and the Transformation of a Turkish Firm from Full-package to Brand Name Manufacturing and Retailing', *Economic Geography*, 80, 221–40.

Van Dooren, R. (2006), La Laguna: Of Exporting Jeans and Changing Labour Relations, *Tijdschrift voor Economische en Sociale Geografie,* 97(5), 480–90.

Woodward, S. (2005), Looking Good: Feeling Right – Aesthetics of the Self, in S. Küchler and D. Miller (eds), *Clothing as Material Culture,* Oxford: Berg, pp. 21–40.

Woodward, S. (2007), *Why Women Wear What They Wear,* Oxford: Berg.

Wu, J. and Delong, M. (2006), 'Chinese Perceptions of Western-branded Denim Jeans: A Shanghai Case Study', *Journal of Fashion Marketing and Management*, 10(2), 238–50.

–1–

The Making of an American Icon: The Transformation of Blue Jeans during the Great Depression[1]

Sandra Curtis Comstock

Introduction

As the chapters in this volume show, at the current conjuncture, an astonishing number of people in a striking number of cultural contexts have come to deploy jeans as a symbol of movement between social worlds and boundary crossing – be it generation, gender, culture, religion or class-inflected boundary crossing. In a world characterized by intensifying exchange and transposable goods, produced by the now 'virtually universal intersection of (cultural) structures', blue jeans seem to epitomize this exchange and intersection.[2] And just as the intersection of cultural structures has lead not to homogenization but to increasingly complex differentiation between seemingly similar practices and products, so too, blue jeans do not so much homogenize as simultaneously translate between and highlight differences among social worlds. A key element permitting this is the now general, cross-cultural *social expectation* that blue jeans are inherently changeable – materially and symbolically. But why do people today believe in and embrace such diversity in jeans styles, looks, and uses? And why do we associate jeans' material and stylistic changeability with social-symbolic ambiguity? This chapter contributes to part of the answer by explaining how and why jeans gained their first, initial layer of material and symbolic protean-ness, and the manner in which this was connected to the emergence of mass-culture in the 1930s.[3]

Prior to the 1930s few thought of blue jeans as ambiguous in meaning or capable of much stylistic variation. However, in just one, short decade, a remarkable shift began to take place. The undistinguished working-class dungaree started to become a gender- and class-blurring icon of 'the American people'. While iconic status would not be fully established until the 1950s, the groundwork for the transformation was laid down in the crucible of the Great Depression. During the Depression, a series of contingent events and circumstances in the US encouraged industry and the public to take up blue jeans as a stylistically and symbolically versatile, class- and gender-blurring national icon. As the idea of the changeable jean was constructed in multiple realms, for multiple reasons, emerging mass-culture industries found growing public interest in the symbolically and stylistically amorphous middle-class jean commercially useful and suggestive. The blue jean's accruing capacity to resonate with an expanding variety of audiences and customers, just as mass-culture was searching for bridges between working and middle class and male and female consumers, made it both alluring and exemplary. So just why did jeans initially take on new, potentially iconic meanings in the late 1930s? How did it come to pass that non-working-class men and women began to embrace what had just a decade earlier been considered the ultimate plebeian garment? And furthermore, why did American clothing makers and retailers so doggedly pursue and embellish upon the newly minted American blue jean, commercially?

Those who have written on the topic take two distinct approaches. Some empha-size 'consumption-side factors', while others emphasize 'production-side factors'. On the consumption side, Leslie Rabine and Susan Kaiser explain these changes in terms of shifts in everyday habits and emulation.[4] They argue that changes in middle-class Americans' everyday activities (such as increased leisure time, wom-en's entry into paid work, greater emphasis on women's sports) led to 'a need' for casual clothing. Given these needs, women then chose dungarees over, for example khakis, because stars like Greta Garbo wore them, and they wished to emulate them. In a different vein, production-centred authors like Ben Fine and Ellen Leopold argue that, in the first decades of the twentieth century, the changes in technologies and strategies of mass-production and mass-distribution created the competition in the women's ready-made garment industry to push manufacturers and retailers to market dungarees and other standardized garments in new ways in order to expand their markets and compete with one another.[5] In this account, Hollywood's uses of jeans and new middle-class leisure activities figure as latent conditions until compet-ing marketers and advertisers activate them by convincing users of their social value and relevance.

The production and consumption approaches disagree on the 'primary factors' explaining the emergence of jeans as a class-ambiguous American icon. However, they both share the belief that underlying conditions (such as shifts in everyday activities, or shifts in production and distribution) and specific mechanisms (such as emulation or advertising) transformed the working-class blue jean into an American icon. These shifts and mechanisms play an important role but these factors alone cannot explain why jeans sellers and consumers made such a radical departure from previous practice, neither can they sufficiently explain why the middle-class jean became such a compelling symbol. In times of stability and continuity it may make sense to think in terms of generalizable forces and mechanisms but William Sewell has pointed out that in moments of crisis and radical departure, relatively slow-changing conditions and static mechanisms cannot adequately explain the drastic reorganization of society's practices and outlooks.[6]

The shift in patterns of jeans production and meanings during the Depression was a radical one, emblematic of deeper political and economic changes in society. It was produced by a breakdown in normal ways of operating, and by a sudden unknowability of the future. Accounting for shifts of this nature requires an enhanced conceptualization of consumption and production – one that pays close attention to jeans consumers' and sellers' experiences and interpretations of disruptive and unexpected events, and one that examines the role of event sequence and conjuncture in shaping interpretations and actions. To be pushed out of deeply ingrained habits of thinking of the blue jean as plebeian, and to embrace the strange idea of blue jean as a class-less American icon, Hollywood, consumers, and jeans sellers had to have their normal ways of doing and thinking substantially disrupted and called into question.

In addition to the factors emphasized by consumption and production schools of thought, two categories of events (regulatory and aesthetic) were crucial in jostling participants' understandings of jeans in the 1930s. The first series of events was regulatory in nature and involved efforts to reorganize clothing consumption and production in a more equitable fashion. These events disrupted the garment trades and inspired unorthodox interactions between previously separate women's and men's work-clothing industries, which often involved experimentation with the middle-class blue jean. The second series of events consisted of spurts of aesthetic activity aimed at making sense of Depression-era calamities and reinterpreting American institutions accordingly. For a variety of reasons, narratives of Depression-era events and experiences repeatedly drew upon blue jeans as a mnemonic leitmotif linking different social categories of people in ways that encouraged the public to see jeans as quintessentially American for the first time.

Neither regulatory nor aesthetic events, nor shifts in the broader conditions of jeans production or consumption produced the transformation of the work dungaree into a class-muting American icon. Rather, it was the particular timing, sequence and conjuncture of disruptive regulatory events and perspective-changing aesthetic events that shaped manufacturers' and retailers' actions, and public tastes. As William Sewell notes, the causal significance of the sequence and timing of disruptions and responses to disruption amplifies and deepens remarkably in moments of serious societal upheaval.[7] Tracing the intricacies of how and why the blue jean became a part of American middle-class and women's clothing repertoires during the volatile 1930s shows just how the timing and sequence of seemingly minor events mattered. It also sheds light on the important role that ordinary elements of material culture like blue jeans can play in helping to connect and reorganize previously separate practices and social categories and tastes.

The Department Store and the Middle-class Women's Dungaree

Prior to 1930, high-end department stores did not offer women's denim dungarees for sale. In fact, a significant portion of the clothing they offered was either manufactured in Paris, or made to order by jobbers from patterns imported from France.[8] The association with French fashion was one of the major sources of the high-end department store's prestige among middle- and upper class customers.[9] Because many of these Parisian designs were based on the French regime of production, a large number of the items were relatively complex in terms of their sewing and required considerable finesse and adjustment of operations by the sewing operator. The quick changes in variety and the complexity of women's clothing encouraged department stores to keep costs down by using agile jobbers, or middlemen, who hired fly-by-night sweat shops or networks of home workers willing to work cheaply and sporadically.[10] All of this started to change in the 1930s as department stores began emphasizing more standardized, simpler, American sportswear for women.

Beginning in 1934 high-end department stores began using dungaree advertisements that emphasized California and Hollywood as a new American fashion frontier. One early Bullock's advertisement made this quite explicit by placing a map with movie set locations and the 'wild west' alongside pictures of men and women in leisurewear. This new realm of American style was defined by its casual sportiness. To emphasize the point, sailor's dungarees were foregrounded to emphasize informality and cosmopolitan travel. Why did department stores start experimenting with dungarees? Why did they decide to offer the unlikely blue jean to middle-class American women who were accustomed to tea dresses and cocktail clothing? Below I will show that shifts in the cultural practices of Hollywood taste-leaders, combined with a series of disruptive regulatory events, motivated department stores to sell dungarees.

Changing Cultural Conditions: Growth in Working-class Women's Consumption of Movies and Magazines, Shifting Working-class Women's Social Roles and the Rise in Visibility of Women's Dungarees in Hollywood

In the early 1930s reports of Greta Garbo, Katherine Hepburn and Marlene Dietrich wearing bell-bottomed dungarees as street clothing crowded magazines and newspapers. For example, male commentators sarcastically declared Katherine Hepburn's dungarees a 'sartorial thrill'. They criticized 'La Hepburn' for wearing dungarees 'like a common farmhand'.[11] Others announced that Hollywood had become 'Trouser-Land' and ascribed the fad to women's 'blind striving ... in a man's field.'[12] In short, actresses' trousers and mannish habits were reviled by journalists, fashionistas, and film producers, alike. What exactly was the public's fascination with actresses' dungarees? And why, if male film makers found mannish actresses in jeans so personally repugnant, did they choose to generate films and publicity that featured these same women, challenging gender and class norms?[13]

To explain this we must take a few steps backwards to understand the changing social context of working-class women, who became the main group driving the production and sales of articles and films on the subject. Going into 1930, working-class households in urban centres tended to subscribe to patriarchal norms that hinged on the idea that, because men were the main breadwinners, they should be given preference over other family members. As working-class men lost their factory jobs, and women's informal work and government relief sustained more and more households, women began to question patriarchy in their homes.[14] As a result, working women began to take a special interest and pleasure in Hollywood news and films that played on the themes of the fragility of gender roles and differences. During this time, the importance of working-class audiences to Hollywood box-office receipts grew as well. As working-class tastes increasingly interested Hollywood, executives commissioned studies that showed working-class women were particularly influential in determining what films their families and friends saw. As a result, while male film producers and directors disliked the strong personas of the dungaree-clad starlets, they produced more and more movies and publicity playing on the gender-troubling themes that working-class women seemed to like best.[15]

Yet, heightened working-class women's interest in these themes did not directly translate into a desire on their part to emulate Garbo's or Hepburn's blue jeans. Working-class women associated jeans with male toil, which made them unenthusiastic about dungarees. Nevertheless, heightened circulation of jeans did capture the interest of a small group of young, elite, college-bound women who wanted to wear less ostentatious forms of clothing in line with the seriousness of the times. This isn't to say it started a fad. In the mid-1930s only a few college women began to wear dungarees in the manner of Kate Hepburn. Detractors persistently described college women's jeans uses as emasculating and used them as an example of how working-class tastes were increasingly degrading an emergent, middle-class American mass-culture.[16]

In this negative context, then, why did *highbrow* department stores opt to carry the dungaree? Careful review of the timing of highbrow department store advertising suggests that the dungaree's status as symbol of gender and class transgression and modern Hollywood style became important as a result of three regulatory events: changes in trade rules, changes in wage rules and the right to organize and the institution of something called the Cotton Code. As I will show, these events, and their interplay with Hollywood meanings, motivated department stores to offer women's dungarees.

Regulatory Events: Disorder, Contingency, and the Active Role of the Dungaree in Nudging High-end Women's Clothing towards Mass Production

As mentioned earlier, prior to the Depression, most women's clothing sold in department stores was derived from samples, or made-up clothing imported from French fashion houses.[17] Beginning in June of 1930, the Smoot-Hawley Tariff Act raised import duties on Parisian ready-made clothing and patterns dramatically. This led to a drastic decline in imports from France.[18] Searching for alternative sources of prestige, stores puzzled over how to develop American sources of distinction.[19] One strategy adopted by department stores was to feature shockingly modern, slightly disreputable, women's dungarees in their newly established ranch and resort shops. Women's dungarees as a signature item in these shops helped stores to propose a new, gender-bending, democratic, American, and Hollywood fashion sensibility against the old, formal, hierarchic, Eurocentric sensibility. Dungarees' plebeian, gender-defying associations provided a shock value that could be profitably used to emancipate department stores from the dominance of Parisian fashion.

By 1935, department stores' assertion that dungarees were markers of an alternate American sartorial space was consecrated when *Vogue* magazine featured 'Lady Levi's' in its summer travel issue. In the article *Vogue* declared: 'True Western chic' is an invention of the cowboy, 'but the moment you stray from (authentic cowboy) tenets, you'll be lost.'[20] Despite the *Vogue* boost, most department stores continued to avoid brand-name, stiff denim jeans, of the straight-legged variety, which were associated with male cowboys. Instead, they offered soft, faded, flowingly feminine bell-bottoms and emphasized the daringly modern, hybrid, gender-blurring qualities of the jean.[21] In emphasizing Hollywood, and back-grounding the cowboy image, the majority of department store advertisements sought to avoid overlapping with the growing associations between Levi's and cowboys. Since the department store's goals were to lower costs and maintain control over dungaree designs, they tended to avoid messages that directly competed with Levi's and which might have compelled them to carry Levi Strauss & Co.'s more expensive jeans.[22]

These dynamics explain how department stores began advertising women's sports dungarees (usually a flowing, sailor-style jean, distinct from the straight-legged, men's Levi's) in the early 1930s. However, they do not sufficiently account for why department stores' dungaree advertisements rose in 1934 and 1935, collapsed in 1936, and then increased significantly from 1938 until military purchases raised dungaree prices in 1941. Understanding this ebb and flow is important because it helps us to identify what really drove department stores' decisions to carry blue jeans. The sudden spike, drop off, and recuperation of denim dungaree advertisements during this period are best understood in terms of the ebb and flow of events altering garment industry regulations.

In 1933 the National Relief Act mandated that the federal government develop codes aimed at stabilizing labour costs and ending competition based on cut-throat pricing in the garment industry.[23] One of the first mandates of the NRA was to require the clothing industry to gather detailed information on garment wages and employment practices throughout the country. These efforts provided unions with information and encouraged new methods for evaluating, comparing, and negotiating piecework regimes and contracts.[24] Many of these methods were borrowed from the far more standardized work-clothing industry, where management and unions had been working on issues of parity in worker compensation for some time.[25] As one labour historian noted:

> The code agencies travelled widely from market to market inspecting shops, examining books, conducting hearings, and comparing labor costs under all types of operations and conditions of employment. A common procedure was to estimate the comparative labor costs of making sample garments ... from market to market. After ... intensive study, these agencies produced the first truly industry wide surveys of production cost factors in their respective trades ...[26]

Armed with new information and tools, unions were better equipped to collectively bargain with the manufacturers, especially in union-resistant labour markets where it had been difficult to gain insider-knowledge of factory practices.[27] At the same time, under new NRA protections of the right to organize, unions finally had the legal room and broad worker optimism necessary to launch highly successful unionizing drives that organized vast numbers of workers across the garment industry.[28] Federal restrictions on homework and the union drive encouraged manufacturers to move to producing within their own inside factories, significantly reducing contractors and home workers.[29] The NRA also required clothing factory owners in different segments of the industry to develop national organizations in order to work with unions to establish codes delineating minimum wage-rates and rules for different segments of the garment industry.[30] This strengthened unions' bargaining power and introduced greater standardization of wages and wholesale prices across regional markets.

However, collaboration between the industry and the state to define the new clothing wage codes also had some unintended effects. Up until the passage of the NRA, union-management bargaining had always recognized a supposed skill differential in the work of sewing operators making garments in different clothing genres. As a result, differences in earnings between industry segments had developed over time. The NRA cotton codes preserved this hierarchal difference in wage rates based on traditional distinctions.[31] The 'Cotton Code' distinguished between appropriate rates for sewing operators making 'women's clothing', 'men's clothing', 'cotton clothing' and 'work clothing', with work clothing wage rates being the lowest of all.[32] As wage rates were standardized and raised, department stores – whose profits had depended on exploiting wage discrepancies by pitting contractors against one another – sought new ways to exploit wage differentials.[33] One option was to develop new garment lines, such as leisure dungarees, that could be made by 'work clothing classified' workers. Because the sportswear genre was relatively novel, rates governing its manufacture were ambiguous, which meant that women's dungarees could be made by workers classified as work-clothing sewing operators, to lower costs per unit. The non-unionized manufacturers in rural areas colluded with this practice to attract business.'[34] Southern and South-Western manufacturers were especially quick to adopt the work-clothing status in order to thwart efforts to raise wages in the South.[35] Thus, strong unionization of the women's clothing industry in the North, increased standardization of regional wage-rates, and special work-clothing wage-rates under the Cotton Code in 1933 explain high-end department stores' increased efforts to sell women's leisure dungarees from 1934 to 1935.

The significance of the NRA codes in shaping department stores' initial decision to offer dungarees is supported by what happened to department store dungaree offerings after three subsequent events. First, generic department-store dungaree advertisements fell after the Supreme Court's 1935 abolition of the NRA clothing codes. Second, department stores' dungaree advertisements recuperated after a wave of new union contracts reinstated Cotton Code-like wage differentials in 1936 and 1937.[36] Finally, the sharp 1941 drop in dungaree advertisements when military jeans purchases raised prices also suggests that department stores' interest in selling dungarees had much to do with wage-differentials.[37] This conclusion is also substantiated by the fact that there was no similar drop in independent stores' advertisements for Levi's until 1943, when material shortages made Levi's unavailable.[38] From this evidence, it is clear that regulations favouring denim work clothing, combined with Hollywood uses of the blue jean, were the key reasons department stores began selling women's dungarees in the second half of the 1930s.

Towards an Event-oriented Explanation of the Department Store Women's Dungaree

The event-centred analysis presented thus far shows that trade and labour-law based disruptions of department stores' usual practices forced department stores to seek alternative strategies of generating fashion prestige and of keeping costs low. The coincidence of these challenges with heightened Hollywood dungaree use, and work clothing wage rules, caused department stores to experiment with selling dungarees. This suggests that jeans were not introduced to middle class women as a result of shifts in norms of production. Rather, women's jeans were introduced as a result of a *breakdown* in norms of production, combined with the advent of the Cotton Code and conditions like new Hollywood meanings and uses of the dungaree. This attention to sequence and timing of events leads us to ask if the Cotton Code and department stores' interactions with the work-wear industry contributed to subsequent tactical shifts in the production of women's wear.

The evidence available suggests that the Cotton Code and the decision to emphasize women's sportswear and dungarees made in work-wear factories were influential in reorganizing department stores women's wear practices. That is, department stores' collaboration with work-wear companies and unions to measure production methods under the Cotton Code, and their subsequent use of work-wear factories to produce sportswear and jeans encouraged those in charge of selecting clothing and managing the production process to adapt the Taylorist principles work-clothing makers had developed from the 1920s through the early 1930s. Department stores' increasing use of work-clothing manufacturers' approaches to clothing design and production is suggested by fashion designer Elizabeth Hawes' description of how the women's wear industry was changing in her 1942 book, *Why Is a Dress?*[39] It is also suggested by letters sent to the United Garment Workers between 1936 and 1942 by factories seeking advice on how to implement new Taylor-based regimes of production.[40] As Elizabeth Hawes points out, once department stores used the new Taylorist strategies of managing garment production, and appreciated the savings involved, they increasingly selected designs that could be easily and efficiently manufactured under this regime.[41] Thus, the Cotton Code and introduction of dungarees and simpler sportswear helped women's wear buyers appreciate the advantages of selling pared-down designs amenable to the Taylorist principles used in the work-wear sector, and led them to think about clothing designs that followed in terms of whether they could be easily made using such principles.[42]

Thus far, I have answered the question why department stores started offering dungarees to middle-class women. This is what an event-centred reworking of Fine and Leopold's production oriented framework does best. However, what it cannot explain on its own is why middle-class consumers finally embraced the blue jean in 1939 and 1940, which will be explored in the next section.

The Manufacturer Designed and Marketed Levi's Brand Blue Jean

In the early 1920s the men's work-clothing industry was quite distinct from the women's wear industry. Levi Strauss & Co. and H. D. Lee ran in-house manufacturing facilities and maintained regional distribution networks of independent community-based stores. As many of these stores were the sole suppliers of clothing and consumer credit in their communities there was little competition from other suppliers. However, by the mid-1920s discount chain stores, like J. C. Penney, and mail order companies, like Sears, began seriously competing with the independent community retailers.[43] While some manufacturer-merchandisers, such as H. D. Lee and the Oshkosh Overall Company, began selling a portion of their clothing to the chain stores, local, independent stores remained their most lucrative clientele. As this happened the increased influence of discount chains depressed manufacturer-merchandisers' jeans prices.

As a result, Levi Strauss & Co. and H. D. Lee began taking a number of measures to lower their costs of production. To do so, they experimented with Taylorist principles, breaking down whole garment production into a series of separate simple tasks, introducing new time and productivity accounting schemes, and experimenting with reorganizing the shop floor to better manage the work flow from one task to the next.[44] Additionally, they increased their advertising, producing their own catalogues, and store cards. These advertisements emphasized the utilitarian qualities of jeans and overalls as work-wear. The care put into manufacturers' hand bills contrasted sharply with the few independent store advertisements, which simply listed blue jeans with a price.[45]

However, in the first half of the 1930s, manufacturer-merchandisers began to experiment not only with lowering production costs but seeking out new markets. Levi Strauss & Co. was the first to introduce jeans oriented toward middle-class dude ranch and frontier themes in 1933, as well as the first to design middle-class women's jeans in 1934. After the 1935 Lady Levi's fashion spread in *Vogue* magazine, several of the other large inside-manufacturer-merchandisers, like H. D. Lee and Oshkosh, followed Levi Strauss & Co.'s lead.[46]

Why did the manufacturer-merchandisers begin pursuing Western, frontier, dude ranch, middle-class meanings in the early 1930s? Why did Levi Strauss & Co. lead the way?

Changing Conditions of Production and Distribution in the Work Clothing Industry

To answer this it is important to first appreciate why Levi Strauss & Co., and eventually other manufacturer-merchandisers, pursued the middle-class market. Consumption-side explanations attribute Levi Strauss & Co.'s campaign to the popularity of Westerns and dude ranches, and the use of Levi's by Hollywood stars. However, the popularity and prestige of the Western film genre plummeted from 1930 through 1938.[47] Furthermore, while a handful of LA, New York, and Chicago news articles mentioned dude ranch uses of Levi's between 1928 and 1930, there were no further mentions until late 1933.[48] Why then did Levi Strauss & Co. begin to allocate scarce resources to advertise the middle-class cowboy concept precisely in 1933? The main reasons have to do with the discount chain stores' growing control over the work-wear market and with the 1934 San Francisco Levi's boycott.

The main crisis that began the shift in manufacturer-merchandisers regime of retailing was the dramatic decline in farmers' and workers' consumption. Between 1929 and 1932, industrial unemployment rose from 1.5 to 15 million persons. At the

LEVI STRAUSS WORK CLOTHES for MEN

XX No. 1 Leather Ticket Waist Overalls

$1.95 per pair, Delivered

WHEREVER HARD WORK AND HARD WEAR GO HAND IN HAND, THERE YOU WILL FIND LEVI STRAUSS OVER-ALLS.

The principal features are: Made of tested selected heavy weight denim; perfect in cut and fit; five pockets; copper riveted at all strain points; do not bind at the crotch; belt loops tacked on; the curved waist band gives a perfect fit over the hips; adjustable back strap; suspender buttons riveted; heavy drill swinging side pockets; over-stitched inside fly. So well made that the manufacturers make this sweeping guarantee: "A New Pair FREE If They Rip."

No. P-3550, as above, Delivered to You, price per pair............ **$1.95**

Cowboy Overall Shirt

Price, $1.95 Delivered

Blue Denim Pleated Blouse

Price $1.95 Delivered

No. P-3551

An open front coat style Shirt or Jumper. Made of extra heavy denim, copper riveted at all points of strain. Has one pocket and matches No. P-3550 Waist Overalls. A shirt built for extra long wear. Like all other Levi Strauss garments, every shirt is rigidly inspected. Only perfect goods are permitted to leave their work rooms.

No. P-3551—Cowboy Over-all Shirt, Price, Delivered to you for **$1.95**

No. P-3552

This pleated blouse is made of extra heavy denim, has one pocket, is copper riveted at all strain points; is usually worn with No. P-3550 Waist Overalls.

No. P-3552 Delivered to You, Price Each **$1.95**

Two-Horse XX Brand No. 1 Cloth Ticket Bib Overalls

Price, per pair, $2.25, Delivered

Here's an overall made of the same quality denim as the famous Levi Strauss Copper Riveted Waist Overalls which have been the leading brand for over 55 years. We show below the principal points of superiority, but words cannot describe the wearing qualities of these overalls. If you buy one pair you will be convinced that they will outwear any other overall made. Each and every pair carries the guarantee "A New Pair FREE if they Rip."

1—XX Quality Heavy Weight Denim.
2—Extra Wide High Bib.
3—Combination Brass Buckles.
4—Buttons Riveted On.
5—Extra Large Seat and Crotch.
6—Two Extra Large Reinforced Hip Pockets.
7—Large Reinforced Rule Pocket.
8—Copper Riveted at all Strain Points.
9—Extra Wide Suspenders.
10—Pencil Pocket.
11—Book Pocket.
12—Watch Pocket.
13—Match Pocket.
14—Comfortable Roomy, Horizontal Side Pockets.
15—Double Sewed.
16—Wide Comfortable Legs.

No. P-3553—Delivered to You, per pair...... **$2.25**

No. P-3553

Men's Khaki Pants

No. P-3554

Price Delivered to You, $1.95

Sizes 30 to 42 Waist

Made of 8 ounce extra heavy Olive Drab Khaki, the best fabric of its kind that money can buy. 18 inch cuff bottoms, 2 side pockets, 2 hip pockets, with button flaps and watch pocket. Belt loops. Matched tacking at all strain points. Quality in every pair and exceptional value at the price.

No. P-3554 Delivered to You, per pair...... **$1.95**

No. P-3554

(See Other Side)

Figure 1.1. Salesman's flyer for Levi Strauss & Co. work clothing, c1926. Courtesy Levi Strauss & Co. Archives, San Francisco.

same time farm income fell from 12 billion to 5.3 billion dollars a year. As a result, workers' and farmers' expenditures on work clothing dramatically declined.[49]

Declines in demand for work clothing affected all players but the well-capitalized discount chain stores suffered far less. In fact, the collapse in work clothing demand allowed discount chains to use their superior purchasing power to obtain unparalleled concessions from workers and manufacturers. This enabled them to cut prices on overalls from one dollar and twenty cents a pair in 1929, to eighty-nine cents a pair in1932.[50] Wielding lower prices and superior cash reserves, the chain stores undercut the independent retailers, upon which Levi Strauss & Co. and HD Lee depended for their most lucrative business.[51] To make matters worse, many workers and farmers not only stopped buying jeans from their local stores – they also stopped making payments on the jeans they had purchased earlier on credit. By the end of 1931 43 per cent of the independent stores in business in 1926 had closed, and those that did survive often lacked the cash to rapidly replenish their work clothing stocks.[52]

As a result, Levi Strauss & Co.'s 1932 sales reached only half of their 1929 levels, and LS & Co., HD Lee and others shortened their work weeks and temporarily shuttered factories.[53] In the meantime, some of their cheapest Southern competitors actually grew, as discount chains increased their purchases from the South.[54] The ability of chain stores to set up distribution regimes linking South to North, and East to West gave them another advantage over the small town retailer, and by 1933 more local stores had closed their doors.[55]

Thus, manufacturer-merchandisers' loss of independent retailers, willing to sell their jeans at a premium price created a strong incentive for them to seek out alternative markets. Levi Strauss & Co., as the only manufacturer-merchandiser not regularly selling jeans to the chain stores, was particularly devastated by these losses. By 1933, concerned about the company's survival without its loyal small-town stores, Levi Strauss & Co. began to tentatively develop a series of advertisements leveraging Hollywood uses of Levi's in the ranch context.[56] However, Levi Strauss & Co.'s commitment to pursuing the middle-class dude ranch theme significantly intensified after San Francisco workers stopped buying Levi's because of the company's non-union status in 1934.

The 1934 Boycott as Decisive Event Propelling Levi's to Devote Substantial Resources to Middle-class Frontier themed Ad Campaign

The catalyst of the event was the labour unrest in California and San Francisco between 1933 and 1934.[57] Working-class agitation and brutal repression of workers in California's fields, factories, and docks bred widespread disgust with industry and bolstered pro-worker sentiment, particularly in San Francisco. This led to a concerted workers' campaign to promote buying union-label consumer items only.[58] While other major manufacturer-merchandisers were already unionized, Levi Strauss & Co. did not sign a union contract until 1937.[59] As a result, the company's normally loyal neighbourhood stores were forced by workers to stop carrying Levi's throughout 1934. In the end, Levi Strauss & Co.'s only San Francisco outlet for its blue jeans in 1934 was a middle-class-oriented saddlery in the suburbs outside the city.[60] From this point forward Levi Strauss & Co. pursued middle-class cowboy and frontier leitmotifs with unusual vigour. As one company manager recalled the period, 'We put a certain imagination into [the Levi's]. It was different from a workman's garment ... We were on the western theme continuously in our advertising.'[61] The continuous advertising paid off with the 1935 *Vogue* article on the Lady Levi. This initial achievement then convinced other manufacturer-merchandisers like H. D. Lee to imitate the Levi's-look and marketing messages in the hopes of freeing themselves from the growing power and control of the chain stores.[62]

The above production-oriented narrative satisfyingly explains how manufacturer-merchandisers began advertising middle-class frontier and cowboy themes. As should be clear, the rise of manufacturer-merchandisers' emphasis on old West themes was particularly contingent upon the specific experiences of Levi Strauss & Co. General conditions, such as the loss of independent retail outlets to the chain stores, and particular circumstances like Levi Strauss & Co.'s special historic relationship with California ranchers and Hollywood stars, encouraged Levi Strauss & Co. to pursue the dude ranch theme, which encouraged others to follow. But the specific event of the 1934 boycott of Levi's in San Francisco enhanced the company's commitment to this idea, before the notion had borne fruit in terms of increased sales. In addition, the *Vogue* feature on Lady Levi's enhanced the legitimacy of the Western jeans theme still further.

These efforts kept the Levi's signature 'Western-style' blue jean with copper rivets, red-threaded seams and the leather patch circulating as a special symbol of the Western frontier in the advertising culture of 1934 and 1935, particularly in California. But nation-wide popularity and desire for this style of blue jean was still four years away, when Eastern stores would begin to regularly carry Levi's. And it was not achieved by advertising alone. As will be evident, California artists uses of the Western-style jean to tell the story of dustbowl migrants and the Great Depression significantly shaped the outcome, as well.

From Mundane Work Pant to Symbol of the Working Class

As many historians have observed, the economic chaos and uncertainty of the Depression brought on a society-wide 'inability to imagine what had happened and would happen next.'[63] Initially, the profound effects of the Depression were hardly reported at all. However, the introduction of pro-worker legislation with the New Deal, encouraged workers who had experienced severe deterioration in working

conditions between 1930 and 1933 to respond with the largest wave of worker activ-
ism and militancy in American history. The intensity of feeling and sense of societal
rupture sent writers, artists and singers out across the byways of the nation in search
of 'the real America'.[64] No image was more repetitively documented or invoked than
that of working people in their overalls and straight-leg blue jeans.

Jeans and overalls appeared on the machine-wedded urban labourers of Diego
Rivera's 1933 Detroit murals of the River Rouge Ford factory; they protected
Charlie Chaplin and his fellows as they were sucked into the relentless pace and
machinery of the assembly line in his 1936 film, *Modern Times*.[65] Newly established
photo-magazines and Sunday news photo-supplements pictured jeans on embattled Southern textile workers, destitute sharecroppers, and striking miners. Many
of these were produced by photographers working for governmental agencies who
circulated these images freely in a bid for public support of their social agendas.[66]
Uniting portraits and panoramas of rural tenant farmers and urban wage-workers,
blue jeans became a mnemonic image that readily evoked the 'new iconography and
rhetoric of class' sweeping the US in the mid-1930s.[67]

*The Role of Aesthetic Events in Transforming 'Working-class Jeans' into
'American Jeans'*

These aesthetic shifts suggest how jeans gained initial purchase on the American imagination, but do not explain why Western jeans and Levi's become so symbolically
powerful, as a sign of 'the American people'. The simple explanation is that advertisements for copper-riveted Western blue jeans that circulated heavily in California
became an attractive symbol and resource for California artists. They drew upon
Western jeans as a symbolic resource as they pieced together a modern frontier
parable that would become the dominant way of making sense of the Depression
years and redefine Americans' understanding of themselves and the nation. The full
story of the political events, artists, journalists, politicians, and state officials that
produced the new frontier parable is another paper in itself. However, below I will
summarize the key events and artistic interpretations that produced the parable, and
helped elevate the Western jean to an American icon.

The contours of the new frontier narrative of the 1930s began taking shape when
photographer Dorothea Lange and economist Paul Taylor were urgently sent by
California and the federal Farm Security Agency to investigate the problems facing
farm workers from the Southwest as they searched for work in California. Lange and
Taylor likened these migrants to modern-day pioneers forging a new life in an unfa-
miliar world of mechanized, industrialized agriculture. Often Lange photographed
migrant workers in the Levi-style blue jeans that were widely worn in California at
the time. Their 1935 article, titled 'Again the Covered Wagon', described refugees'
westward migration as a search for 'individual protection in the traditional spirit of

Figure 1.2(a). Drought Refugees Stopped Along the Highway. Dorothea Lange 1936. Library of Congress, Prints & Photographs Division, FSA-OWI Collection, LC-USF34-016739-E.

Figure 1.2(b). Towards Los Angeles. Dorothea Lange 1937. Library of Congress, Prints & Photographs Division, FSA-OWI Collection, LC-USF34-016317-E.

Figure 1.2(c). Near Meloland. Imperial Valley. Large Scale Agriculture. Gang labor, Mexican and White. Lange FSA1939. Library of Congress, Prints & Photographs Division, FSA-OWI Collection, LC-USF34-019195-E.

the American frontier'. They warned, however, that what refugees found when they arrived was a modern frontier 'of social conflict' and insecurity.[68] Lange and Taylor advocated government aid to these worker-pioneers as a modern solution for taming the 'wilderness' of social conflict, just as the Homestead Act had tamed the physical wilderness of the nineteenth-century old West. This analogy was driven home by combining such statements with cowboy movie-like images of Southwestern migrant workers in Western, Levi-style cowboy jeans leaning alongside canvas-covered jalopies and walking down the lonely road in their Stetsons.[69] The story struck a chord in more progressive circles and generated numerous articles, pamphlets, and books.[70]

However, it was Archibald MacLeish's epic 1938 photo-poem narrating the Depression that proposed a transformative pioneer myth explicitly linking the massacres of Eastern industrial workers to the struggles of sharecroppers and farmer-workers in the agricultural fields of the West.[71] Using many of Lange's images, MacLeish proposed that during America's expansionist period the allure of frontier land had produced blindness to the evils of concentrated wealth in the East. The Depression, for him, represented both a reckoning with this illusion and a new wilderness of social conflict that workers of all backgrounds and classes had to resolve through focus on their common humanity.[72]

Both Lange's and MacLeish's versions of the dustbowl migrant as working-class pioneer were picked up in Steinbeck's March, 1939 novel, *The Grapes of Wrath,* and John Ford's 1940 film adaptation of the novel.[73] The popularity and notoriety of Steinbeck's book made his dustbowl family, the Joads, a metaphor for the times, and inspired thousands of articles and photo spreads.[74] At the same time, John Ford's film emphasizing the story's utopian agrarian impulses, and support for legitimate outlawry against monopoly capital, tied the story to a new Western movie formula that Ford had successfully proposed the previous year in his film, *Stagecoach,* starring John Wayne.[75] Following this model other film-makers rehabilitated the prestige Western as parable of the Depression.[76] As they did, prominent use of Western jeans became the preferred way for Western films to gesture toward working-class, Western, and populist rhetorics and America's past and present all at once.[77]

The Interpretive Contexts of the Eastern Dude Ranch and War: Bringing Together Women's Fashion Jeans and Western Frontier Jeans Meanings

The events discussed above not only multiplied commercial and state-sponsored narratives invoking the Levi-clad cowboy as totem of American egalitarianism. They encouraged middle-class men and women to join in the myth. By 1940, 25,000 families a year visited Western dude ranches to pursue their own frontier fantasies.[78] Simultaneously, many Eastern farms and resorts established vacation dude ranches near large cities.[79] Travel articles lauded the Eastern dude ranch for the access it

Figure 1.3(a). Dudes and cowboy from Quarter Circle U Ranch. Marion Wolcott 1941. Library of Congress, Prints & Photographs Division, FSA-OWI Collection, LC-USF34-058898-E.

Figure 1.3(b). Production. B-17F Heavy bombers. Alfred T Palmer 1942. Library of Congress, Prints & Photographs Division, FSA-OWI Collection, LC-USE6-D-007811.

provided white-collar workers to the Western experience. Now secretaries, office clerks, bankers, and tycoons could enjoy the equalizing experience of addressing one another on a first name basis, wearing the same Western jeans, participating in the same demanding physical activities, and eating around a common table.[80] Anxious to mix appropriately with the leisure elite, white-collar women purchased the flowing jeans touted by department stores and the Western jeans proscribed by fashion mavens and Eastern equestrian shops. Once on the dude ranch, white-collar and middle-class men's and women's uses of Western-style and department store-style jeans to act out their equalizing frontier dreams bonded their intimate fantasies to the larger State- and Hollywood-promoted ideas of the Western jean as symbol of Americans' 'natural' distaste for elitist pretension and greed.

Meanwhile, another shift was also afoot in general women's dungaree use. While writers had consistently condemned women's jeans in the 1930s, the symbolic use of the dungaree to delineate American clothing style and tastes gained legitimacy as the looming war shifted public understandings. By 1940 journalists were writing about college women patriotically dressing in jeans to train for the jobs left vacant by male soldiers. Through the lens of war, college women's choice of jeans suddenly seemed patriotic, practical, frugal, and in keeping with the national shift from consumerism to wartime conservation and military production.[81] In addition, the liberty of American women to choose what suited them best (for the war effort or just plain comfort) was contrasted with the absolute prohibition of pants-wearing imposed on French and German women.[82] As Marlene Dietrich put it:

> The idea (that women's slacks) ... are not respectable ... is old fashioned and European ... I am reminded of my last visit to France when it was unlawful for a woman to appear in trousers in public ... Here the freedom to wear slacks at all is a little liberty we women cherish ... Girls are entitled to more freedom in dress ... because of the part many play in national defense ... Slacks are more sensible ... They are a great economy ... (and save) on the expense of ... underclothing (and) hose ... I'd say the American way would be to let girls dress as they please.[83]

The war years encouraged many to see women's work and jeans as patriotic and emblematic of American pragmatism and democracy. The war context legitimated department stores' use of women's jeans as a symbol of American style. Contrasts between American and European attitudes towards women's clothing especially encouraged people to associate the gender-egalitarianism of the fashion dungaree with the class-egalitarianism of the predominantly male Western blue jean. Whether for or against women in jeans people began to see jeans as a sign of youthful America's repudiation of gender and class hierarchies, and distaste for elitist, wasteful ostentation. Through everyday use and the new interpretive context of war, previously separate meanings of women's fashion jeans, and men's frontier jeans began to blend into one contradictory, protean, symbol that artists and everyday people would return to again and again.

Conclusion

To conclude, at the general level this chapter has presented an event-centred approach to explaining the broad shifts in jeans consumption and production that took place during the Great Depression. This has helped identify the regulatory and aesthetic events that most contributed to this transformation. An event-centred approach is, in my view, particularly necessary for understanding dramatic shifts in material culture that occur in moments of societal upheaval and crisis. This is because the approach highlights the transformative importance of interactions between processes of production and consumption, as well as the transformational effects of exchanges between distinctive regimes of production or strategies of meaning making, for example between women's and work clothing industry networks, or working- and middle-class oriented film and photo-magazines. It shows that, in fact, economic, political, and cultural events are the contingent forces that push different groups to link and rearrange these processes and regimes in ways that fundamentally change them.

At a more specific level, while this chapter has shown that the emergence of blue jeans as a boundary-blurring sign of American egalitarianism was a fragile, event driven outcome, it also suggests why inventing class- and gender-bridging artefacts and symbols like the dungaree was an integral part of how commercial entities and state reformers sought to resolve the economic and political crises of the period. That is, declines in consumption among all social groups during the 1930s encouraged commercial entities from Levi Strauss & Co. to Twentieth Century Fox to search and foment the kinds of material culture and tastes that might extend the appeal of their products to new social groups and bolster sagging sales.[84] At the same time, the collapse of public confidence in the American capitalist system in the early 1930s sent reform-minded intellectuals and state bureaucrats alike in pursuit of narratives, symbols and artefacts with the resonance to speak to and draw together diverse groups and sensibilities in order to encourage the broadest numbers to identify and favour their society-changing projects and agendas.[85]

In a short, while the emergence of the socially transposable blue jean in the 1930s was unique and contingent, it was also the expression of a general, crisis-inspired turn toward intensified mass-forms of consumption and mass-forms of political culture that would define the century to come. Once a certain potential and allure became evident, experiments with social-category-transcending blue jeans became highly useful to the mass-culture industries and mass-oriented politics, and were reproduced with aplomb. While the chapter cannot make any bolder claim as to why blue jeans have spread so intensively and extensively beyond their Depression-era home, the unusual protean-ness with which blue jeans emerged from the peak Depression years certainly made it a highly attractive resource in the nascent mass-cultural industries and mass-politics of the time. The chapters that follow suggest that blue jeans' protean-ness and association with boundary crossing have remained their most important and compelling qualities. The question remains as to what extent the remarkable persistence of these qualities is still as intimately intertwined with the spread and deepening of localized mass-culture industries and mass-forms of political mobilization and culture.[86]

Notes

1. I would like to acknowledge the University of Western Ontario's internal Social Sciences and Humanities Research Council Internal Grants for funding a portion of the archival research in the Southern Labor Archives. In addition UWO's Sociology Department and Michael Carroll, Sam Clark and Laura Huey in particular, provided a supportive environment in which to write. I would also like to acknowledge the enthusiastic and invaluable assistance of Traci JoLeigh Drummond, Archivist at the Southern Labor Archives at Georgia State University. Finally, Leah Stevenson-Hastings' indefatigable work copying and organizing materials for analysis was also essential to this chapter.
2. Sewell (2005: 150).
3. There is disagreement over when mass-culture industries emerged in the US. These disagreements have to do with the conflation between popular culture and mass culture, as Michael Kammen points out. Here I am asserting that mass culture industries emerged between the 1930s and 1950s. This is when photo magazines came into their own, when films began to strive for the broadest audiences possible, and when well-to-do women's wear became most generally mass produced. (Green 1997; Hawes 1942; Kammen 1999; May 2000).
4. Rabine and Kaiser (2006).
5. Fine and Leopold (1993: 87–147).
6. Sewell (2005: 225–70).
7. See *Logics of History* (Sewell, 2005: 219, 225–70). Philip McMichael explores the methodological implications of this world view in terms of how it changes the comparative strategies we must employ when comparing periodically or steadily interacting phenomena (McMichael 1990).
8. Ley (1975).
9. Hawes (1942: 12).
10. Hawes (1942: 6); Green (1997).
11. Mann (2006: 199).
12. Berry (2000: 154–60).
13. Berry (2000); Denning (1996); 'Detective Lends Motif to Fashion' (1941).
14. Cohen (2008); Crane (2000); Mann (2006); ; May (2000); McComb (2006); Robertson (1996).
15. Welters and Cunningham (2005); Thomas (1935); Berry (2000); May (2000).

16. 'Article 10 – No Title' (1941); 'Detective Lends Motif to Fashion' (1941); 'She is Not Sure Where She is Heading in This Angry World …' (1941); Warner and Ewing (2002).
17. Lipovetsky (1994: 58–60).
18. Ley (1975: 88).
19. Best & Co. (1933); Bullock's (1934); Green (1997: 114); Macy's (1933).
20. Downey (2007: 62).
21. These advertisements emulated the popular bio-pieces highlighting Hollywood stars' idiosyncratic tastes, habits, and transgressions. According to Michael Kammen, by the late 1920s entertainers' biographies gained prominence and emphasized their private lives, consumption, and tastes (Kammen 1999: 57). These consumption-focused articles were bolstered by merchandisers' distribution of photos of stars wearing their clothing in national magazines (Gledhill 1991: 34–5).
22. Although Macy's and Best's briefly experimented with Levi's for a few weeks following the Vogue articles.
23. Carpenter (1972: 634).
24. Carpenter (1972: 600–24).
25. Abernathy (1999: 28–32); Howarth et al. (2000).
26. Carpenter (1972: 619–20).
27. Braun (1947).
28. The ILGWU alone went from 50,000 members in the spring of 1933 to 200,000 members in 1934 (Herberg 1952: 47–8).
29. 94 per cent of the men's clothing industry was brought into inside factories by 1940 (Green 1997: 63–71).
30. Cobrin (1970: 200).
31. By 1934, 85 per cent of the men's clothing trade was unionized. The ILGW, in less than three years, had multiplied eightfold from 23,876 in 1932 to 198,141 in 1934 (Carpenter 1972: 649).
32. Carpenter (1972: 734–5).
33. Cobrin (1970: 181–2).
34. Cobrin (1970: 181).
35. Cray (1978: 88); Marsh and Trynka (2002: 24–38); Staff (1933, 1936); Box 268, United Garment Workers of America Records, L1992-17/L1997-08. Southern Labor Archives. Special Collections and Archives, Georgia State University, Atlanta (hereafter referred to as UGWAR SLA).
36. This was then reinforced by the Fair Labor Standards Act of 1938 which strengthened unions by establishing nation-wide minimum wages and reducing clandestine clothing production (Blackwelder, 1997: 39–44, 102–3, 16; Monroy 2006; Wolensky, Wolensky and Wolensky 2002).
37. 'Plants Here Speed Clothing for Army' (1941); 'Pay Rises Sought in Cotton Trades' (1941).

38. 'Clothes Shortage Found in 25 States' (1943); Fear Textile Drain in Relief Programs, (1943); Gritz (1943).
39. Hawes (1942: 12–24).
40. Braun (1947: 1–91); Gomberg (1948); Production Systems. Box 83, Folder 14: UGWAR SLA.
41. Hawes (1942: 87–99).
42. Hawes (1942).
43. Cobrin (1970); Fraser (1983).
44. Cray (1978); Howarth et al. (2000).
45. Cobrin (1970: 117–24, 146–9); Cray (1978: 67, 77, 80–2); Fraser (1983: 540); Howarth et al. (2000); 'Penney Spends 2,250,000 Annually' (1928); File 2, Box 4: UGWAR SLA; 12/12/1921 J.C. Penney, Box 391: UGWAR SLA, Staff (1925, 1928). See also HD Lee Boxes 372, 377, 384, 386, 394: UGWAR SLA; Marsh and Trynka (2002: 34–7); Little (1996: 23, 32) and Fraser (1983: 539).
46. Downey (2007: 60–4); Marsh and Trynka (2002: 34–55).
47. Anderson (2008); May (2000: 283); Scott (1939); Slotkin (1992: 254–7).
48. 'Correct Clothes for Feminine "Dudes"' (1930); 'Melancholy Days?' (1929).
49. 'Business World' (1932); Cray (1978: 80); 'Great Depression', *Encyclopedia Americana*; 'Work Clothing Sales Pointed to Employment Turn March 1' (1930).
50. UGWA correspondence with J.C. Penney. Folder 2, 3, and 4, Box 2: UGWAR SLA.
51. Cray (1978: 82); Staff (1930, 1931, 1932).
52. Burd (1941); 'Twenty Percent of Small Town Stores are Chains' (1933).
53. Cray (1978: 84); 'Business World' (1932); *New York Times,* 20 July 1932, p. 14; *New York Times,* 30 August 1932, p. 37.
54. Cray (1978); 'Business Notes' (1933); 'Garment Company Plans Five-Day Week' (1930); Organizer Notes, Boxes 386, 389: UGWAR SLA.
55. 1930 Articles. Box 2, Folder 4: UGWAR SLA; 'Twenty Percent of Small Town Stores are Chains' (1933).
56. Downey (2007: 62); Harris (2002: 14).
57. Denning (1996).
58. Cray (1978: 85–8); Glickman (1997).
59. Box 377: UGWAR SLA.
60. Cray (1978: 85–8).
61. Cray (1978); Downey (2007: 62).
62. Downey (1995, 2007: 59–60); Marsh and Trynka (2002).
63. Denning (1996: 264).
64. Stott (1973).
65. Sheeler, 1978; Hurlburt, 1989; Chaplin, *Modern Times,* 1936 (film).
66. Finnegan (2003: 170–90).
67. Denning (1996: 8–9).

68. Taylor (1936a: 350).
69. Taylor (1936b).
70. Denning 1996 (268–70); Lorentz, *The Plow That Broke the Plains,* 1936 (film); McWilliams 1939; Steinbeck (1936, 1938).
71. MacLeish (1977).
72. Meltzer (1978: 105).
73. Loftis (1998: 134–49); Denning (1996: 262); Steinbeck (2002); Ford, *The Grapes of Wrath,* 1940 (film).
74. Finnegan (2003: 2); 260-8: Denning (1996: 260–8); Loftis (1998: 163).
75. Grant (2003); Slotkin (1992: 281–303).
76. Slotkin (1992); May (2000).
77. Increased use of Western blue jeans and down play of more vaudevillian cowboy costumes was noted by commentators of the time in more female and family oriented singing cowboy films, as well as the new Western epic (Scott, 1939).
78. "More Ranches for Dudes," 1936; Zimmerman, 1998.
79. Zimmerman (1998).
80. Markland (1939, 1940, 1941, 1942a, 1942b); Ray (1941).
81. 'Barnard Girls Get Auto Repair Study' (1941); 'College Girls Ask for "Sense" in Clothes, and they Get It at Mary Lewis Showing' (1942); 'Coming Fashions. Defense Activities Influence Fashions' (1942); 'Duty Duds and Other Practical Things are Worn at Showing of College Fashions' (1942); Gardener (1941); 'Girls Will be Boys' (1942); JTH (1940); Pope (1941); Schnapper (1939).
82. Hawes (1942: 63–6).
83. Godychaux (1941).
84. Hawes (1942); Kammen (1999); May (2000); Slotkin (1992).
85. Denning (1996).
86. On extensification and intensification see Mintz (1986).

References

Abernathy, F.H., Dunlop, J.T., Hammond, J. and Weil, D. (1999), *A Stitch in Time: Lean Retailing and the Transformation of Manufacturing – Lessons from the Apparel and Textile Industries.* Oxford: Oxford University Press.

Anderson, C. (2008), The Western Film … by the Numbers! Retrieved 27 January 2009, from http://www.b-westerns.com/graphs.htm (accessed 27 January 2009).

'Article 10 – No Title' (1941). *Washington Post,* 31 August.

'Barnard Girls Get Auto Repair Study' (1941), *New York Times,* 14 February.

Berry, S. (2000), *Screen Style: Fashion and Femininity in 1930s Hollywood,* Minneapolis, MN: University of Minnesota Press.

Best & Co. (1933), Display Ad 7. *New York Times,* 11 June, p. 7.

Blackwelder, J.K. (1997), *Now Hiring: The Feminization of Work in the United States, 1900–1995.* College Station, TX: Texas A&M University Press.

Braun, K. (1947), *Union-Management Co-operation. Experience from the Clothing Industry,* Washington, DC: Brookings Institution.

Bullock's (1934), Display Ad 14, *Los Angeles Times*, 22 January.

Burd, H.A. (1941), 'Mortality of Men's Apparel Stores in Seattle, 1929–1939', *Journal of Marketing,* 6(1): 22–6.

Business Notes (1933), *New York Times,* 20 June, p. 35.

Business World (1931), *New York Times,* 22 December, p. 43.

Business World (1932), *New York Times,* 4 February, p. 37.

Carpenter, J.T. (1972), *Competition and Collective Bargaining in the Needle Trades 1910–1967,* Ithaca, NY: New York State School of Industrial and Labor Relations.

'Clothes Shortage Found in 25 States' (1943), *New York Times,* 4 January, p. 14.

Cobrin, H.A. (1970), *The Men's Clothing Industry. Colonial Times through Modern Times.* New York: Fairchild Publications Inc.

Cohen, L. (2008), *Making a New Deal: Industrial Workers in Chicago, 1919–1939.* Cambridge: Cambridge University Press.

'College Girls Ask for "Sense" in Clothes, and They Get It at Mary Lewis Showing' (1942), *New York Times.* 6 August.

'Coming Fashions. Defense Activities Influence Fashions' (1942), *Hartford Courant,* 25 May.

'Correct Clothes for Feminine "Dudes"' (1930), *New York Times,* 6 July, p. 96.

Crane, D. (2000), *Fashion and Its Social Agendas: Class, Gender, and Identity in Clothing,* Chicago, IL: University of Chicago Press.

Cray, E. (1978), *Levi's,* Boston, MA: Houghton Mifflin.

Denning, M. (1996). *The Cultural Front: The Laboring of American Culture in the Twentieth Century,* London: New York: Verso.

'Detective Lends Motif to Fashion' (1941), *New York Times,* 27 August.

Downey, L. (2007), *Levi Strauss & Co. & Co,* Charleston, SC: Arcadia Pub.

'Duty Duds and Other Practical Things are Worn at Showing of College Fashions' (1942), *New York Times,* 11 August.

'Fear Textile Drain in Relief Programs' (1943), *New York Times,* 11 November, p. 33.

Fine, B. and Leopold, E. (1993), *The World of Consumption,* London: Routledge.

Finnegan, C.A. (2003), *Picturing Poverty: Print Culture and FSA Photographs,* Washington, DC: Smithsonian Institution Press.

Fraser, S. (1983), 'Combined and Uneven Development in the Men's Clothing Industry', *Business History Review,* 57(4), 522–47.

Gardener, J. (1941), 'The Young Crowd Design Their Own Fashions', *Christian Science Monitor,* 31 July.

'Garment Company Plans Five-Day Week' (1930), *New York Times,* 11 December, p. 2.

'Girls Will Be Boys' (1942), *Hartford Courant,* 9 August.

Gledhill, C. (1991), *Stardom: Industry of Desire*, London: Routledge.

Glickman, L.B. (1997), *A Living Wage: American Workers and the Making of Consumer Society,* Ithaca, NY: Cornell University Press.

Godychaux, M. (1941), 'History in the Making. Front Door Ballot Box Forum', *Los Angeles Times,* 10 August.

Gomberg, W. (1948), *A Trade Union Analysis of Time Study,* Chicago, IL: Social Science Research Associates.

Grant, B.K. (2003), *John Ford's Stagecoach,* Cambridge: Cambridge University Press.

Green, N.L. (1997), *Ready to Wear, Ready to Work,* Durham, NC: Duke University Press.

Gritz, E.D. (1943), Agency Says Needs Will Be Met, *Washington Post,* 26 May, p. 15.

Harris, A. (2002). *The Blue Jean,* New York: Power House Cultural Entertainment Inc.

Hawes, E. (1942), *Why Is a Dress?* New York: Viking Press.

Herberg, W. (1952), 'The Jewish Labor Movement in the United States', *Industrial Labor Relations Review,* 5(4): 501–23.

Howarth, G., Martino, T., Melton, S., Miegel, A., Morley, J. and Weissman, M. (2000), 'Levi's a Company as Durable as its Jeans', http://shakti.trincoll. edu/~ghowarth/levi.html (accessed 22 September 2004).

Hurlburt, L.P. (1989), *The Mexican Muralists in the United States.* Albuquerque, NM: University of New Mexico Press.

JTH (1940), 'Coeds Tell What They like at Boston Clothes "Parade"', *Christian Science Monitor,* 25 July, p. 9.

Kammen, M. (1999), *American Culture, American Tastes: Social Change and the Twentieth Century,* New York: Knopf.

Ley, S. (1975), *Fashion for Everyone. The Story of Ready-To-Wear,* New York: Charles Scribner's Sons.

Lipovetsky, G. (1994), *The Empire of Fashion: Dressing Modern Democracy,* Princeton, NJ: Princeton University Press.

Little, D. and Bond, L. (1996), *Vintage Denim,* Salt Lake City: Gibbs-Smith.

Loftis, A. (1998). *Witnesses to the Struggle: Imaging the 1930s California Labor Movement,* Reno: University of Nevada Press.

MacLeish, A. (1977), *Land of the Free,* New York: Da Capo Press.

Macy's (1933, 06/07), Display Ad 6, *New York Times,* 7 June, p. 5.

Mann, W.J. (2006), *Kate: The Woman Who Was Hepburn,* New York: Macmillan.

Markland, J. (1939), 'Dude Ranch Comes East', *New York Times,* 11 June, p. XX5.

Markland, J. (1940), 'Ranges in the East', *New York Times,* 26 May, p. XX1.

Markland, J. (1941), 'The East Goes West: A Tenderfoot Gets Tough Riding a Dude Range Not Far from City', *New York Times,* 25 May.

Markland, J. (1942a), 'Eastern Dude Ranches Busy Amid Colorful Autumn Scenes', *New York Times,* 18 October, p. D7.

Markland, J. (1942b), 'Eastern Dude Ranches Offer Outdoor Life near Big Cities', *New York Times,* p. D9.

Marsh, G., and Trynka, P. (2002), *Denim: From Cowboys to Catwalks. A Visual History of the World's Most Legendary Fabric,* London: Aurum Press.

May, L. (2000), *The Big Tomorrow: Hollywood and the Politics of the American Way,* Chicago, IL: University of Chicago Press.

McComb, M.C. (2006), *Great Depression and the Middle Class: Experts, Collegiate Youth, and Business Ideology, 1929–1941,* New York: Routledge.

McMichael, P. (1990), 'Incorporating Comparison within a World-Historical Perspective: An Alternative Comparative Method', *American Sociological Review,* 55 (June), 385–97.

McWilliams, C. (1939), *Factories in the Field,* Boston: Little, Brown & Co.

Melancholy Days? (1929), *Chicago Tribune,* 1 September.

Meltzer, M. (1978), *Dorothea Lange: A Photographer's Life,* New York: Farrar, Straus, Giroux.

Mintz, S. (1986), *Sweetness and Power: The Place of Sugar in Modern History,* Middlesex, UK: Penguin Books.

Monroy, D. (2006), 'Los Angeles Garment Workers' Strike', in V. Ruiz (ed.), *Latinas in the United States,* Minneapolis: Indiana University Press, pp. 408–10.

'More Ranches for Dudes' (1936), *New York Times,* 14 June.

'Pay Rises Sought in Cotton Trades' (1941), *New York Times,* 21 March, p. 23.

'Plants Here Speed Clothing for Army' (1941), *New York Times,* 12 January, p. 40.

Pope, V. (1941), 'Defense Workers Inspire New Mode', *New York Times,* 8 August.

Rabine, L. and Kaiser, S. (2006), 'Sewing Machines and Dream Machines in Los Angeles and San Francisco: The Case of the Blue Jean', in C. Breward and D. Gilbert (eds), *Fashion's World Cities,* New York: Oxford, pp. 235–50.

Ray, G.E. (1941), 'Down the Long Pack Trail', *Independent Woman,* 22 (July): 202–4.

Robertson, P. (1996), *Guilty Pleasures: Feminist Camp from Mae West to Madonna,* Durham: Duke University Press.

Schnapper, B.M. (1939), 'Recruits are Ready for War', *Washington Post,* 8 October.

Scott, J. (1939), 'Current Film and Play Productions … Hollywood Today', *Los Angeles Times,* 5 March, p. C4.

Sewell, W. (2005), *Logics of History: Social Theory and Social Transformation,* Chicago: University of Chicago Press.

'She is Not Sure Where She is Heading in This Angry World …' (1941), *New York Times,* 7 December.

Sheeler, C. (1978), *The Rouge, the Image of Industry in the Art of Charles Sheeler and Diego Rivera,* Detroit: Detroit Institute of Arts.

Slotkin, R. (1992), *Gunfighter Nation: The Myth of the Frontier in Twentieth-century America,* New York: Atheneum.

Staff. (1925), 'Chain Store Expanding', *Los Angeles Times,* 21 July, p. 16.

Staff. (1928), 'Penney to Show Gain in Earnings', *Los Angeles Times,* 21 December, p. 7.

Staff. (1930), 'Penney Cuts Prices to New Cost Basis', *New York Times,* 22 June, p. N18.

Staff. (1931), 'Many Sears Prices Back to 1913 Level', *Wall Street Journal,* 22 May, p. 4.

Staff. (1932), 'Sears Cuts Prices, Stresses Quality', *Wall Street Journal,* 16 July, p. 11.

Staff. (1933), 'Two Men's Clothing Codes'. *New York Times,* 18 July, p. 9.

Staff. (1936), 'AFL Strikes Back', *Wall Street Journal,* 23 November, p. 4.

Steinbeck, J. (1936), 'The Harvest Gypsies', *San Francisco News,* 5–12 October.

Steinbeck, J. (1938), *Their Blood is Strong,* San Francisco: Simon J. Lubin Society of California.

Steinbeck, J. (2002), *The Grapes of Wrath,* New York: Penguin.

Stott, W. (1973), *Documentary Expression and Thirties America,* New York: Oxford University Press.

Taylor, P.S. (1936a), 'Again the Covered Wagon', *Survey Graphic,* 24: 349.

Taylor, P.S. (1936b), 'From the Ground Up', *Survey Graphic,* 25: 526–9.

Thomas, D. (1935), 'Katie Gets a Haircut', *Washington Post,* 29 September, p. SM3.

'Twenty Percent of Small Town Stores are Chains' (1933), *Wall Street Journal,* 29 November, p. 6.

Warner, P.C. and Ewing, M. (2002), 'Wading in the Water: Women Aquatic Biologists Coping with Clothing, 1877–1945', *BioScience,* 52(1): 97–104.

Welters, L., and Cunningham, P.A. (2005), *Twentieth-Century American Fashion,* Oxford: Berg.

Wolensky, K.C., Wolensky, N.H. and Wolensky, R.P. (2002), *Fighting for the Union Label: The Women's Garment Industry and the ILGWU in Pennsylvania,* University Park, PA: Pennsylvania State University Press.

'Work Clothing Sales Pointed to Employment Turn March 1' (1930), *New York Times,* 30 March, p. N22.

Zimmerman. (1998), 'Western Beginnings', unpublished Master's thesis, American Studies Program, University of Virginia, http://xroads.virginia.edu/~MA98/zimmerman/duderanch/front.html (accessed 14 June 2010).

Films cited

Chaplin, C. (prod.) (1936), *Modern Times,* United Artists.

Lorentz, P. (prod.) (1936), *The Plow that Broke the Plains,* Resettlement Administration.

Zanuck, D. (prod.) (1940), *The Grapes of Wrath,* 20th Century Fox.

–2–

Diverting Denim: Screening Jeans in Bollywood

Clare M. Wilkinson-Weber

Introduction

During a research visit to Bombay in 2008, I asked a young costume assistant, as we sat talking in a suburban Bombay coffee house, how often she had sourced jeans for films. She replied: 'Denim is big in films. Our actors are wearing denim throughout the film. They have to have jeans, unless they are wearing a suit. I cannot think of a film where we haven't used jeans, even actresses.'

There is nothing particularly striking about this statement until one considers that as recently as the late 1980s it would have been inconceivable. It is possible to watch several popular Hindi films from the 1960s and 1970s in their entirety, even those films with a reputation for being fashionable for their time, and not see a single blue jean or denim jacket.

Only with the transformation in the Indian economy of the late 1980s and 1990s did denim begin to make a more frequent and prominent appearance in Indian media.[1] Since then, in the midst of Bollywood's undimmed enthusiasm for spectacular costume, jeans have made a remarkable and somewhat quieter shift towards costume normativity. The increasing momentum of a consumerism that began in the 1980s has vastly expanded opportunities for, among other things, ready-made clothes consumption (Mazumdar 2007: xxi; Vedwan 2007: 665; Virdi 2003). The quickening pace of the appropriation of denim for film costume directly coincides with this phenomenon, and film remains an influential and in some cases the dominant visual source for the artefacts and practices of consumerism in the sub-continent (Mazumdar 2007:18 and Miller, this volume).

The first part of this essay sketches shifts in the occurrence and meaning of jeans in film costuming in the tradition of the majority of film costume studies (e.g. Berry 2000; Bruzzi 1997; Dwyer 2000; Gaines and Herzog 1990; Moseley 2005; Street 2001). If jeans, as Miller and Woodward (2007) argue, are a prism through which to examine some of the anxieties associated with modernity, the 'career' of jeans in popular Hindi film elaborates and seeks to resolve the lingering anxiety about 'what to wear' that has vexed Indian consumers since colonial times (Tarlo 1996). In the second half, I go beyond conventional analyses to show that the screen images at issue are predicated on material practices that make judicious and tactical use of brands, fakes, and copies both in Bombay and in other market places. In the subculture of Bombay media production, these practices illustrate and respond specifically to the anxieties of Bollywood stars who are the most prominent models of jeans-wearing for the Indian public. Even in Bollywood films, despite the fantastic settings which remain exotic and remote to most South Asian viewers, jeans have emerged as everyday clothing (Miller and Woodward 2007; Sassatelli this volume) that lack the existing cues to sartorial distinction associated with most Indian garments (Banerjee and Miller 2008; Tarlo 1996). Jeans on film are not like couture items that 'speak' on their own terms (e.g. Bruzzi 1997). Instead left to themselves they would 'speak' in largely uniform tones about sexuality, relationships, and personal autonomy in ways that supersede their particular use in any given narrative context. This is because they first designate their sameness and predictability (Miller and Woodward 2007: 343) – the same range of colours, the arrangement of rivets, the subtle variations on one form. But to the individuals who wear them, for whom dress is a critical signifier of their personal charisma and celebrity, all this is insufficient. In order to emphasize their own distinction (Bourdieu 1984) stars will try to display brands publicly; if they cannot, they strive for distinction through fusing their personal jeans choices with their portrayal of characters – choices that are delegated to designers and their assistants to actualize. This is a power that stars wield, which is denied to character actors, extras – even the star's double.

These brand assertions implicitly articulate the limits of Bombay's retail ecology, placing a firm constraint upon the extent to which a mere film fan can emulate the stars. Those disappointed at not looking like their film idols when they buy their clothes may feel that 'what one sees is not what one gets' but, conversely, from the point of view of the costumer, 'what one gets is not necessarily what one sees'. The game of illusion, effacement and manipulation starts long before the film hits the theatres.

Jeans and the Spectacular: Denim on Screen

The film industry in Mumbai (still referred to in film circles and in this chapter as Bombay) has the distinction of being the best known nationally and globally of all the various film centres in India (Dwyer and Patel 2002: 8; Ganti 2004: 3; Mazumdar 2007: xviii; Rajadhyaksha 2003). Since its earliest years, costume has been one of the distinct visual pleasures associated with film going (Bhaumik 2005:90; Dwyer 2000; Dwyer and Patel 2002: 52; Wilkinson-Weber 2005: 143). If what is spectacular is in part what can either not be appropriated or only appropriated with considerable qualification, then jeans indeed belong next to the lavish costume displays that few Indians would dream of copying without considerable modification; as Miller points out in his study of denim in Kannur in this volume, jeans in India remain the clothing choice of a few rather than, as in other countries of the world, the many. On the other hand, urban middle and upper classes, both male and female, and young people across an even wider social span, find it easier than ever to buy jeans now that domestic or imported (often fake) versions from elsewhere in Asia provide a range of price and quality alongside foreign high-priced labels. When these consumers judge a costume's 'wearability' as clothing, they are now making assessments of cost as much as whether it complies with social standards of attire (Berry 2000: xiv). Jeans unlike almost any other garment are thus tenuously poised between the spectacular and the mundane.

That the clothed celebrity body inspires aspiration and emulation is a widely accepted maxim, holding that clothing possibilities are imaginatively anticipated via film viewing before being actualized in shopping and wearing practice (Berry 2000; Dwyer and Patel 2002; Eckert 1990; Stacey 1994; Street 2001: 7; Wilkinson-Weber 2006). For viewers to be able to anticipate their own, comparable experiments in dress, a certain naturalism in the depiction of characters and settings is needed so that costumes can seem minimally 'wearable'. More than this, though, the materials, practices and institutions (social and ideological) to foster emulation must exist, or otherwise film viewers would not dream of 'dressing up' like their favourite actors. In India, the personal tailor or menswear store until recently had the almost exclusive ability to facilitate the customer's desire to emulate movie costumes until the relaxation of curbs on foreign imports and an exploding market in consumer goods in the 1990s (Sheikh 2007; Wilkinson-Weber 2005). From this point began a growth of new shopping practices, spaces and dress conventions. Hindi film has arguably, via its fascination with the material accoutrements of status and power, long been making the case for what Berry (2000: xiii) terms a 'symbolic economy' in which the management of appearances amounts to a complex set of moral statements about selves in class, caste, and patriarchal contexts. Film not only models (in every sense of the word) the kind of clothes that are central to these locations and experiences, but costume itself is central to the definition of occupations, lifestyles and identities that distinguish the new, globally-aware, Indian citizen, be these corporate executives, ganglords, reporters, even NASCAR (US based stock-car racing) drivers, and a host of others.[2]

Male Hindi movie actors – 'heroes' or stars, and some supporting or character actors – began wearing denim jeans and jackets in their films in the early to mid-1970s. By the later 1970s female film stars – 'heroines' – were doing so as well. Despite the apparent naturalism of the contexts in which jeans were worn, the wearing of denim by stars bore little resemblance to the actual reality in which the film was imaginatively located. Still comparatively scarce, and by no means shared by all the stars in the star pantheon, film uses of denim came well in advance of when jeans and jackets began to be accepted even among the middle classes, as appropriate apparel for Indian bodies.[3]

Jeans, when they appeared, were typically signifiers of characters exploring new forms of identity and social mobility. It is perhaps not entirely coincidental that denim came into Bollywood film just as the major tropes and themes of mainstream film shifted towards a focus on subaltern subjects and the pursuit of justice, and away from romance. Theorists have associated the emergence of the action film and action heroes, chief among them the iconic star Amitabh Bachchan, with social and political upheaval in India (Ganti 2004: 32–3; Prasad 1998). Other scholars have pointed to the emergence of homoerotic subtexts in the focus on *dosti* or male relationships that overshadow heterosexual pairings (Kavi 2000; Rao 2000). Connected to both is the wearing of denim, which, in the words of Rabine and Kaiser (2006: 236), can be 'endlessly adapted to the creation of new genders and sexualities'. Jeans, unlike suits or tailored outfits, destabilized conventional sartorial distinctions of elite versus subaltern. The star's jeans were visually central, of course, but he – like some of the minor characters or extras played by junior artists – could well be a lower class or socially marginal character (for example, Dharmendra in denim jacket and jeans as the petty criminal turned hero of the iconic 1975 film, *Sholay*).

For men, jeans were an extension of a Western-style wardrobe (shirts and trousers for the most part), an Indian version of which was already widely in use. Jeans on women, on the other hand, were a clearly transgressive deviation from Indian styles. Anxiety about the propriety of women wearing jeans in public life has only slowly and partially given way to the preferences among the affluent – but certainly not among lower class women – for this kind of attire. As a style of clothing imported from overseas, worn by both men and women, and replete with countercultural and sexual implications, jeans exemplified the 'un-Indian'. In addition, the way they both concealed and revealed the body, the way they were to be worn, was problematic. Unlike skirts that were rejected by many women because they boldly exposed the legs, jeans covered them, following the function, if not always the form, of existing clothing types. *Churidar* (tight-fitting trousers) and *salwar* (loose-fitting trousers) were universally regarded as suitable for women, albeit coded by their specific religious, regional, and age associations. Indeed, an advertisement for a fabric company in a 1969 Filmfare shows a very fair-skinned woman wearing the fabric stitched into a *kameez* (tunic-blouse), with jeans as a kind of *churidar* beneath. But wearing a long shirt over jeans, while still very popular in India, does not rule out wearing jeans with a shorter garment on top, allowing the body's form from the knee up to the waist to be revealed, even shown off (see Sassatelli this volume). Mould-breaking heroines like Parveen Babi and Zeenat Aman pushed the boundaries in their films of the 1970s and early 1980s when they wore jeans with short or tucked-in blouses. These costume choices signalled and substantiated their playing of roles that expanded the boundaries of what defined the archetypal film heroine. To what extent their roles as fashion leaders tended to destabilize the sartorial orders of dress for ordinary men and women, and thus the hierarchies associated with them, is debatable, because very few women could emulate their styles, and for the most part, even film heroines continued to cleave to Indian clothes (occasionally veering off into respectable professional outfits like police uniforms). In separate research among young males and females, Derné (1999: 559) and Banaji (2006) reported that jeans were counted among the types of provocative clothing that heroines only wore to 'please' the film hero. As recently as 2002, a ban on jeans among young women in Delhi universities exemplified an embattled institutional morality even as cable television was offering more and more models of the new femininity in the form of jeans-wearing by MTV India VJs (Cullity 2002: 421). In addition, until recently the threat of reprisals for female autonomy in occupation, behaviour and dress were rarely far from the surface in Hindi films, and emerged straightforwardly in B.R. Chopra's *Insaaf ke Tarazu* (1980). In this loose remake of the American film *Lipstick*, Zeenat Aman plays a model who must deal with the consequences when her rapist is found innocent of the crime. Casting Aman as a model allowed the film makers to make her non-conformist wardrobe central to her identity and in effect a party to her assault; in the rape scene, her clothes, including a pair of jeans, are metonymically disarrayed and discarded by her attacker.

The sheer increase in jeans-wearing among the middle classes in metropoles in the last five years alone surely contradict any notion that women find jeans on screen to be on the same level as attractive but 'unwearable' costumes like the revealing outfits typically worn in song and dance 'item numbers'. On the contrary, jeans now appear to be colonizing domains previously dominated by the *salwar-kameez* as the habitual dress of the youthful, fashionable, yet still socially respectable 'college girl'. This is made obvious in Madhur Bhandarkur's recent film *Fashion* (2008), about sex, betrayal, and venality in the contemporary Indian high fashion world. Having suffered some accumulated indignities from being a top model, Priyanka Chopra, as the heroine, makes a recovery in her modest home in Chandigarh, where she wears jeans as the outfit of the demure, contrite *beti* (daughter). Thus, contemporary jeans on film actresses are simultaneously body-hugging items that communicate autonomy and desirability, at the same time as they speak of pliant youth and wholesomeness, allowing for a certain multivocality in the depiction of screen heroines.

Bollywood Sells: Brands, Desire and Film

The normativity of jeans on female stars represents a significant adjustment in the status of denim as film costume. However, it is on male stars that the potential of jeans to communicate assertiveness and sexuality is most developed, in arguably proportional terms to the degree that women's jeans have been 'domesticated'. Meticulously choreographed and beautifully mounted film song sequences are prime 'advertising' space for clothing commodities, where the perfected body and costume combine in motion. As the opening song for Sanjay Gadhvi's 2006 film *Dhoom 2* unfolds, the viewer is treated to full-length shots of Hrithik Roshan, a star well known for his dancing, undulating in a pair of ripped jeans. In an even more striking example, the lengthy sequence 'Dard e Disco' ('Disco Fever'), from Farah Khan's *Om Shanti Om* (2007) features Shah Rukh Khan in no fewer than four changes of jeans (culminating in the curious – but critical from a plot point of view – choice of a refinery worker's carpenter jeans and a hard hat). Earlier in the song, Khan emerges from a pool of water wearing nothing but a pair of D&G jeans (in a scenario not un-like Ursula Andress walking out of the sea in *Dr No*).[4] The intent is for the viewer to admire Khan's toned physique (whose acquisition is tirelessly described in promo-tional material for the film) in the same way that the female star is made the object of gaze in conventional 'item numbers'.

Such unapologetic display of the body unclothed but for a pair of jeans continues into two current advertising campaigns that employ male film stars. In both cases, it is noteworthy that the copy emphasizes the highly personal nature of denim clothing (see Miller and Woodward this volume) to assure the viewer of the authenticity of their testimonials. Wrangler's recruitment of star John Abraham was part of its 'brand overhaul' to accentuate its appeal to urban youth (Kannan 2007). Abraham models Wrangler jeans in a series of electronic and print advertisements where he essays a languorous sensuality, reclining in an outdoor bathtub, riding a motorbike, stretched out shirtless in his jeans on a beach, or even posing as a pool boy. In a steamier video, he tangles with the less well-known actress Jiah Khan in her own Wrangler denims, ending up in the same bathtub only this time apparently naked (with the jeans discarded on a nearby tree branch).[5]

Akshay Kumar meanwhile was paid around $1.5 million (£900,000) to take part in an extensive campaign for Levi's jeans (Joshi 2008). Its provocative signal image could be seen in late 2008 over the Levi's store in Bandra (a suburb of Bombay, home to several movie stars as well as a favourite shopping area) wherein Kumar engages the viewer with a knowing smirk while a woman reaches around to unbut-ton his jeans.

The campaign as a whole relentlessly alludes to Kumar's screen image of asser-tive sexuality, but the ads nevertheless constitute a fairly complex sexual portrayal wherein Kumar is as important for making himself available for seduction as seduc-ing. His appearance, in other words, is enough to incite women to 'unbutton' him, a sign not just of his own carefree attitude to these sexual overtures but an entirely new message about the acceptable limits of female sexual expression The campaign included Indian and non-Indian female models, some better known than others, but most partially concealed by the Kumar body displayed primarily for the imagined viewer, starting to attend to the fly buttons that are the distinctive design hallmark of Levi's.

For all the pleasures these song sequences and advertisements presumably provide for female viewers, and the vicarious experience of feeling desirable that they extend to heterosexual males, these are not just occasions for the celebration of straight desires (Kavi 2000: 309). Indeed, Gopinath (2000: 285) argues that song sequences

Figure 2.1. Billboard over the Levi's Jeans outlet on Linking Road, showing Akshay Kumar in one of the signature images of his Levi's advertising campaign.

– and the more extended performances that the Wrangler and Levi's campaigns include – are 'place(s) of fantasy that cannot be contained or accounted for in the rest of the narrative' in which 'queer desire emerges' (Gopinath 2000: 285), suggesting that the 'outrageous eroticism' of denim first explored by gay men in the US in the 1970s and 1980s (Rabine and Kaiser 2006: 244) has now travelled without much interference into new cultural contexts. Nevertheless, the subversiveness of new forms of heterosexual desire remain the most likely to provoke 'pushback'. To revert to the example of Akshay Kumar's Levi's campaign, there is a statement attributed to him that explains the appeal of the campaign's signature theme: 'The word unbuttoned appealed to me. Unbuttoning is not an act but an attitude.' He is also said to 'have told the brand manager that not just the physical aspect of unbuttoning but the entire campaign could be woven around the slogan live life unbuttoned or liberate yourself. The concept is about freedom.' Such an unbridled expression of rebellious autonomy went largely without comment in a jaded city like Bombay until the 2009 Lakme Fashion Show, when Kumar invited his own wife, Twinkle Khanna, to do the unbuttoning honours. All at once, one Anil P. Nayar filed suit against Mr Kumar for 'indecent display in public', an ironic accusation in light of the fact that this was the first time he was being openly unbuttoned by a woman with a legitimate claim to do so (BBC 2009). Evidently the emancipatory and erotic associations of the campaign (and by extension of jeans) are at odds with moral stances that, while ridiculed by many in the middle and upper classes, still exert influence over Indian public culture. Given the fairly explicit link between the structure of Levi's jeans and their presumed erotic function that is part of the campaign itself, the lawsuit (unresolved at the time of writing), no matter its implications for Mr Kumar, only strengthens the message about the sexual connotations of jeans, particularly when they enclose (and threaten to expose) the fetishized body of a celebrity.

Emulation and Creation: Jeans In and Out of Film

In her introduction to a seminal volume on the feminist reading of film costume, Jane Gaines (1990: 17) writes that the fashion 'tie-up' in Hollywood costuming (or the translation of film costumes into 'cinema styles' offered for sale in retail establishments) 'prefigures the postmodern symptom of image-reality collusion: the real dress becomes the counterfeit to the movie fictional original.' Gaines is entirely correct to point to the complex relation of the 'real' copy with the 'authentic' image but she omits an earlier sleight of hand by which even yet another original may be co-opted to 'play' a part as a costume during the film's shooting. The pre-shooting life of costume opens up a new critical dimension on the 'ecology' of filmmaking, for ever since ready to wear clothing has been available in either the West or, more recently India, it has replaced at least in part the making of costume from raw materials. The clothing and textile elements that go into the creation of a costume are factors of production, subject to both aesthetic and practical considerations – whether it is obtainable, whether it fits, whether it furthers the commercial and rhetorical goals of interests besides those of designer and director (for example, the actor, the advertising company, the fashion house, the brand). What one can buy for a film constrains what one can film, just as what one can buy after seeing a film constrains the extension of identity into realms that film defines. In other words, costumes are not simply the tangible outcome of a designer's imagination, but of material practices that implicate a far greater range of social actors.

What the affluent Bombay shopper can buy is the same as what the assistant costume designer or assistant director responsible for costume sees when they go 'shopping' for a film. The difference is that only one is shopping for him or herself; the other is consuming on behalf of actors whose look they must imagine in an entirely different way. From the lean times of the early 1990s, denim is now easy to find in India's metropoles. In Bombay the affluent have the luxury of the greatest choice in department stores like Shopper's Stop, where they can find entire floors filled with denim jeans, shirts and jackets. In the Bandra branch in 2008, jeans were stocked on two floors: 'Fashion wear' and 'Denims wear.' Significantly, men's and women's clothes were displayed together by label, deviating from the usual pattern in Indian wear of segregating apparel by gender. The 'Fashion wear' floor included international labels in men's and women's jeans like Guess, Esprit, Benetton, Calvin Klein and Gas. All the models in the advertisements that ringed the space – both male and female – were white, except for the inevitable Akshay Kumar, whose same Levi's ad as an almost lifesize cut-out graced the top of the staircase. Ambient music included classic rock standbys from Dire Straits and Jefferson Airplane, underscoring the American connotations that still appeared to cling to denim.

The 'Denims wear' floor displayed Indian brands including Provogue, AND (the brand belonging to designer Anita Dongre), Remanika, Vibe, and Kraus. The foreign brands on this floor were stalwarts like Wrangler, Pepe, Levi's and Lee. On the same floor was non-denim sportswear from Puma, Adidas, and Nike. On the walls this time were several more photos of Indian stars like the actress Esha Deol endorsing Provogue, but the models photographed in the foreign brands section were again overwhelmingly white. The taste for non-Indian models is apparent in magazine and newspaper advertising as well, suggesting that the associations of exoticism and superior value continue to be attached to non-Indian bodies, even as a new, young generation of attractive 'Bollywood' stars makes itself available for advertising.

Prices for jeans varied widely and showed the cachet of designer products. Thus Indian jeans in 'denim's wear' began at around Rs 850[6] and climbed to around Rs 1,600, whereas Wranglers, Levi's and Lee began at around Rs 1,800 and went as high as Rs 3,000. At the very top of the order were Calvin Kleins, which began at Rs 3,500 and went upwards from there. Glancing at the labels inside the foreign brand jeans showed they were generally imported from manufacturing centres in south-east Asia.

Figure 2.2. A section of the Lokhandwala shopping area where shops selling jeans and other off-the-rack items proliferate.

Boutiques and brand outlets for denim also punctuate the Mumbai landscape. A stretch of the Linking Road in suburban Bandra is a popular shopping district that sprouts shop fronts for Pepe Jeans, Wrangler, and Levi's. In smaller markets like Lokhandwala, another suburb of Mumbai and a favoured shopping area for middle-class consumers and film sourcers, small shops teem with shelves of sharply folded denim jeans, and salesmen pull them out and toss them on the counter one after another after in the familiar way of small retailers.

These jeans all averaged from around Rs 700 to 1,200. In these shops one finds Asian imports, Indian-made jeans and, above all, fakes, like a pair of Diesel jeans that I was told, in straightforward and only mildly apologetic tones, were knock-offs. The jeans were not a particularly good fake, with poor quality stitching and the product labels sewn in at what one can only call a 'jaunty' angle. Their cost was Rs 1,200 – obviously cheaper than real Diesel jeans (which retail for around $250 on average in the US) although I cannot tell whether this was a good price for a fake. Far cheaper jeans come from street markets where prices drop to around Rs 200.

Despite the remarkable growth of the clothing market in Bombay, it is not regarded by designers and stylists for the biggest Bollywood productions as the place to buy clothes for leading characters and top stars. In this regard, Bombay is very different from Los Angeles, which, although not a fashion 'city' on a par with New York and Paris, is nevertheless its own fashion hub by virtue of the images of style it produces, and as a centre of textile production (Rabine and Kaiser 2006). There are also the carefully cultivated relationships in fashion and textile retail that facilitate the complex reciprocities involved in giving clothes on a 'trial' basis with the option to return, granting permission to cart away multiple copies of single items, and so on and so forth, without which the business of making costume would grind to a halt. All these chains and connections necessitate vast numbers of cultural 'brokers' in the industry to mediate between production and shop front or fashion house, and between designers, directors, actors and so forth. More recently, Los Angeles has emerged as the key location for 'premium' jeans manufacture, where production sits cheek by jowl with the star bodies on which the apparel appears.

In comparison, Mumbai has several failings. First, there are the limitations of Mumbai as a commodity market. When costumes are bought for major characters, or if the same costume is to be worn several times in the film, with variations in wear or damage, then copies matching these states have to be obtained. In the North American industry, the costume team can either pick up several copies of a garment, or take it to a seamstress for copies to be made. In India, the first option is complicated by the fact that the stock of duplicates within a store is limited.[7] Admittedly a tailor can make duplicates but there may be insufficient fabric, or the actor may insist upon ready-made – not stitched – copies (see Wilkinson-Weber 2010). I have also been told that stitching is becoming a more expensive option and that ready-mades are likely to be cheaper, illustrating the impending crisis for film tailors if the global sweatshop continues to undercut them.

The second problem is that Bombay does not have the full range of designer and high-end label clothing that well-paid Bollywood stars have come to expect. Jeans today are fast becoming the daily clothing of choice among stars, corresponding to heightened awareness of and access to brand label jeans, as well as an upheaval in dress codes that now favour an entirely new aesthetic in how stars present themselves in public (and in private as well). This is most striking in the case of male stars, for whom jeans are now entirely appropriate attire in the most informal as well as formal settings, taking to the extreme the potential of denim to allow the person to both 'dress up' as well as 'dress down' (Woodward this volume).

The attachment of actors to certain kinds of clothing labels is formally incorporated into costuming practice in North America. When an actor signs a contract for a picture, his or her measurements and brand preferences are immediately communicated to the costume designer. If demands are disproportionate to the actor's relative position in the acting ranks, then they are ignored. On the other hand, the star with a sheaf of product endorsements brings not just a list of brand labels, but the physical garments themselves as 'free' costumes. Several times I have heard designers in North America mention jeans by name when they are discussing the actors' label preferences. The powerful can, and do, get almost whatever they want: 'it gets to be $300 jeans. And all labels.' They may even ask for jeans for their friends who accompany them on set. Sometimes this is because actors blatantly 'want to take home clothes at the end of the movie' for their own personal wear after the film is over, and jeans make for more adaptable, useful articles than excessive or spectacular costumes. As a result, 'the first thing an actor tells us is what type of jean he wears so he can take it home.' No other item of clothing is mentioned as frequently in this context, showing that jeans are uniquely positioned to span the professional and the personal, the gap between character and actor, in part because of their easy movement on and off set.

In India, stars who have long been accustomed to the personal attention of the designer, or the personal service of tailors, now construct a personal association with particular brand labels. Coming to a production with a list of brands may not yet be common practice, but because stars favour having their own personal designer for their film work, the designer is the one most likely to be entrusted with obtaining their brand preferences. Jeans are mentioned more than any other item when an actor's likes and dislikes are discussed. One actor, I was told, 'wears nothing but Calvin Klein, he wouldn't wear anything else. If I were to take Levi's to him he would throw it in my face, that he won't wear it.' In fact, 'our actors are not used to wearing Indian brands at all, if there is a tie-up with Indian brand, what do you do? You need to use Diesel brands, you never descend that far.' True, denim production goes on in India – indeed, Arvind Mills, based in Ahmedabad in the state of Gujarat was at one time the third largest manufacturer in the world of denim cloth and finished jeans in the world (as well as the 'ready-to-stitch' Ruff-n-Tuff kit for rural dwellers (Baghai et al. 1996: 47)). Many global labels are sold in India as franchised products of Arvind (McCurry 1998). There are and have been several Indian brands of jeans – Flying Machine is among the best known and oldest – and others have sprung up in recent years. All these though are regarded as inferior to non-Indian brands, even though they find endorsements from stars (for example, Provogue has been endorsed for several years by actress Esha Deol).

In fact, so stubborn is the conviction among actors (and some directors and producers) that foreign is better that combing overseas markets for clothes sourcing comes first in any big budget Hindi movie. Diesel, a favourite jean brand that is globally well regarded, cannot currently be bought in India, for example (see Yan 2004): 'For guys, they love Diesel, because it does look and fit very well. We work with Diesel quite a lot', said one designer. The speed of global commodity flows notwithstanding, designers and actors view Bombay fashion as less 'up-to-date' than European or American fashion. Top designers prefer sourcing from London or New York, but if time is scarce, Dubai or Bangkok are the next locations of choice. To quote another assistant designer: 'For women, jeans we get from Bangkok, they are probably copies but fabric is really good, they are stretch jeans, is good for all our actresses. They are well made with a good fit. Bangkok is very nice, very street, very SE Asian. All of the designers are there, DKNY, really cheaper, cheaper than Dubai.'

While the actor-as-star demands costumes that may merely masquerade as the character's clothes, as opposed to constituting them, it is important to note that the character is not played by only one person. For example, there may be a stunt double. It is highly unlikely that stunt doubles will wear costumes made to the same standard, or of the same label as the star. Sometimes different materials have to be used to suit the rigours of the stunt, but more often it is not worth spending the same amount of money on a stunt man or woman's costume. The need for the stunt double to match the star has been only loosely approximated in Hindi films in the past, in part as a result of the exigencies of filming on tight or uncertain budgets, as well as less stringent commitment to the codes of realism by which the various manifestations of the character body should be seamlessly integrated. But in big budget films that increasingly emphasize a 'professionalized' practice in which costume is more carefully pre-planned, and the codes of realism are adhered to, a more flawless integration of these 'versions' of the character is essential. Where the designer and costumer used to go to the tailor for all duplicates, now they simply buy items like t-shirts and shirts. The same is true of jeans. Designers do not always feel confident that a tailor can perfectly render a product like jeans: 'Sometimes you make things, they don't look good. When I pick up clothes, it does look natural. Like a pair of jeans, if I make it's not going to be as good as picking it up at a store.' In other words, the capacity of a local tailor is downgraded relative to (most likely) a sweatshop worker. The same considerations are unlikely to deter the use of a tailor to make a duplicate for a stunt actor, although I have no data to determine how often this is done (using seamstresses to make duplicates of all kinds of clothing is freely acknowledged by American costume producers). In both settings, it is the star who insists on the label jeans with all of the 'branding' marks that confirm its provenience (labels, motifs, stitch pattern). In an inversion of the usual pattern in which the personalized garment is more highly valued, stars – in their desire for a brand label that differentiates a subset of manufactured jeans into an exclusive (although not singular) category – get a standardized, mass-manufactured product, while the stunt double who has a pair of jeans stitched gets a made-to-measure item.

Stitched duplicates are fakes of a kind, albeit fakes that have been integrated into film costume practice for a very long time. If designers do turn either to fakes or to cheap brands, this is not exclusive to stuntmen or junior artists. With the greater availability of ready-made clothes it is not unheard of for stars to be 'tricked' (not by designers, but by set workers like assistant directors and dressmen) into wearing fakes instead of brand label clothes, and costumers may resort to all kinds of devious practices, even sewing in false labels to convince the actor that the garment is authentic. These measures may be necessitated by either limited time or a limited budget, but the evident glee with which 'faking' stories are told speaks to the antagonism that often exists, even if below the surface, between cast and crew, and pleasure at severing the connection between star and brand that is otherwise axiomatic. In this light, demanding an overseas provenance for their jeans – whether for personal use or for wearing as a costume – may be the stars' counter-strategy to the possibility of accidentally wearing a fake. This kind of trickery depends not upon the craftiness of a local tailor, but instead the simple fact that, as Miller and Woodward point out (2007: 338) 'jeans leap from $30 to $230 with little instantly discernable difference in texture and style'.

Conclusion

From the sporadic appearances of the early 1970s to the flood of images of the present, denim has become a central signifier in popular Hindi film. Disrupting the previous sartorial regimes in which men's and women's costume was sharply differentiated, jeans are worn today by both film heroes and heroines, and conform to a range of expressions and characterizations from the demure to the openly erotic. Jeans of almost all varieties – stone-washed, stretch, distressed – are by now familiar components in the presentation of actor bodies (simultaneously as a character and as a celebrity persona) as modern, desirable, free – 'unbuttoned' in the language of Levi's – and yet unashamedly Indian. In tandem with the broadening uses and meanings of denim in film costume is the sheer availability of jeans in the Indian marketplace, culminating in the past several years with the arrival of Western brand labels in urban retail outlets. At the same time, jeans have become an essential part of the actor's off-screen wardrobe, where they strive for distinction from the mass of their viewing fans by selecting expensive, foreign-bought brand labels. Overlaying for the moment Woodward's (this volume) differentiation of habitual versus non-habitual clothing on to the categories of the actor's personal versus their screen wardrobes, it becomes apparent that denim plays a similar function in both systems. Only jeans span the two categories on a recurring basis, blurring the lines between what is the actor's and what is the character's clothing. And only jeans can extend out of the intimate domain of the actor's own clothing collection to claim a presence on the set. If the actor insists upon brand label jeans, and is threatened by the use of a substitute, it is because – as elsewhere – of the unique familiarity and comfort denim has to offer in comparison to other kinds of clothing.

Film costume is thus poised between the personal and the iconic; between the demands of the label and the demands of the designer or the star (whose singularity is simultaneously supported and subverted by the label); and between the mass-manufactured brand and the devalued duplicate that is made to measure. Jeans on film may dissimulate as well as simulate, since the high-priced brand is as likely to take on the appearance of a common article as the opposite (in fact, it is more likely to do so). On set, brands masquerade as the ordinary and ordinary jeans masquerade as brands. Together they generate apparently stable, compelling images that elicit corresponding consumption acts that themselves draw on a range of material alternatives to recreate the desired 'look'. Through their consumption and acting practice, designers, their assistants, and of course actors (from stars to junior artists) serve as cultural brokers for the consuming audience, anticipating their consumption choices even as they prepare to shape them. Just as their professional equivalents did for the dissemination of the powerful image of denim via Hollywood, so they are doing in a new setting, for a new, transnational audience. Unless, however, the viewer is an affluent globetrotter (and only a very few are) the means to copy the star is removed by means of the star claiming unattainable forms of sartorial distinction, asserting their position at the top of a starkly differentiated consumption hierarchy (Fernandes 2000).

Acknowledgements

Research for this chapter was funded by the American Institute of Indian Studies and Washington State University Vancouver. I have benefited from comments on this article by the editors. I am also grateful to friends and colleagues who have taken photographs or otherwise reported back to me on sightings of denim in India. Finally I thank Heather Lehman for her work on preparing the photographs that illustrate this chapter.

Notes

1. Indirect evidence comes from analysis of the ubiquity of jeans in advertisements and feature photographs in *Filmfare* magazine from 1969 to 1994. This research confirms that depictions of denim dramatically increase from 1988 onwards.
2. For representative films in which these kinds of characters appear see, for example, *Guru, Maqbool, Lakhsya* and *Ta Ra Rum Pum*.
3. The 'dungarees' defined and described in Hobson-Jobson (Yule 1903: 330–1) do not appear to be related culturally to the appearance of denim since the 1960s in India, whose visual and sartorial influence – if not necessarily manufacture and fabric – come from outside the country.
4. The same allusion is also apparent in Daniel Craig's emergence from the water in *Casino Royale*, demonstrating the evident cross-cultural appeal of transposing eroticized images of women on to male bodies.
5. Pitching for Macroman casual wear (an Indian brand), film star Hrithik Roshan appears in promotional photographs modelling one of their singlets (vest). However, the most striking part of the photograph is the tagline of the manufacturer that appears to issue from the crotch of his distressed jeans. Whether this is intentional or otherwise I am unable to tell since I have not found any more adverts for this brand.
6. The exchange rate at the time was approximately 50 rupees to the dollar, and about 77 rupees to the pound.
7. I have been told by designers in Vancouver, Canada that the US is without peer in the sheer size of the stock one can find in department stores.

References

Baghai, M., Coley S., White, D., Conn, C. and McLean, R. (1996), 'Staircases to Growth', *McKinsey Quarterly*, 4: 39–61.

Banaji, S. (2006), 'Loving with Irony: Young Bombay Viewers Discuss Clothing, Sex and their Encounters with Media', *Sex Education*, 6(4): 377–91.

Banerjee, M. and Miller, D. (2003), *The Sari*, New York: Berg.

BBC News/South Asia. 'Bollywood Star in Obscenity Case', 3 April 2009, http://news.bbc.co.uk/2/low/south_asia/7981081.stm (accessed 27 July 2009).

Berry, S. (2000), *Screen Style: Fashion and Femininity in 1930s Hollywood*, Minneapolis, MN: University of Minnesota Press.

Bhaumik, K. (2005), 'Sulochana: Clothes, Stardom and Gender in Early Indian Cinema', in R. Moseley (ed.), *Fashioning Film Stars: Dress, Culture, Identity*, New York: Routledge, pp. 87–97.

Bourdieu, P. (1984), *Distinction: A Social Critique of the Judgement of Taste*, Cambridge, MA: Harvard University Press.

Bruzzi, S. (1997), *Undressing Cinema: Clothing and Identity in the Movies*, London: Routledge.

Cullity, J. (2002), 'The Global Desi: Cultural Nationalism on MTV India', *Journal of Communication Inquiry*, 26(4): 408–25.

Derne, S. (1999), 'Making Sex Violent: Love as Force in Recent Hindi Films', *Violence Against Women*, 5(5): 548–75.

Dwyer, R. (2000) 'Bombay Ishtyle', in S. Bruzzi and P. Church-Gibson (eds), *Fashion Cultures*, New York: Routledge, pp. 178–90.

Dwyer, R. and Patel, D. (2002), *Cinema India: The Visual Culture of Hindi Film*, New Brunswick, NJ: Rutgers University Press.

Eckert, C. (1990), 'The Carole Lombard in Macy's Window', in J. Gaines and C. Herzog (eds), *Fabrications: Costume and the Female Body*, New York: Routledge, 110–121.

Fernandes, L. (2000), 'Restructuring the New Middle Class in Liberalizing India', *Comparative Studies of South Asia, Africa, and the Middle East*, 20 (1–2): 88–112.

Gaines, J. (1990), 'Introduction: Fabricating the Female Body,' in J. Gaines and C. Herzog (eds), *Fabrications: Costume and the Female Body*, New York: New York, 1–27.

Gaines, J. and Herzog, C. (1990), *Fabrications: Costume and the Female Body*, Routledge, New York.

Ganti, T. (2004), *Bollywood: A Guidebook to Popular Hindi Cinema*, Routledge, New York.

Gopinath, G. (2000), 'Queering Bollywood: Alternative Sexualities in Popular Indian Cinema', in A .Grossman (ed.), *Queer Asian Cinema: Shadows in the Shade*, New York: Haworth, 283–298.

Joshi, T. (2008), Akshay Unbuttoned, *Mid-day*, Mumbai, 22 August 2008, http://www.mid-day.com/entertainment/2008/aug/220808-akshaykumar-steamy-commercial.htm (accessed 27 July 2009).

Kannan, S. (2007), Wrangler's Urban Legend. *Business Daily*. 27 September 2007, http://www.thehindubusinessline.com/catalyst/2007/09/20/stories/2007092050010100.htm (accessed 27 July 2009).

Kavi, A.R. (2000), 'The Changing Image of the Hero in Hindi Films', in A. Grossman (ed.), *Queer Asian Cinema: Shadows in the Shade*, Binghamton, NY: Haworth, pp. 307–12.

Mazumdar, R. (2007), *Bombay Cinema: An Archive of the City*, Minneapolis, MN: University of Minnesota Press.

McCurry, J.W. (1998), Arvind aims at denim supremacy, *Textile World*, 148(3): 42.

Miller, D. and Woodward, S. (2007), 'Manifesto for a Study of Denim', *Social Anthropology*, 15(3): 335–51.

Moseley, R. (ed.) (2005), *Fashioning Film Stars: Dress, Culture, Identity*, London: BFI.

Prasad, M.M. (1998), *Ideology of the Hindi Film: A Historical Construction*, Delhi, Oxford University Press.

Rabine, L.W. and Kaiser, S. (2006), 'Sewing Machines and Dream Machines in Los Angeles and San Francisco', in C. Breward and D. Gilbert (eds), *Fashion's World Cities*, London: Berg, pp. 235–50.

Rajadhyaksha, A. (2003), The 'Bollywoodization' of the Indian Cinema: Cultural Nationalism in a Global Arena', *Inter Asia Cultural Studies*, 4(1): 25–39.

Rao, R.R. (2000), 'Memories Pierce the Heart: Homoeroticism, Bollywood-style', in A. Grossman (ed.), *Queer Asian Cinema: Shadows in the Shade*, Binghamton NY: Haworth, 299–306.

Sheikh, A. (2007), Film Merchandising Comes of Age in India. In *Rediff India Abroad*, 9 November, http://www.rediff.com/money/2007/nov/09films.htm (accessed 27 July 2009).

Stacey, J. (1994), *Star Gazing: Hollywood Cinema and Female Spectatorship*, London: Routledge.

Street, S. (2001), *Costume and Cinema: Dress Codes in Popular Film*, New York: Wallflower Books.

Tarlo, E. (1996), *Clothing Matters: Dress and Identity in India*, Chicago, IL : University of Chicago Press.

Vedwan, N. (2007), 'Pesticides in Coca-Cola and Pepsi: Consumerism, Brand Image, and Public Interest in a Globalizing India', *Cultural Anthropology*, 22(4): 659–84.

Virdi, J. (2003), *The Cinematic Imagination: Indian Popular Films as Social History*, London: Rutgers University Press.

Wilkinson-Weber, C. (2005), 'Tailoring Expectations: How Film Costume becomes the Audience's Clothes', *South Asian Popular Culture*, 3: 135–59.

Wilkinson-Weber, C. (2006), 'The Dressman's Line: Transforming the Work of Costumers in Popular Hindi Film', *Anthropological Quarterly*, 79(4): 581–608.

Wilkinson-Weber, C. (2010), 'From Commodity to Costume: Productive Consumption in the Making of Bollywood Film Looks', *Journal of Material Culture*, 15(1): 1–28.

Yan, J. (2003), 'Branding and the International Community', *Journal of Brand Management* 10(6): 447–56.

Yule, S.H. (1968), *Hobson-Jobson: A Glossary of Colloquial Anglo-Indian Words and Phrases, and of Kindred Terms, Etymological, Historical, Geographical and Discursive by Henry Yule and A.C. Burnell,* Delhi: Munshiram Manoharlal.

Films cited

Akhtar, F. (dir.) (2004), *Lakshya*, UTV Communications.

Anand, S. (dir.), *Ta ra rum pum,* Yash Raj Films

Bhandarkar, M. (dir.) (2008), *Fashion*, UTV Communications.

Bhardwaj, V. (dir.) (2003), *Maqbool*, Yash Raj Films.

Campbell, M. (dir.) (2007), *Casino Royale*, Sony.

Chopra, B.R. (dir.) (1980), *Insaaf ka Tarazu*, B.R. Films.

Gadhvi, S. (dir.) (2006), *Dhoom 2: Back in Action,*Yash Raj Films.

Johnson, L. (dir.) (1976), *Lipstick*, Paramount.

Khan, F. (dir.) (2007), *Om Shanti Om*, Eros.

Ratnam, M. (dir.) (2007), *Guru*, Madras Talkies.

Sippy, R. (dir.), *Sholay*, Sippy Films.

Young, T. (dir.) (1962), *Dr No*, United Artists.

–3–

How Blue Jeans went Green: The Materiality of an American Icon

Bodil Birkebæk Olesen

First they built the country's infrastructure,
then they populated it with a collective identity

(Sullivan 2006: 6)

In his book from 2006, James Sullivan traces the history of jeans in America, or what he terms 'the American uniform' (Sullivan 2006: 8), from their humble nine-teenth-century work-wear origins to their present status as 'the best-selling and most volatile garment of them all' (Sullivan 2006: 10). His comprehensive account, rang-ing from discussions of the origins of the name denim to its only recently terminated recycled use in American dollar bills, from the ascension of 'lifestyle brands' like Diesel and Lucky to their role in advertising, demonstrates the multitude of ways in which 'jeans have come to embody two centuries worth of the myths and ideals of American culture' (Sullivan 2006: 3). As his account makes clear, this particular iconic relationship between a garment and a culture encompasses both the past and the present, the symbolic and the material, imbuing any individual act of wearing jeans with significance that transcends the act itself.

This relationship between jeans and American identity is a dynamic one that keeps changing and expanding, and it is not restricted to the iconic repertoire described by Sullivan. In this chapter I move beyond a predominantly semiotic perspective by taking as my starting point the role of jeans in consolidating and transforming American normative values, and more specifically their significance in transforming such values as they include issues of ethical consumption and environmentalism. My specific focus is on the so-called denim drives, organized by Cotton Incorporated since 2006. In these drives American consumers are given the opportunity to donate their old pairs of jeans, which are processed into eco-friendly insulation material and used in charity projects. Discussing these campaigns in some detail, I place them in a context of environmental concerns, a growing interest in ethical consumerism as well as the increasing attention of corporations to improve and promote their public image. I suggest that jeans constitute an ideal object of donation in these campaigns because of their multivocality, and their well established role in materializing and performing normative American values. I also trace the material transformation of jeans into insulation material, more specifically the political and economic circumstances that influence the applications of such reclaimed fibre material. By doing so, I show how the success of these campaigns also depend on the material properties of the American uniform, and, ironically, on the popularity of the garment itself. This account thus offers further insight into jeans' significance in America while also illustrating that in order to understand the contemporary dynamics of jeans metamorphosis from blue to green we have to work with the entire range of its properties, which include material propensities, social and economic contexts, and symbolic and cosmological meanings of this material.

Symbolic Ubiquity and Material Omnipresence

As indicated by Sullivan in the epigraph that opens this chapter, one of the most interesting aspects of the history of jeans in America is that while originally their adoption rested in their use value, their continued popularity instead tied to their sign value. It was the robustness, durability and availability at a low price that made jeans the work wear of choice with nineteenth-century frontier miners and farmers, and this early adoption became articulated in advertisement as originality and authenticity that continue to be important to the Levi's as a brand. But while the garment's original, utilitarian status may be well suited for articulating an emerging national identity, what is equally remarkable about jeans in America is the garment's ubiquity as a signifier in conjunction with the diversity of what it signifies (Davis 1989: 347–52; Rabine and Kaiser 2006: 236). The 'basic building blocks of all hippie wardrobes' (Melinkoff 1984: 163), an expression of gender equality for 1960s American feminists, of 'gang mode' for hip-hoppers, the donning of the garment has symbolized anti-establishment or alternative identity as often as it has symbolized a national one. And the reference to the garment in virtually every American music genre, in fiction, art, cinema and poetry – not to mention advertisement (Botterill 2007) and the growing body of quasi-academic and journalistic literature on jeans (Finlayson 1990; Gilchrist and Manzotti 1992; Marsh and Trynka 2005; Snyder 2008) – has made jeans a signifier that is particularly good to think with in American culture.[1] This symbolic ubiquity is matched by the garment's omnipresence in American's wardrobes. According to Cotton Incorporated's Lifestyle Monitor research, Americans own an average of seven to eight pairs of jeans. In 2008, 37 per cent reported that they have bought a pair of jeans last month and 35 per cent stated that they planned to buy a pair next month.[2] Moreover, Americans wear jeans four days per week on average,[3] and 75 per cent state that they love or enjoy wearing denim. A slightly higher number of men and women (78 per cent) recently stated that they 'prefer to go places where I can wear jeans.'[4]

From a sociological point of view what is equally fascinating, yet somewhat less explored, about the ubiquity of jeans in American cultural and social life, is the central role of jeans in the production and reproduction of a number of distinctively American normative values that its omnipresence helps engender and maintain. Here I am not simply referring to the way in which jeans constitute the ideal garment for solving the conundrum of individualism and conformity in America (Spindler and Spindler 1983: 64) (although a visit to any American college campus will confirm how this solution works for pretty much every American college student) but rather to the existence and contents of an explicitly stated dress code. Not only do Americans attach great importance to being correctly dressed in a number of different contexts, but the explicit reference to such a dress code – often, for example, included in the official invitations to professional and academic conferences – works to ensure that everyone can be properly dressed on socially significant occasions. Remarkably, on informal social occasions such as weekend picnics with friends, family, or even colleagues, despite the apparent lack of constrains regarding proper attire, jeans seem to be not just what everybody wears but almost what everybody should wear. While the inclination towards jeans on such informal occasions may spring from the individual's anxiety about 'blending in' or 'dressing right' on occasions that lack explicit rules, the donning of jeans also materialize the conceptual distinction between work and leisure, as well as one's adherence to the lifestyle and moral values that the distinction entails in an American context. This role of jeans as a marker of collective values is perhaps even clearer in another American practice: a number of American workplaces allow a so-called causal dress day, most often Fridays, on which employees can wear jeans at work. The seemingly 'subversive' nature of this dress practice, by being so tightly regulated, simultaneously acknowledges the legitimacy of a dress code and the necessity of social regulation, but also articulates a particular relationship between work and leisure – and one's voluntary adherence to it – that the purpose of work, after all, is not the individual's selfish pursuit of material possessions, but rather the means to realize core collective values in one's leisure time.[5]

The connotations of work, leisure and the ultimately moral relationship between them, as well as the central role of jeans as the materialization of one's adherence becomes even clearer when considering how this casual dress code has recently been made an occasion for so-called community service. A growing number of American workplaces engage in various schemes for which employees can wear jeans on specified dates in exchange for a small donation to charity. To give a few examples, since 2004 the employees at Sauk Valley Bank, a small bank in Illinois with three branches and 171 million dollars assets, have participated in its Jeans for Charity every Friday, donating two dollars to a pre-selected charity or organization.[6] The Jeans Day Charity Initiative at accounting firm Deloitte & Touche's Chicago office allows its 2,500 employees to wear jeans on the last Friday of every month when purchasing a five dollar sticker. The money collected is donated to a new charity every month, chosen by the employees, a setup that, according to a spokesperson, 'really helps create a sense of community' and 'give employees a voice' within the corporation while simultaneously 'creating connections to the Chicago community'.[7] Deloitte & Touche's Jeans Day Charity Initiative was inspired by the March of Dime's Blue Jeans for Babies program. March of Dimes, a North American health charity working to improve the health of babies, conducts this annual fundraising event in partnership with companies across the United States. Like Deloitte's programme, Blue Jeans for Babies affords employees the opportunity to dress casually at work by purchasing a sticker, button or t-shirt to benefit the March of Dimes. Since 1996, Lee, a leading American brand of jeans, has run the National Lee Denim Day, on which it raises money for the Breast Cancer Charity. Under the slogan that, 'hope starts with your favorite jeans' employees at any workplace can register a team for the Denim Day, upon which they receive a free participation kit intended to make the Denim Day a 'fun and successful event' and wear jeans to work in exchange for a donation of five dollars.[8] Jeans' unique ability to materialize and sustain normative values, however, is not restricted to the donning of the garment. Below I shall describe a number of campaigns in which the individual donation of the garment *itself* has become a new, innovative way of doing charity.

'Interactive Charity'

In 2005 Cotton Inc., the American cotton growers' and exporters' interest organization, launched their 'Cotton's Dirty Laundry Tour'. Part of a $27 million advertising and promotion push it intended to sow loyalty among young consumers by positioning cotton as a versatile, easy-care option that is ideally suited for the demand of young American college students.[9] Organized as one-day campus events at ten colleges across the country, and spiced up with music, fashion shows and games, the tour provided basic information and activities about cotton garments and their care to American youngsters who, as the organizers put it, 'may be doing their own laundry for the first time in their lives.'[10]

When this promotional push was repeated in 2006 it included an additional campaign under the trademark name of 'Cotton. From Blue to Green.' Also known as the 'denim drive' the idea of the programme was simple: students were asked to donate a pair of old jeans to the campaign and in return were given a five dollar discount voucher that could be used when purchasing a new pair of jeans in local participating stores. The more than 14,000 pairs of jeans collected in the campaign were subsequently processed into Ultra Touch denim insulation, a so-called eco-friendly insulation material made of recycled cotton, primarily denim, and used by the Baton Rouge branch of Habitat for Humanity, a Christian charity organization, in the construction of 30 new homes designated for families that were displaced by the Hurricane Katrina in 2005.[11] Through this campaign, Cotton Inc., according to a press release, showed its commitment to the environment by 'producing and participating in … special projects that communicate the importance of minimizing harm on the environmental footprint by being natural, sustainable, responsible and renewable.'[12] By creating this opportunity for college students to donate their jeans, a representative explained, the denim drive showed students the benefits of a natural, renewable fabric as well as how easy it is to do something for the environment and contribute their own bit.

In 2008, the denim drive expanded to include retail partnerships. On 8 April 2008, veteran retailer National Jean Company and Earnest Sewn hosted a fashion show in New York – admission requiring the donation of a pair of jeans at the entrance – to mark their Make an Earnest Difference five day charity denim drive in National Jean Company's New York stores, inviting jeans donations in return of a 20 per cent discount on any new pair of jeans at National Jean Company. The campaign culminated with in-store events at National Jean Company's Long Island and Manhattan locations – described as a 'further incentive to drive in-store denim donations and awareness of the Cotton. From Blue to Green denim drive initiative' – on the following weekend where fashion experts and celebrities offered advice and played judge for various fashion games for customers hoping to win a National Jean Company gift card. The retailer partnership also included Guess by Marciano, who throughout April 2008 gave a 10 per cent discount towards the purchase of new jeans to all customers donating a piece of old denim at any of the store locations. Guess by Marciano's participation in the denim drive, according to vice-president David Chiovetti, 'symbolizes our commitment to the people and groups we interact with … it illustrates the Guess by Marciano brand's true DNA as being more than just about fashion.'[13]

In 2005, prior to the denim drive, a somewhat similar campaign was run by the Polo Ralph Lauren Foundation, the philanthropic foundation of Polo Ralph Lauren Corporation, a leading design, marketing and distribution corporation of apparel, including the well-known brand Polo jeans, home accessories, accessories and fragrances. Under the umbrella of the foundation's G.I.V.E. (Get. Involved. Volunteer. Exceed) programme, which provides employees with volunteering opportunities, the foundation launched its G.I.V.E. Your Jeans a New Home initiative to collect denim from employees, college students and from celebrities and musicians. While the campaign's campus events offered Polo Jeans at a discounted price to students who donated their used jeans, campaign organizer Maria Tilley explained, a major concern of the drive was 'trying to get the message (of volunteering) out to students and the community … to inspire and encourage community service through volunteerism.' Whether or not Tilley considered donation itself an act of volunteerism (and some students apparently volunteered quite a lot, donating four pairs of jeans at a time), many students seemed to have been encouraged to volunteer because, as one student put it, '60 dollars is a pretty good deal for jeans.'[14] The campaign collected more than 19,000 pairs of jeans, which were processed into Ultra Touch insulation. A team of Polo volunteers, including Senior Vice President of Advertising, Marketing and Communications David Lauren, helped install the insulation in a nineteenth-century building in the South Bronx, which it sponsored in partnership with Habitat for Humanity New York City and Bonded Logic, a partnership that gave much pride to Ralph Lauren, according to David Lauren in a press release prior to the install-ment, as 'this effort is consistent with the Company's commitment to volunteerism and to contributing in a meaningful way to underserved communities.'[15]

In March 2002, prior to its G.I.V.E. your Jeans a New Home Campaign, Polo Jeans had run its 'Red, White & New' campaign, in which college students at twenty US campuses could exchange an old pair of jeans for a discount on a new pair of Polo Jeans from Macys.com. The donated jeans were given to Swift Denim for recycling, and the profits donated, via the Lauren Foundation, to the American Red Cross Disaster Relief Fund, the September 11th Fund, the Twin Towers Fund, and the American Heroes Scholarship fund.[16] According to Senior Vice President of Corporate Management Ross Klein, '"Red, White & New" is our way of thanking our college consumer and at the same time give something back to the community. The interactive element allows the individual students to make a contribution and be rewarded for their charitable act.'[17]

Charity, Strategic Philanthropy and Cause-related Marketing

As already mentioned, there is a strong moral undercurrent to American individual-ism and to the understanding of work and leisure that it entails. And while, as I de-scribed above, this implies that work really is a means to an end, so leisure activities often include charitable elements. Church activities of various kinds, ranging from bake sales, volunteering in soup kitchens, are among the more obvious examples, but such activities also include sports events and activities such as bike races and runs, in which part of the entry or participation fee is donated to various charities (Myerhoff and Mongulla 1986). While certainly related to such charity, philanthropy has also played a comparatively large role in the US in the twentieth century due to the generous tax relief granted to corporate philanthropy (Bremner 1988; Friedman and McGarvie 2003). A number of scholars have pointed to significant changes in corporate approaches to philanthropy and marketing since the 1990s (McMurria 2008; Stole 2008). As corporations have realized the potential benefits of making philanthropy part of their marketing efforts, a growing number of businesses now try to integrate a social cause or issue into a brand's personality or identity as a way of accommodating to the desires of consumers to be generous and civic-minded citizens, although in a way that is profitable for the corporations (King 2001: 116). One of the fastest growing trends within such strategic philanthropy, as it has been termed, is cause marketing or cause-related marketing, a type of marketing involv-ing the cooperative efforts of a for-profit business and a non-profit organization for mutual benefit. A well-known and early example of such cause-related marketing is American Express' campaign to help restore the Statue of Liberty and Ellis Island in 1983. The credit card company promised to donate 1 cent for every card transaction and $1 for every new card issued during the last three months of 1983 to the cause, and collected $1.7 for the restoration. While the monuments benefited, the effort also gained enormous publicity, and following the campaign the company experienced a 28 per cent increase in the use of its credit cards (Stole 2008: 26).

In these pursuits of strategic philanthropy, the general trend has been for companies to use a narrow focus or theme to both maximize the impact of giving and to align contributions with the company's business goals and brand characteristics (King 2001: 122). Such themes are often chosen for their broad appeal and uncontroversial nature, and they are often based on consumer research, in order to align companies to causes that will make them look as good as possible in their consumers' eyes, while avoiding any potential for looking bad through this alignment. From a branding perspective, however, a corporate alignment with an ideal cause may potentially turn out to be counterproductive to the establishment and consolidation of the brand itself. For example, several companies have used the term 'dream cause' about breast cancer as a subject of cause-related marketing. The cause has broad appeal: breast-cancer does not seem to have socio-economic factors that could potentially entail discussions of race and class; it is easy to work with the Susan G. Komen Breast Cancer Foundation as a partner, and the pink ribbon has already 'branded' breast cancer. However, the growing number of corporations that have chosen to align themselves with breast cancer and research also face the problem of differentiating themselves and their brands from all those others who target the same cause (King 2001: 129).

Cotton Inc.'s alignment with environmental concerns may at first seem to entail the kind of problems described above. Environmental concerns currently have unusually broad appeal but a large number of corporations have already aligned themselves with environmental issues (including Wal-Mart's Acres for America programme and General Motors' partnership with the Nature Conservancy) As the number increases, and an institution's or corporations' demonstrated effort to minimize their environmental impact is to be expected as part of good business conduct, the expectations of a corporate commitment to improving the health of the planet may in itself be insufficient basis for brand differentiation. In this light, Cotton Inc.'s denim drive may not so much be a dream cause as a dream medium for a great cause, with the additional benefit of simultaneously branding one's product as a great product. The collection of used jeans rather than money, and the donation of these jeans to a good cause, not only allows Cotton Inc. to demonstrate its concern for environmental and social issues, but also to position the product it promotes as 'natural' and therefore 'good for the environment' at the same time.[18] While the relatively innovative interactive component of jeans donation may contribute to establishing the brand, it also dramatizes the notion of charity to the consumer by facilitating an embodied experience of being an ethical consumer by literally 'doing something for the environment' in the sense of bringing a pair of jeans and handing them over on location. Moreover, this compassionate act of environmentalism requires minimal effort and sacrifice as it takes place in a context of music and game events on college campuses or in clothes stores, and the sacrifice of giving up an old pair of jeans is instantly rewarded with the opportunity to replace them with a brand new pair – at a bargain price.

I would argue that an equally significant element of the drives' efficacy is the multivocality of the meaning of jeans themselves, as well as their ability to index normative value. The ubiquitous evocations of jeans in films, advertisements, music, and fiction simultaneously provides a repertoire of symbolic meaning to draw upon in a dynamic way, allowing them to resonate broadly with, and simultaneously unify, issues of personal identity, patriotism and charity/good moral conduct. And their material presence, and the lived experience of belonging that wearing them facilitates, amplifies the experience of personal compassion and engagement that arises from giving them away in the denim drives. In other words, while they are the ideal garment for these campaigns because everyone has a pair to donate, their centrality in normative rallying serves to amplify the idea that participating in these campaigns is important, good, and productive. The multivocality of the American uniform and its normative significance thus continue to inform the practices involving jeans even as they become objects of exchange.[19]

From the Sociology of Clothing to the Engineering of Fibrous Materials

However, this act of exchange also entails a transition for jeans from a garment to a generic material. In the following, I describe the qualities of jeans that are central to their utility as an insulation material. The main constituent of cotton and other vegetable fibres is cellulose, a polymer, or macromolecule. It is the particular arrangement of these polymers into long chains in a fibre that determines its chemical, physical and mechanical properties such as strength, elongation and absorbance (Collier and Tortora 2000: 34). When a garment ceases to have use value for a consumer and is discarded, and when garment production generates large quantities of trimmings and clippings with no utility for production, which are thus classified as waste, from an engineering point of view such discarded items remain fibrous materials and therefore have potential for further applications. Cost is often paramount to these applications. Although the range of applications is limited by the fact that the fibres have been used for clothing, they often constitute a cheaper material than virgin cotton fibre and they are therefore valuable in cases where the novelty of the fibre is not crucial.[20]

The economic and material potential of pre-consumer waste, consisting of clippings and thread, is often unleashed by returning such waste to its original fibrous state. The fabrics and thread are subjected to the action of disintegrating machines, which pull the rags apart and break them up followed by a succession of garnet machines of increasing fineness whereby the threads that composed the original textile are unravelled into their constituent fibres. This process compromises the mechanical properties of the fibre, making it better suited for applications exploiting a variety of cotton fibres' other properties including stuffing in mattresses and pillows, carpet underlay, and floor padding. For many of these applications the reclaimed fibre is processed further into so-called nonwovens, which are sheets, webs or bats of fibres that are bonded to each other by adding an adhesive such as resin, fusing the fibres thermally or chemically, or by stitching them.[21]

In addition to the properties of the particular fibre and the technological possibilities for tailoring them to particular ends, possible applications are equally subject to social values, supply and demand, and national and international legislation. The use of reclaimed cotton fibre in various applications, for example, has changed continuously since the mid-1970s due to various political and economic factors. Cotton fibre was a common content in carpet underlay and door panels in the automotive industry until the early 1970s when it was replaced by synthetic fibre in an attempt to reduce the weight of vehicles, thereby making them more fuel-efficient. However, as the cost of landfill and the concern with environmental implications (and recycling) are rising, so are concerns to find biodegradable and recycled solutions in the automotive industry. The sound-absorbing properties of carpet underlay is important: noise inside passenger compartments can be reduced by attaching sound-absorbing materials to various components such as floor-coverings, package trays, door panels, headliners and trunk liners. One recent development has been the research into floor coverings using natural fibre nonwovens, among them waste cotton, whose acoustical absorption properties are at par with existing products but that are bio-degradable and therefore more environmentally benign (Parikh, Chen and Sun 2006).

Ultra Touch Insulation

This interconnectedness of fibre properties and political economic factors in determining the potential applications of reclaimed cotton fibre is important when considering the Ultra Touch insulation material made out of jeans collected in the denim drives. Manufactured by Bonded Logic in Chandler, Arizona, Ultra Touch is a non-woven insulation material made with 85 per cent reclaimed cotton, mainly from denim waste from the Mexican blue jeans industry. It is described as an eco-friendly insulation material that is free of the carcinogens and formaldehyde found in conventional fibreglass insulation. The reclaimed cotton fibre, processed by an independent American garnetter prior to its manufacture at Bonded Logic, is subject to a treatment process that treats each fibre with a fireproofing solution. The material is then mixed with polyolefin fibres, which, when the mixture is heated, melts and bonds it together as a bat. It is then extruded for the engineered density and thickness prescribed by the so-called R-value, a measurement expressing its insulation properties as its ability to resist heat flow, as the recommended insulation properties vary for walls, ceilings and floors.[22]

While Ultra Touch has the same thermal qualities as conventional insulation material, as well as superior acoustical qualities, it is 30 to 50 per cent more expensive than such conventional materials. As in the case with cotton insulation for automobiles, it is growing environmental concerns that ensure a market for Ultra Touch, including a growing segment of consumers who have a desire to build homes using materials that in various ways put fewer strains on the environment, as well as some with a concern for the state of the indoor climate in their home: the formaldehyde and other toxic elements in conventional fibreglass insulation are believed to trigger asthma and allergies and, although such rumours remain unconfirmed, it is believed that in-house research carried out by insulation manufacturers confirming this has been kept from the public.

Such concerns are also embraced by a growing number of institutions, and while they may be equally informed by concerns over their public image or the need to put in good business conduct, it is now common practice among organizations and institutions to highlight the eco-friendly materials of buildings whenever and wherever possible. To give but a few examples, Hackensack University Medical Center made sure that it included, in its press release announcing the construction of its new Women's and Children pavilion, that it was made with blue jeans insulation.[23] A growing number of American colleges are now using their environmental awareness as a way of attracting incoming students and, in 2005, Lewis and Clark College – a private liberal arts college in Portland, Oregon – used Ultra Touch insulation, among a number of other eco-friendly building materials, for its new social science building as did University of Texas School of Nursing and Student Community Center.[24] Likewise, the Organic Valley headquarters in Wisconsin and the recently built William and Flora Hewlett Foundation headquarters in California were both insulated with Ultra Touch, the eco-friendliness of the buildings and materials a major emphasis in the concomitant press releases.[25]

As mentioned earlier, it is the trapping of air within the material that gives it its insulating qualities. A crucial property of the fibre for doing this is the length and the fineness of the fibre, as it is the interconnected loops and curls that will trap the air. This prerequisite favours the use of denim and other fabrics with a relatively small number of rather tightly twisted fibres in their yarns. Extracting the fibres of such coarser and less twisted yarns is also less costly than is the case with yarns with more and finer fibres in their cross-section. Another factor is the compressional resilience, of loft, of the fibre – the ability of fibre assemblies to return to their original thickness after being flattened or compressed. The particular yarn and weave used for denim has a less compromising effect on the loft of the reclaimed fibre compared to other weaves and yarns, and the ability to return to the thickness of the original virgin fibre. Denim is not the only fabric containing fibres with these qualities. Wool fibres, as well as fibres in a number of other cotton fabrics, can have similar qualities. But the worldwide production of wool is marginal compared to that of cotton, making supplies of cotton waste larger and cheaper.[26] Moreover, mixing fibres that are reclaimed from different types of fabrics makes it difficult to control the properties of the insulation product, a fact that favours using only one type of fabric waste, consequently favouring a fabric for which supplies are readily available in large enough quantities.

As it turns out, denim fits these criteria perfectly. Not only does the garment's popularity mean that a staggering number of jeans are produced annually but the particular process for cutting the fabric for jeans also generates a lot of clippings: denim is woven in long pieces and rolled into long rolls. Then identical shorter pieces are cut and stacked and cut in the exact shape needed, producing a lot of trim waste. On the other hand, the manufacture of other cotton garments such as t-shirts generates much less trimming. Additionally, as garnetters try to source their textile waste from nearby countries in order to minimize transportation costs, and Bonded Logic sources all its fibre material from one single garnetter in the US, again to reduce costs, there are also currently a large number of jeans manufacturers in Mesoamerica, some of them producing more than 20,000 pairs of jeans a day.[27] In other words, the successful self-alignment of environmental concerns and jeans donation that is central to the denim drives may be informed by a variety of commercial and ethical concerns, but it is equally sustained by the material propensities of the fibrous phenomenon in question. While the previously existing environmental awareness has sustained a market for Ultra Touch and thereby provided a medium for a highly successful campaign, the chemical, physical, and mechanical properties of cotton fibre is what enabled the product in the first place. But, ironically, the popularity of denim and the multivalence of its embodied meanings also ensure the necessary quantities of pre-consumer denim waste that sustains the production of Ultra Touch.

Conclusion

In their manifesto for a study of denim (2007), Miller and Woodward suggest that the ubiquity of denim – its global presence – is key to its anthropological significance and relevance for ethnographic investigation. While its global presence speaks to the socio-economic forces shaping our contemporary world, the specificity and plethora of its local appropriations allows us to probe, perhaps with more depth and sophistication than would be provided by any other study of a single commodity, the condition of global modernity. This chapter has shown that, as we move beyond a narrow focus on representation or the scrutiny of a singular domain or genre in which jeans are found to inquire into their dynamic relationship with everyday, sartorial practices, we can begin to see an additional dimension of such ubiquity, which is particularly significant for jeans in America. This significance, as Miller and Woodward also contend, is not simply that people everywhere wear the same garment, but rather that within regional boundaries this ubiquity can become the very medium through which specific values are created and sustained, contested and circumvented. But what is worth highlighting here is perhaps the historical depth and cultural breadth that is so unique to jeans in America, coupled with their moral dimension and the manifold aspects of American-ness that wearing them entails. There is, I believe, something unique, a unique capacity perhaps, to objects with a very long and diverse cultural history and the significance, meanings, and value they can create and sustain. Not only do almost all Americans wear jeans – this ubiquity has considerable time depth, since they have worn them pretty much since the birth of their country as a nation-state. And as my introductory quote by Sullivan suggests, this capacity is rooted in the fact that the garment is worn – that it is a material entity. It was worn because it was durable and comfortable, then it was worn because it once was worn by people who appreciated its durability and comfort, or because James Dean wore it, or because so many people wear it that it makes you feel 'safe' and comfortable. And, as described earlier, the ubiquity of references to jeans in America – in songs, in movies, fiction, ads, poetry, the arts – as well as their ubiquity in particular social contexts – on campuses, at Sunday picnics, on Fridays in workplace charity events – has made jeans in America particular sedentary objects. That is to say they are simply there, ready and present, for actors to draw upon in their own expressive practices. As I have suggested, one implication of this sedentary nature of jeans is that the normative values that are expressed through jeans in so many contexts give it a unique mobilizing capacity for new projects that relate to core American values. Values that figures such as Al Gore (2006) are working hard to ensure will increasingly include environmental concerns.

In the case of the jeans-donation campaigns that I have described here, the concern with charity – containing varying elements of patriotism, victims of natural disasters or poverty, doing good for environment, and concerns with the practices of large corporations – the attempt to resonate or link up with values and ideals that are central to American culture, and that such charity takes place through jeans is in no way a coincidence. If one is trying to make charity appear as natural and ubiquitous as a practice then it makes for a ready link to jeans. Having stressed the materiality of jeans as key to their efficacy throughout this chapter, emphasizing their status as a piece of material culture (Küchler and Miller 2005) and following this through by focusing also on the trajectory of the garment once it is no longer worn, it is perhaps only adequate to conclude that even when transformed to a fibrous insulation material, the iconicity of the American uniform continues to impinge on the material and shape its agency.

Notes

1. On the ubiquity of jeans in American music, see http://www.cottoninc.com/lsmarticles/?articleID=168 (accessed 7 June 2010).
2. Denim Jeans – the US Wardrobe Stable. Cotton Inc. supply chains insight brief, November 2008 http://www.cottoninc.com/SupplyChainInsights/Denim-Jeans-US-Wardrobe-Staple/Denim-Jeans-US-Wardrobe-Staple.pdf?CFID=13608758& CFTOKEN=98847703 (accessed 7 June 2010).
3. Cotton Inc. Lifestyle Monitor Trend Magazines Denim Issue Summer/Fall 2000, http://www.cottoninc.com/LifestyleMonitor/LSMDenimIssue/?Pg=16 (accessed 7 June 2010).
4. Denim Jeans – the US Wardrobe Stable. Cotton Inc. supply chains insight brief, November 2008 http://www.cottoninc.com/SupplyChainInsights/Denim-Jeans-US-Wardrobe-Staple/Denim-Jeans-US-Wardrobe-Staple.pdf?CFID=13608758&CFTO KEN= 98847703 (accessed 7 June 2010).
5. Whether questioning the historical origins of individualism in America (Shain 1994), criticizing the tendency to homogenize such individualism (Kusserow 1999), or depicting how it informs social practice (Bellah, Madsen et al. 1985; Gable and Handler 2006; Varenne 1977) a number of scholars nevertheless argue that although individualism is a dominant value in America – and one that is often considered an antithesis to collective values or aspirations – such individualism is subject to normative values about the good life, i.e. it is seen as the means for working hard for the benefit of one's family and one's community.
6. See http://www.saukvalleybank.com/Jeans%20For%20Charity20-%20August.htm (accessed 25 March 2008).
7. See http://www.winningworkplaces.org/library/features/blue_jeans_day.php (accessed 7 June 2010).
8. See www.denimday.com (accessed 7 June 2010).
9. See http://promomagazine.com/news/cotton_tour_091505/index.html (accessed 7 June 2010).
10. See http://www.accesscotton.com/ (accessed 7 June 2010).
11. See http://promomagazine.com/news/cotton_tour_091505/index.html (accessed 7 June 2010).
12. See www.cottoninc.com/PressReleases/?articleID=460 (accessed 7 June 2010).
13. See http://www.cottoninc.com/PressReleases/?articleID=461 (accessed 7 June 2010).
14. See http://www.dailyfreepress.com/news/used-jean-sale-helps-insulate-homes-1.926892 (accessed 7 June 2010).
15. See http://findarticles.com/p/articles/mi_m0EIN/is_2006_May_26/ai_n26878043 (accessed 7 June 2010).
16. See http://www.fashionwiredaily.com/first_word/media/article.weml?id=614 (accessed 7 June 2010).

17. See http://media.www.centralfloridafuture.com/media/storage/paper174/news/2002/03/27/Entertainment/Jeans.Were.Traded.In.Towards.The.Purchase.Of.A.New.Pair-224062.shtml (accessed 7 June 2010).

18. According to a press release by Cotton Inc., a factor behind the 'Cotton. From Blue to Green' campaign was extensive in-house research showing that many consumers wished to 'do something for the environment' but were unsure regarding how and what to do. In addition to the denim drive, the press release explained, the organization had also worked hard to brand its well known (recognized by 85 per cent of Americans) Seal of Cotton logo as a 'natural' product that therefore is renewable and good for the environment (www.cottoninc.com/PressReleases/?articleID=460, accessed 7 June 2010). See also Jacobson and Smith (2001: 162–5).

19. The engagement of corporations and organizations whose vested interests in the continued demand for the commodities they produce or promote has of course been subject to critique (for example, Smith 1996; Smith 1998; Todd 2004). It is worth noting that in the 'Cotton. From Blue to Green' campaign environmentalism is presented as entirely compatible with consumerism as the eco-friendliness of consumers' behaviour depends entirely on how they choose to get rid of a single piece of castoff clothing. What is conveniently left out of this articulation of environmentalism is the strains that consumption puts on the environment in various forms – natural resources, pollution and post-consumer waste – and the 68 lbs of clothing that the average American consumer throws away every year (http://www.textilerecycle.org/facts.pdf, accessed 7 June 2010).

20. The best known use of castoff clothing is, of course, its use as second-hand clothing and various scholars have already discussed the way in which such castoff clothing constitutes a cheap alternative for a number of third world countries (Hansen 2000; Norris 2005).

21. See http://www.inda.org/Glossary.pdf (accessed 7 June 2010).

22. R-value is measured in Kelvin square meters per watt.

23. The goal, the press release explained, is 'to keep patients healthier'. The press release emphasizes the institutions 'holistic approach' to health, mentioning also that only non-toxic cleaners are used in the institution, that floors are rubber instead of laminate and that hand rails are made without PBC. http://www.sciencedaily.com/videos/2006/0507-blue_jean_insulation.htm (accessed 7 June 2010).

24. See http://www.schoolconstructionnews.com/ME2/Audiences/dirmod.asp?sid=86E03AC2EC4B4A00843270C8C92B5A9D&nm=Archives&type=Publishing&mod=Publications%3A%3AArticle&mid=8F3A7027421841978F18BE895F87F791&tier=4&id=F0AFF79F084B449085C11BBFEA307590, http://www.bondedlogic.com/news.htm (accessed 28 April 2009).

25. See http://www.homegreenhome.biz/, http://www.bondedlogic.com/ultratouch-features.htm (accessed 28 March 2008).
26. The world, annual wool and cotton production in 2007 was 2.1 million tons and 25 million tons, respectively http://www.naturalfibres2009.org/en/fibres/index.html (accessed 7 June 2010).
27. Interview with American garnetter, 23 April 2008. In 2000, jeans manufacturing firms in the region surrounding the city of Torreon in northern Mexico produced an average of more than four million pairs of jeans a week (Bair and Gereffi 2001: 1889). Columbia, Honduras, and Nicaragua are also home to jeans manufacture.

References

Bair, J. and Gereffi, G. (2001), 'Local Clusters in Global Chains: The Causes and Consequences of Export Dynamism in Torreon's Blue Jeans Industry', *World Development,* 29(11): 1885–903.

Bellah, R. N., Madsen, R., Sullivan, W. M., Swidler, A. and Tipton, S. M. (1985), *Habits of the Heart: Individualism and Commitment in American Life,* New York: Harper & Row.

Botterill, J. (2007), 'Cowboys, Outlaws and Artists: The Rhetoric of Authenticity and Contemporary Jeans and Sneaker Advertisements', *Journal of Consumer Culture,* 7(1): 105–25.

Bremner, R.H. (1988), *American Philanthropy,* Chicago: Chicago University Press.

Collier, B. J. and Tortora, P. G. (2000), *Understanding Textiles,* Upper Saddle River, NJ: Prentice-Hall.

Davis, F. (1989), 'Of Maid's Uniforms and Blue Jeans: The Drama of Status Ambivalences in Clothing and Fashion', *Qualitative Sociology,* 12(4): 337–55.

Finlayson, I. (1990), *Denim: an American Legend,* New York: Simon & Schuster.

Friedman, L.J. and McGarvie, M.D. (eds) (2003), *Charity, Philanthropy, and Civility in American History,* Cambridge: Cambridge University Press.

Gable, E. and Handler, R. (2006), 'Persons of Stature and the Passing Parade: Egalitarian Dilemmas at Monticello and Colonial Williamsburg', *Museum Anthropology,* 29(1): 5–19.

Gilchrist, W. and R. Manzotti (1992), *Cult: A Visual History of Jeanswear: American Originals,* Zug, Switzerland: Sportswear International.

Gore, A. (2006), *An Inconvenient Truth: The Planetary Emergency of Global Warming and What We Can Do about It,* New York: Rodale.

Hansen, K.T. (2000), *Salaula: the World of Secondhand Clothing and Zambia,* Chicago: University of Chicago Press.

Hawley, J.M. (2006), 'Digging for Diamonds: A Conceptual Framework for Understanding Reclaimed Textile Products', *Clothing and Textiles,* 24(3): 262–75.

Jacobson, T.C. and Smith, G.D. (2001), *Cotton's Renaissance: A Study in Market Innovation,* Cambridge: Cambridge University Press.

King, S. (2001), 'All-Consuming Cause: Breast Cancer, Corporate Philanthropy, and the Market for Generosity', *Social Text,* 69(4): 115–43.

Kusserow, A.S. (1999), 'De-Homogenizing American Individualism: Socializing Hard and Soft Individualism in Manhattan and Queens', *Ethos,* 27(2): 210–34.

Küchler, S. and Miller, D. (eds) (2005), *Clothing as Material Culture,* Oxford: Berg.

Marsh, G. and Trynka, P. (2005), *Denim: From Cowboys to Catwalks: A History of the World's Most Legendary Fabric,* London: Aurum.

McMurria, J. (2008), 'Desperate Citizens and Good Samaritans', *Television and New Media,* 9(4): 305–32.

Melinkoff, E. (1984), *What We Wore: An Offbeat Social History of Women's Clothing 1950 to 1980,* New York: Quill.

Miller, D. and Woodward, S. (2007), 'Manifesto for a Study of Denim', *Social Anthropology,* 15(3): 335.

Myerhoff, B. and Mongulla, S. (1986), 'The Los Angeles Jews' "Walk for Solidarity": Parade, Festival, Pilgrimage', in H, Varenne (ed.), *Symbolizing America,* Lincoln: University of Nebraska Press, pp. 119–35.

Norris, L. (2005), 'Cloth that Lies: The Secrets of Recycling in India', in S. Küchler and D. Miller (eds), *Clothing as Material Culture,* Oxford: Berg, pp. 83–106.

Parikh, D.V., Chen, Y. and Sun, Y-L. (2006), 'Reducing Automotive Interior Noise with Natural Fiber Nonwoven Floor Covering Systems', *Textile Research Journal,* 76(11): 813–20.

Rabine, L.W. and Kaiser, S. (2006), 'Sewing Machines and Dream Machines in Los Angeles and San Francisco: The Case of the Blue Jean', in C. Breward and D. Gilbert (eds), *Fashion's World Cities,* Oxford: Berg.

Shain, B.A. (1994), *The Myth of American Individualism: The Protestant Origins of American Political Thought,* Princeton, NJ: Princeton University Press.

Smith, N. (1996). 'The Production of Nature', in G. Robertson, J. Bird, B. Curtis and M. Mash (eds), *FutureNatural: Nature, Science, Culture,* London: Routledge, pp. 35–55.

Smith, T. (1998), *The Myth of Green Marketing: Tending our Goats at the Edge of the Apocalypse,* Toronto: University of Toronto Press.

Snyder, R.L. (2008), *Fugitive Denim: A Moving Story of People and Pants in the Borderless World of Global Trade,* New York: W.W. Norton & Company.

Spindler, G. and Spindler, L. (1983), 'Anthropologists View American Culture', *Annual Reviews in Anthropology,* 12: 49–78.

Stole, I.L. (2008), 'Philanthropy as Public Relations: A Critical Perspective on Cause Marketing', *International Journal of Communication,* 2: 20–40.

Sullivan, J. (2006), *Jeans: A Cultural History of an American Icon,* New York: Gotham Books.

Todd, A.M. (2004), 'The Aesthetic Turn in Green Marketing: Environmental Consumer Ethics of Natural Personal Care Products', *Ethics and the Environment,* 9(2): 86–102.

Varenne, H. (1977), *Americans Together: Structured Diversity in a Midwestern Town,* New York: Teachers College Press.

–4–

The Limits of Jeans in Kannur, Kerala

Daniel Miller

Not Global Denim

Within the context of a study of global denim, South Asia is significant in represent-ing perhaps the only remaining major region of the world where the wearing of jeans remains relatively uncommon. No one place can stand for South Asia, but an advan-tage of Kannur, a town in northern Kerala, is that at least for that state, it represents in the minds of its inhabitants, a clear position midway between the cosmopolitan-ism of the metropolis and the conservatism of the countryside. As such, many people in Kannur view it as on the brink of further change that may well see the demise of much that is local and traditional, replaced by the inevitable rise of more cosmopoli-tan influences represented by cultural forms such as jeans. However, as this chapter will argue, there are grounds for thinking that such developments are not inevitable and Kannur may remain poised at this brink for a considerable time to come. This chapter is not primarily concerned with the spread of jeans wearing but with the rise of a conservatism that constrains such wearing.

The relative scarcity of jeans wearing does not constitute a relation or reaction to Americanization because jeans have no such association. When asked where jeans originally came from, or which region of the world was most associated with jeans today, only a very small number, mainly from the elite of the town, or with relatives living in the West, made any link to the US. As far as the vast majority of people were concerned, jeans are an Indian phenomenon. Many people suggested they were developed as especially tough strong trousers for mining purposes. Most as-sumed this was within India, but if not then Germany was the favoured location, or sometimes the UK, very rarely the US.

Kannur is first and foremost part of Kerala, and the news and debates that take place are dominated by the state which also represents the region where Malayalam is spoken. From Kerala the next horizon is south India, especially neighbouring Tamil Nadu, whose more impoverished population is the source of current migration to the state. Most people have very limited understanding of Hindi, the language most associated with the Indian state, and state politics certainly comes second to local politics. There are many studies now concerned with the rise of a wider cosmopolitanism or sense of Indianess such as Mazzerella (2003) in relation to commerce and advertising and by Favero (2005) in a study of young men in Delhi (see also Wilkinson-Weber, this volume), and some have applied this to Kerala (Lukose 2005). But in Kannur, the dominant image of foreign lands is the Gulf, where many of them have found work. Kerala is a comparatively well educated state and the wider world is well known, even to those who have not worked abroad. There is a global Diaspora and in certain areas, other than blue jeans – for example cricket and football – there is considerable knowledge and interest in this wider world.

The town of Kannur, with a population of approx 63,000, is divided into approximately 50 per cent Hindu 35 per cent Muslim and 15 per cent Christian, though sources differ. The population is dominated by the Tiyyar caste (the same as the Izara, excellently documented by F. Osella and C. Osella 2000). The traditionally dominant caste, in hierarchical terms, is the Nayar (Fuller 1976). Muslims and Christians tended at least in the past to be just as associated with caste hierarchy as Hindus. Historically the older city of Kannur was ruled by a Muslim raja, or quite often a female Bibi, while the modern town was developed by the British as an administrative district of the Madras Presidency, including an army cantonment, railway station and large jail. All of this has been cross-cut by dramatic political and economic transformations. Kerala has democratically elected a Communist government regularly although usually alternately with other parties since 1957. Kannur, as all of Kerala, is festooned with the flags and wall frescos of the CPI(M) (Communist Party of India, Marxist) whose influence extends to almost every local organization from women's groups to trade unions to village self-governing panchayats. This domination by communism, with its emphasis on land redistribution and relative equality, led to the development of the economic Kerala Model (Jeffrey 1992; Desai 2007) which produced a higher life expectancy than the US and better literacy rates relative to most of India. It has, however, also created inefficient and moribund state-subsidized enterprises and bureaucracies. There also remain considerable problems of unemployment and suicides amongst farmers (mainly low caste and tribal) faced with mounting debt.

Ironically, the most important consequence of higher levels of education was that, combined with its own Muslim traditions, it qualified Kannur workers for relatively well paid work in the Gulf. In turn this money has fuelled a construction boom, rising land prices and flourishing local capitalism and consumption, conspicuously evident in the palatial nature of many of the houses built by these returned workers (see Whilete 2008 for Kerala consumption more generally). The tension between these new forces of modernity whether communist or capitalist and traditional social and religious differences, has made Kannur the main site within Kerala for political violence. Killings at a low, but regular, level occur between the cadres of the CPI(M) and mainly the RSS or extreme wing of Hindu traditionalist parties.

Kannur Clothes

There are virtually no families where jeans do not have a presence or where they are not contested for one reason or another. In contrast to most regions of the world outside of South Asia, where adult jeans wearing stands today at close to 50 per cent, in Kannur around 5 per cent of the adult population wears jeans when walking in the town (based on my own counts) – made up of 10 per cent of the male adult population and 0 per cent of the adult female population. Male dress is dominated by the classic casual 'pants' that are the clear result of tailoring being simple straight-sided trousers, typically in a dull brown, worn with a short-sleeve shirt in white or beige. There are just a few named categories of trousers: casual, cargo, jeans, tracksuit, and, for length, Bermuda, short and three-quarter. The word 'denim' is unknown except as a textile. Denim jeans may include colours other than blue, with black and brown as the most common alternatives (my street statistics, however, are based only on the more distinguishable blue jeans). Around 25 per cent of men still wear a *dhoti* or *lunghi,* that is an unstitched cloth, when walking in the centre of town. Women's wear is divided: with 43 per cent wearing *sari,* 33 per cent *churidah* (the local name for shalwar-kamiz), 21 per cent *burkha* and 3 per cent a veil/large head-scarf that is more than an ordinary scarf but not a full *burkha* (as they are known in the north). On festive occasions a much higher percentage of *dhotis* are worn by men and *saris* by women. At home, women tend to wear a rather shapeless 'maxi' dress over a petticoat.

The exception here is children's wear, in which a combination of cargo pants with jeans is the dominant style of clothing for young boys. This is a very florid version of jeans, with any number of pockets, which can appear in any part of the jeans. Many of the items, which tend to be sold in sets of matched top and pants, are in bright colours and include elaborate embroidery work, or printed detail. Some of those that look like jeans are not actually made of jeans material, but in general, the kiddie jeans of Kannur take the jeans genre to new gaudy extremes. This is the start of a very evident generalization which is that denim jeans are graded largely according to age. Jeans for young children are the most elaborately decorated, but young teenagers still show a tendency towards embroidered patterns that stands out in reds and white especially around the back pocket. They may display additional cargo pants-style pockets and every kind of fading and distressing. This gradually becomes muted, until plain jeans with limited decoration around the back pocket dominate at the university and post-college level. After this jeans themselves become relatively scarce, until by the age of 35 to 40 they lose out almost entirely to plain casual trousers either, the lower price stitched pants or the high-class 'executive' and pleated forms, including chinos, that are found in most offices amongst the higher paid. This executive wear is often a formal government or company dress code. This correlation with age, as almost everything in this chapter, is a generalization with exceptions. Even a baby might wear entirely plain jeans (as was found in one expensive and elite shop in the city of Kozikhode) and one can find older men still wearing jeans. This age correlation, however, does seem warranted in the main.

At the earliest age, young girls' dress includes jeans, such as the cargo-style denim used by boys, but also skirts in jeans materials and jeans trousers with very bright embroidery, often in flower patterns with additional sequins. From around 9 to 12 years these include the distressed jeans that boys of that age are also wearing, as well as feminized versions where the fading becomes, in effect, a two-tone combination based around a bright colour such as pink or green denim. Jeans as a material is never as common for girls as for boys. As girls become older teenagers and potential brides, jeans fade from the public arena of town. Jeans wearing continues in certain contexts, however. For example at one school around 20 per cent of 13–15 year-old girls wore jeans on the rare days when they were allowed to appear in non-uniform. This decreased for those of 16 plus years. An exception is known to be the engineering college where it is said half the girls wear jeans, although on the day I visited it was 100 per cent *churidah* because this was a non work day and in effect jeans had become working clothes. This is compatible with not seeing them in town wearing jeans, because most schools and colleges have buses that pick them up from near home. Almost all girls possessed jeans, however, and would expect to wear them on any occasion when they left Kannur, whether this was a school excursion or family travel to other towns in India.

Learning from the Osellas

My analysis of this pattern is derived largely from analogy with the far more extensive research presented in the book *Social Mobility in Kerala* by Filippo and Caroline Osella (Osella and Osella 2000, see also 1999) based on over three years intensive fieldwork in a village in the middle of Kerala. This book documents the way the numerically dominant Izava caste (equivalent to Tiyyar in Kannur) accomplished a gradual rise in relative caste status, partly through differentiation from lower castes such as the Christian Pulaya caste. The Pulaya readily colonized new fashions such as the raga-influenced street styles of the local Malayalam film industry. In response, the Izava become more conservative in dress, associating themselves thereby with some higher castes.

Similarly I found that in Kannur it was the Muslim population that had become associated with fashion, brighter colours and shiny materials and were also inordinately fond of jeans. Notwithstanding a growth in the use of black and purdah in recent years, a woman in public wearing shiny materials, outside of a wedding, would be thereby recognizable as Muslim. In contrast, Hindus, outside of weddings, had become associated with dull and subdued styles. There has been considerable interest recently in Muslim fashion but once again the situation in Kannur seemed less connected to global Islamic fashion (e.g. Tarlo and Moors 2007), or indeed to

Islamic theology (compare Sandikci and Ger 2006, 2007 on Turkey, Abaza 2007 on Egypt). This aesthetic of shining, bright and glittering styles seemed more associated with the 'new money' coming from the Gulf (Osella and Osella 2007a: 244).

For young Muslim men this relatively gaudy style was particularly evident in their jeans. They tended to possess both more jeans and jeans of the latest styles. These included low-waisted jeans, various forms of distressed jeans, including crushed and faded jeans, and jeans with extensive colourful embroidery on the back pocket or legs. Clothing retailers talk in terms of four seasons, comprising two Hindu festivals of Vishu and Onam and the two Muslim festivals of Eid ul-Fitre and Eid Bakrid. It is Eid that dominates clothing sales, amounting to between four and twelve times the sales of non-festival weeks. They note that it was at Muslim, not Hindu, festivals when they sold imported jeans, expensive and fashionable jeans, including the most elaborately decorated jeans. My evidence was not sufficient to properly consider the internal differences within young Muslim male dress (for which see Osella and Osella 2007a: 245–8 on *freak* style and chinos).

Traditionally, disparagement by taste and accusations of vulgarity were more associated with caste than religion per se. Today Hindus are clearly trying to imply that this Muslim preference for bright colours is more like the vulgar taste of villagers, rather than town sophisticates. This becomes associated with an implied disparagement that almost amounts to infantalization, in that Muslim dress, and in particular the more gaudy variety of jeans, is also thereby rather more like children's wear and less like that of responsible adults in the eyes of the Hindus. As the shops report, it is not just that Hindus buy less expensive or fashionable clothes at festivals, but they are also more likely to buy jeans and fashionable clothes for their children, whereas the Muslim population buys these for adult males. Fashion certainly affects the clothes of young children as in the influence of Bollywood and other film styles. For example, in January 2008, the most recent Malayalam cinema hit film, *Chocolate,* had led to a fashion for buttons in the form of open copper colour discs, which a few months later were a trend in clothing for 4 and 5 year olds.

To some extent then it is then possible to transpose the Osellas' arguments from their village context to this town. One community may have refrained from following certain kinds of fashionable dress in order to retain distance from another community, now closely associated with such fashions. Jeans are implicated in this, where they are fashionable or elaborately decorated and distressed. There are, however, a number of significant differences and consequences when one looks in more detail at the Kannur situation. The Christian Pulaya remain relatively impoverished and oppressed in the village situation. By contrast, in Kannur, while the Hindu population, and especially the Tiyyar are numerically dominant, the Muslims are gaining advantage in every other respect. Muslims traditionally ruled the region itself. They are favoured for Gulf employment. They are now the conspicuously wealthy population of Kannur. When eating out at the expensive hotel restaurants in town, Muslims clearly outnumber all other diners, but then they are in general the more outgoing population and are more visible in parks, and other sites where families can go out for an evening for a stroll.

Notwithstanding that many Muslim women are either entirely or partly robed in black, the rest of their clothing is often extremely bright and festooned with shiny materials such as metallic embroidery and sequins. Given that, in addition, the men are more likely to wear bright shirts, such as yellow and embroidered jeans, it is Muslims that stand out as the mobile decoration of the town itself. It is not that jeans per se are associated with Muslims. Curiously even the shalwar-kamiz has largely detached itself from any such association (see Bahl 2005; Banerjee and Miller 2005), though not entirely for Kerala as noted by Osella and Osella (2007a: 239). Rather, jeans are subsumed within this larger aesthetic, so that more expensive, more gaudy and decorated jeans are associated both with youth and with Muslim taste. When Kannur Hindus make these associations there is some ambivalence to the gaze, since these jeans were until recently a conspicuous marker of success and wealth and public presence. This may well also be the reason why the Muslim population see no reason not to flaunt their presence or an aesthetic that shines to the world. So in listening carefully to conversations amongst Hindus it was clear that discussions of jeans and shiny clothing expressed ambivalence and resentments which are growing.

Today everyone recognizes that the possession of brand labels, and clothing associated with the celebrities of the Bollywood film industry (see Wilkinson-Weber this volume) represents a form of aspiration too dominant in the larger world, to be ignored, or lightly dismissed as merely vulgar. After all, it is not just the young blades of the Malayalam cinema, but also the venerable patriarch of Bollywood, Amitabh Bachchan, who is likely to be sporting faded denim in a film role. It is his son Abhishek Bachchan, who recently married Aishwarya Rai in the 'wedding of the century', who appears in adverts for jeans. So, for example, a conservative 23-year-old Hindu, who knew that she would be married as soon as she finished her MA, was starting to receive potential suitors. She assumed that '90 per cent' of these would come visiting wearing jeans. She would see this as a sign of their economic stability and good character, as long as these were relatively plain jeans with a brand. Although she knew little of the details of such brands, she would certainly try and get a sight of these labels if she had the opportunity. As such this early interpretation of an implied infantalization may be too simple. After all, children are mainly the projection of aspiration and it is perhaps more reasonable to see the Hindu emphasis on children's jeans/cargo style and other fashionable wear as more a sign of their general ambivalence.

A deeper understanding of this ambivalence surrounding jeans can be gleaned from the more recent work of the Osellas. In their work on masculinity they discuss the kind of teenager who wears highly distressed and elaborated jeans. They may be dismissed as just typical teenage behaviour, but they may also be granted an element of 'rude boy' status; viewed as the kind of men who would try and 'hang out' with women – a more forward and potentially aggressive masculinity associated by

Hindus with young Muslim men. The Osellas' analysis of various sites of masculinity (Osella and Osella 2001, 2007b), for example the two main male heroes of the Malayalam cinema (Osella and Osella 2004), suggests that the various ideal type models of masculinity found in Kerala should not be seen as a simple opposition. Rather they are analytically more a form of alterity. The various symbolic distinctions and stereotypes found expressed through religion, caste and gender form a larger structure of possibilities that are pertinent to all (compare Miller 1998 on ethnicity and consumption). Given the new Gulf money, there are now several potential routes by which these same young men can move towards the more responsible images of adulthood and fatherhood. As the Osellas show in the analysis of narratives of progress (Osella and Osella 2006), these are often contradictory and cross-cut by various factors.

What the material from Kannur so far presented highlights is an ambivalence to jeans that partly reflects the way a single sartorial dimension is caught up in a much more multidimensional matrix of possibilities. We start with a simple relationship between men and stitched pants. We then find a general correlation between age and jeans wearing. We now see the realm of trousers elaborated to signify this increasing diversity of masculine images, including the contrast of jeans with pants as executive style, but also between plain and highly decorated jeans. Unlike other trousers, highly decorated jeans can be elaborated to match these more complex and fluid internal complexities of male trajectories, as compared with the older conventional plain brown stitched pants. At the same time jeans are incorporated in such a way that there is still an overall and dominant trajectory. This allows jeans to remain as a vehicle for the repudiation of irresponsible youthfulness by responsible working adults enacted through a separation from, first, elaborated jeans and then jeans wearing itself.

This ambivalence about jeans is also captured in various instances where what people say about them is clearly contradicted by other evidence. One example of this is discussion of cost, although this also reflects the sheer speed of change in the market. Virtually all informants describe jeans as the more expensive style of trousers. Hindus inevitably explain that Muslims have more jeans simply because they have more money. There was a time when this would have been the case, and when possession of jeans would have indicated a specific link with Gulf resources. Today, however, jeans are probably the single cheapest option in trousers. Unbranded jeans in the market can be found for 200 or 300 rupees (there were approximately 80 Indian rupees per pound sterling in January 2008). This is the reason why jeans sold as cut material that still has to be stitched have largely disappeared, since a tailor would likely charge around 170 rupees just for the stitching, which now is mainly reserved for wealthy Gulf-based clients who find difficulty with the standard sizes of ready-made wear. By contrast, casual pants are still often stitched. While branded jeans can also be found in price ranges right up to 2,000 rupees, so would other branded trousers. So jeans are as cheap, if not cheaper, than alternatives.

Other factors make jeans considerably better value. Almost everyone believes that jeans last longer than other trousers; perhaps twice as long. Jeans are said to improve in appearance over time: both fading and even tearing might enhance their appearance. By contrast, all other trousers look best when brand new, and if faded or torn should be given away to the poor, or if cotton, can be torn for rags. Yet the discourse remains that Muslims have more jeans because they have more money. This essentially reflects a situation where Muslims do spend a great deal more on clothing in general and have considerably more money as would be manifest in other measures, such as, houses prices or expenditure on gold for weddings.

Although the source of this wealth is Gulf work, there is no concept of Gulf jeans. Many who brought jeans in the Gulf assume they were originally produced in India, although those inspected were mainly of Thai or Chinese manufacture. Most people still claim that Gulf clothing was more expensive and of higher quality but some are starting to admit that they were actually often cheaper, and of lower quality than at least branded Indian jeans. Things have changed considerably since the time of the Osellas' fieldwork, when fashion came from the Gulf. No one in Kannur saw the Gulf as having any influence at all upon current men's fashions.

The Legend of the Married Woman in Jeans

This ambivalence about jeans is even clearer if we turn from caste and religion to women, which dominated the question of who could and should wear jeans. Kannur was generally presented as lying midway between rural areas where jeans wearing amongst adult women would be largely forbidden and Indian metropolitan areas such as Bangalore or Mumbai where they would be largely uncontentious. There was a bit more uncertainty about larger towns in Kerala such as Ernakulam and Kozikhode. For people in Kannur, the critical image was that of a married woman wearing jeans in public. I was able to sit with people in the city centre who asserted that if we were to walk outside we would immediately be accosted by such an image. Similarly almost everyone could name some specific individual woman who wore jeans in public, by reference to which village she lived in, or some distant relative. Although no such women were ever seen walking in Kannur, the image of the married jeans-wearing woman had achieved an almost legendary status.

There was no consensus about this symbol of imminent change. Older teenage girls at a relatively wealthy English medium school were split 50/50 as to whether they thought it should be permissible for a married woman to be seen wearing jeans in public. A young unmarried woman discussing the situation a mere five years previous when she was eighteen described how upset her father had been when she first wore jeans. College principles, guardians of women's hostels and in-laws were among the many, apart from parents, who were specifically mentioned as actively intervening in this control over women's dress. A wife, whose husband was in the

Gulf, wore his jeans, but only in the privacy of her home. Unmarried older teenage girls almost all said they possessed jeans but only wore them when travelling outside of Kannur, which was now almost entirely accepted, depending upon how they are worn. Jeans, partly covered with a long loose kurta/blouse was fine. But jeans with a short blouse and certainly any kind of tight blouse, especially if a woman has medium to large breasts, is seen as a sign of potential 'loose' behaviour,

These concerns make sense as part of more general control over women's behaviour. It may help to imagine these traditions as analogous to Jane Austen's novels, (though a better guide would be *Ancient Promises,* a novel by Jaishree Misra). Unmarried women are not expected to walk unaccompanied after nightfall, or to be seen too often in association with the same male – even a college friend from the same neighbourhood travelling together to school is likely to be warned off after a while. Anything that might lead to innuendo, and therefore affect marriagability, is an issue. For higher castes, or middle and high-income women, marriage follows immediately after education and is usually arranged. After marriage, women may still be forbidden work, even when their husbands are increasing away for decades in the Gulf. In as much as love marriage as against arranged marriage has provided the mainstay of cinema drama now for decades, so too the tension between tradition and change in women's roles is clearly present within most families.

This mythic image of the married woman in jeans objectifies both a threat and promise. Some men reported that their main sexual fantasy remained the ideal of the demure, innocent female, in traditional dress, who finally achieves and appreciates sexual experience, thanks to the fantasist. But a man who preferred sex with women on top noted that he and others with similar preferences tended also to have erotic dreams of women in jeans. Jeans signifies both a loose woman but also a strong woman, potentially both repellent and attractive to men, and most likely both. This male ambivalence is compounded by the number of young men who, at least in their youth, were active within communist cadres, or were told by their parents only to study and win a place in college; both of which situations favoured austerity in relation to sexuality, but also repressed desire. In the conclusion, I will return to the question as to whether this means that further change is imminent.

Jeans, Brands and Functions

These larger associations between social parameters and jeans represent historical forces, some longer term, some of the last few decades. At the same time, jeans are subject to all sorts of short term dynamics. The shops are as much concerned with fashions that last a year, if not less. Jeans in general were not much in fashion in early 2008. The current trend is a form of casual pants with single colours but textured fabric. Some forms of distressing and fading are very 'last year' while other styles of back-pocket embroidery are trendy for certain age groups. Bollywood, and to a less extent the local Malayalam and neighbouring Tamil film industries are the main influences on fashion, along with current TV series.

There are no enclosed air-conditioned malls in Kannur, given the cost of electricity, but the town is dominated by a three-storey pink palace known as City Centre, which at least has an escalator, even if it never works. Here is found Citymart, which sells the most expensive jeans to be found in Kannur. Citymart was originally established as a franchised outlet for Arvind Mills (Paul 2008: 107–15) founded in 1931 in Ahmedabad, Gujerat, the centre of India's textile production. In 1987 the company decided to concentrate on denim and by 1991, with production at 100 million metres per annum, it had become the world's fourth largest producer of denim. It also became India's largest textile producer. As an international denim producer it manufactures a very wide variety of blended cotton, forms of fabric, and the range of distressed treatments that make up much of the contemporary jeans market. Yet between 2000 and 2004 the company was in financial crisis, from which it is only now recovering.

Seen from Kannur, while denim is now an established part of local clothing, it still remains at 5 per cent of the adult population, around a tenth of what would be found in most countries. The vast majority of jeans sold in Kannur are cheaper than Arvind brands and indeed unbranded. Arvind ventures such as Ruf & Tuf, a pack of jeans material for local stitching, worked well for a time and are still well know to lower income groups, until all such stitching became uneconomic compared to cheap unbranded jeans. Citymart has now gone multi-brand. Arvind remains an important example of what Mazzarella (2003) documented as the Indianization of branding. Since at Citymart one finds Wrangler, Pepe and Lee, all of which apparently compete, but are in fact all Arvind Mills brands, and are thought of by consumers as Indian brands. These sell for around 1,600 rupees, and it is mostly only wealthy families who have even heard of them. Another section of the shop is devoted to less expensive jeans of 600–900 rupees. These are again divided into three main brands including Newport, another Arvind Mills brand. Advertising for Newport by the Bollywood film star, Akshay Kumar (the same star discussed by Wilkinson-Weber), was the campaign most recalled by consumers. Otherwise they mainly mentioned Indian labels such as Killer, Live-In, Sturdy or Hard Currency, which are found in many more shops, including other shops in city centre that are less expensive than Citymart and sell at around 500–700 rupees. In the case of Live-In, there is a shop exclusive to that brand. Most of these brands come out of Mumbai or Bangalore. The situation is confused since virtually every pair of jeans is sold with a label that looks like a brand. In many shops there are almost as many different labels as there are jeans and so these labels are essentially meaningless. Jeans in the ordinary shops of the bazaar and the bulk of jeans for those who had no direct link to Gulf money sold at around 400, but jeans could be found even below 300 if one searched. These are probably made in the Erode and Tirupur areas of Tamil Nadu.

The most fashionable shop in town, was experimenting in new styles of display, augmented by t-shirts from heavy metal groups such as Iron Maiden. Its entire stock was imported from Bangkok. They claimed no brand, but provided different and elaborate styles of distressing and embroidering. Brand itself may be localized. For example, one business sells a brand at full price in some shops. But most of its trade is based on materials bought as textile from the same source, locally stitched, with the addition of a cheap fabric version of the original metal brand label. These cheaper local copies are made with the agreement of the brand itself. This strategy for stretching the market seemed more common than the production of fake label jeans, but most low-income consumers showed little interest in brands. Women and children almost all wear unbranded jeans.

I had thought that no denim was produced in Kerala, but the region of Kannur is well known as a centre for handloom production. One local company, Ambadi, has for many years produced high-value handloom furnishing fabrics for companies such as the Designer Guild. Companies have used their fabrics for furnishing at both Buckingham Palace and the White House. Ambadi had used conventional jeans material in some of these products, although it had a problem locally sourcing enzyme-washed fabric with sufficient consistency for furnishing. Recently, it had experimented with handloom denim. If a market could be found, it is capable of producing handloom, organic, fair trade, plant Indigo dyed denim. A stark contrast with the appalling conditions that I was told were associated with some of the Tamil sites that manufacture the cheapest jeans.

The final discourse, pertinent to constraints on jeans wearing, concerned functionality and suitability. Kerala has several months of intense monsoon during which it seems almost impossible to dry any clothes at all. Jeans were notoriously slow to dry and uncomfortably heavy when wet. Similarly jeans were seen as thick and heavy and not well suited to the hot season. They were said to be more appropriate for the cold season, but Kerala doesn't really have a cold season. There are a just few weeks in December to January when the weather is a few degrees lower than usual. Jeans are worn despite such issues.

Jeans washing has become the site of more open conflict between men and women and between young and old. The problem is evident to anyone who has spent any time in travelling in India. Along with bird calls and train whistles there is the common distant *thwack* of clothes being beaten against rocks as part of what seems an endless task of clothes washing. The problem of jeans is that they are heavy when wet. So almost every woman who doesn't have a washing machine suggests that she suffers now from permanent back ache as a result of the introduction of jeans in particular. Most young men shrugged this off as simply an unfortunate but inevitable effect of fashion. Some men stated clearly that they never wore jeans, or no longer wore jeans out of deference to the health of their mothers. In only one case it was because the man was doing his own clothes washing.

Conclusion

There is a particular significance of a site such as Kannur for the global denim project. Even if there are a hundred and more countries that can be properly characterized as subject to processes that we term 'globalization' or 'Americanization', the majority of the world's population live in the two regions of China and South Asia. These are both of such size and internal integrity that they cannot easily be subsumed under this generalized discourse. Similarly the colonial legacy concerning indigo in India has faded entirely from memory and is unknown to people today. At this highest end there is some influence from Bollywood and this use of branding by Arvind Mills, which mediates global trends. To understand the constraints upon jeans in Kannur we need largely to focus on Keralan social dynamics.

I have taken my cue from the exemplary anthropology of the Osellas. Both their original model of groups repudiating fashion in order to distance themselves from others, and their recent work showing the complex intersection of factors such as age, Gulf money, masculinity and modernity. My own fieldwork is of much smaller compass and less nuanced but there are some possible contributions to be made by concentrating on this single genre of jeans and its relationship to Kannur specifically.

The first is the general association between jeans and movement. I don't want to imply a coherent cosmology or simplified symbolic system applicable to all, but there is clearly a consistent linkage between jeans and the movement from local to external space. As usual there is a pragmatic legitimation for this. Jeans are said to be ideal as travel wear. They are relatively tough and may be worn several times before being cleaned. Jeans tend to dominate at the annual school excursions. They are what younger women wear when going out of Kannur; however, this argument linking jeans to pragmatism only goes so far. They are almost invariably seen as the appropriate wear when visiting a larger metropolitan site such as Bangalore and Mumbai, more because they are viewed as sites of jeans wearing. Then they may be worn when going out to visit relatives. An ideal time to wear jeans was said to a party for someone about to go abroad.

The linkage to movement and mobility implies a temporal as well as spatial dimension. Many clearly assume that there is some inevitable trend towards modernity in which Kannur is set to emulate more metropolitan Indian sites and jeans become eventually as common here as there. Perhaps – but there seems to be another side to this coin. The more impressive evidence comes from the various forces that work in the opposite direction. The resistance constituted by the differentiation of Hindus and Muslims in which the fashion following of the latter reinforces the conservatism of the former. Also there is the degree to which women wearing jeans remains this significant absent presence in Kannur itself. So that, even if most younger women have them, even if they wear them at college, thanks to special buses and surveillance they manage not to be wearing them in the public space of the town. This became almost a leitmotif of my work, such that by the end of fieldwork, friends were constantly 'looking out' for this jeans-wearing adult woman in town for me to speak to, with promises to phone in any sightings.

As in many parts of the world there are political, religious and other discourses that respond to imaginations of modernity by moving in the other direction towards the revitalization of tradition and custom. Kannur is clearly positioned as the site of a certain grounded tradition. A smallish town, nowhere special, Kannur, is ideal as a place that people come from; a home that, even if they never return, since Kannur has little to offer to those that have seen the world, remains important as this point of origin. This is not as extreme as Olwig (1996) found in one Caribbean island that is increasingly constructed for its visiting diaspora. But in Kannur the positioning works well even for the population that never leaves. The specific location between rural and metropolitan gives Kannur its particular structural position as a place where change stops. As a female schoolteacher put it, 'so far no one could change from our culture. Even though people wear anything in the Gulf, when they come back they change to our traditional dress.'

People allow Kannur to exercise such discipline over them because in return it provides a relatively simple and stable objectification of something that is perhaps more valuable, given the increasing complexity and nuances of possibility that lies in the jeans-wearing world that they travel to. In South Asia, where men have worn shirts and trousers for more than a century, it has obviously been women who have remained the objectification of tradition in dress (Banerjee and Miller 2003). As a result most women, whatever their desires and beliefs, continue, at least for now, to feel very uncomfortable with the idea of actually wearing jeans within Kannur. For men the situation is parallel to that described by Johnson (1997) for the Philippines, in that local distinctions act to limit the sense of being penetrated by outside forces. By creating a clear gradation of jeans wearing and jeans varieties based on age, and making the repudiation of jeans an evident sign of growing maturity, the overall percentage of jeans wearing for men as well as women, remains relatively slight.

So this chapter was largely concerned not with why people wear jeans in Kannur but why they don't. It started with an insight from the Osellas about how the acceptance of Western fashion by lower caste groups creates conservatism amongst those who seek to differentiate themselves from such cases. The chapter expanded from that example to suggest a series of analogous cases where dominant groups use their repudiation of jeans to repudiate what they see as problematic dynamics within previously dominated groups. This is evident in the gradual simplification and then rejection of jeans by older established men, seeking to assert their new status of responsibility and security. It is also there in the distancing from the most fashionable and flamboyant jeans associated with Muslim men, by the numerically dominant Hindu population, who also try and associated such brightness and decoration with the vulgarity of rural bumpkins and with infants. Finally, we see this in the constant policing of the potential eruption of the-jeans-wearing-married-woman by the dominant male population. The issue is not that of an outside, which is represented by a distant America or West. As so often, that symbolic potential can be mediated and mutated into something far more pertinent and local – here combining the potential of youth, women and Islam within the single genre of blue jeans and the capacity of this garment to assert and to disrupt.

Acknowledgements

Many, many thanks to Lucy Norris and her family Dirk and Florian for their help and hospitality during this fieldwork, which took place during December 2007 and January 2008. Also to Seema, Shibin and Venu, plus the many people of the town of Kannur who agreed to give their time to discuss jeans. A photo essay based on this research may be viewed at www.ucl.ac.uk/global-denim-project. Thanks to Lucy again for her detailed comments upon a draft of this paper. I also thank Sophie Woodward for her comments.

References

Abaza, M. (2007), 'Shifting Landscapes of Fashion in Contemporary Egypt', *Fashion Theory* (special issue edited by E. Tarlo and A. Moors), 11(2/3): 281–97.

Bahl, V. (2005), 'Shifting Boundadies of "Nativity" and "Modernity" in South Asian Women's Clothes', *Dialectical Anthropology,* 29: 85–121.

Banerjee, M. and Miller, D. (2003), *The Sari,* Oxford: Berg.

Chopra, R., Osella, C. and Osella, F. (eds) (2004), *South Asian Masculinities,* Delhi: Kali for Women/Women's Unlimited Press.

Desai, M. (2007), *State Formation and Radical Democracy in India,* London: Routledge.

Favero, P. (2005), *India Dreams: Cultural Identity among Young Middle Class Men in New Delhi,* Stockholm: University of Stockholm.

Jeffrey, R. (1992), *Politics, Women and Well-Being, How Kerala became a 'Model',* London: Macmillan.

Olwig, K. (1996), *Global Culture, Island Identity,* London: Routledge.

Fuller, C. (1976), *The Nayar Today,* Cambridge: Cambridge University Press.

Johnson, M. (1997), *Beauty and Power,* Oxford: Berg

Lukose, R. (2005), 'Consuming Globalization: Youth and Gender in Kerala, India', *Journal of Social History* 38: 915–35.

Mazzarella, W. (2003), *Shoveling Smoke: Advertising and Globalization in Contemporary India,* Duke University Press.

Miller, D. (1998), 'Coca-Cola: A Black Sweet Drink from Trinidad', in D. Miller (ed.), *Material Cultures,* Chicago: Chicago University Press.

Osella, F. and Osella, C. (1999), 'From Transience To Immanence: Consumption, Life-Cycle and Social Mobility in Kerala, South India', *Modern Asian Studies*, 33(4): 989–1020.

Osella, F. and Osella, C. (2000), *Social Mobility in Kerala: Modernity and Identity in Conflict*, London: Pluto.Osella, C. and Osella, F. (2001), 'Contextualising Sexuality: Young Men in Kerala, South India', in L. Manderson and P.L. Rice (eds), *Coming of Age in South and Southeast Asia: Youth, Courtship and Sexuality,* Curzon Press: London.

Osella, C. and Osella, F. (2004), 'Malayali Young Men and their Movie Heroes', in R. Chopra, C. Osella, and F. Osella (eds), *Masculinities in South Asia*, Kali for Women: Delhi.Osella, F, and Osella, C. (2006), 'Once upon a Time in the West: Stories of Migration and Modernity from Kerala, South India', *Journal of the Royal Anthropological Institute,* 12(3): 569–88.

Osella, C. and Osella, F. (2007a), 'Muslim Style in South India', *Fashion Theory* (special issue edited by E. Tarlo and A. Moors), 11(2/3): 233–52.

Osella C. and Osella, F. (2007b), *Men and Masculinities in South India,* London: Anthem Press.

Paul. J (2008), *International Business,* New Delhi: Prentice Hall of India

Sandikci, O. and Ger, G. (2006), 'Aesthetics, Ethics and Politics of the Turkish Headscarf', in S. Küchler, and D. Miller (eds), *Clothing as Material Culture,* Oxford: Berg.

Sandikci, O. and Ger, G. (2007), 'Constructing and Representing the Islamic Consumer in Turkey', in *Fashion Theory* (special issue edited by E. Tarlo and A. Moors), 11(2/3): 189–210.

Tarlo, E and Moors, A. (eds) (2007), *Fashion Theory* (special issue edited by E. Tarlo and A. Moors), 11(2/3).

Whilete, H. (2008), *Consumption and the Transformation of Everyday Life: A View from South India,* Basingstoke: Macmillan.

–5–

'Brazilian Jeans': Materiality, Body and Seduction at a Rio de Janeiro's Funk Ball[1]

Mylene Mizrahi

The '*Calça da* Gang', or 'Brazilian Jeans' are a specific style of trousers that has been widely recognized in cosmopolitan contexts. Expanding upon the general symbolism of Brazilian culture, 'Brazilian Jeans' are thought of not just as sexy, but as having an ability to make the wearer more sexy. The foundations for this idea lie in the original context from which these particular jeans arose. They were and they remain the main female attire at Rio de Janeiro's Funk parties. In confronting the jeans in this context and looking at media discourse that surrounds them, we can see what it is about them that gave rise to this wider belief in their power and potential. Media discussion of jeans at Funk Balls is quite clear that the object itself could in and of itself produce a body. More particularly they explain the success of the style: these trousers could 'give a bum' (*bunda*), a much-valued part of the female body in Brazilian culture as a whole. This feature became its most conspicuous attribute when it subsequently developed as a global style through its consumption by upper class people to be appropriated by hegemonic Brazilian denim manufacturers and finally exported as Brazilian jeans (Mizrahi 2003). Having in mind this mythology built around the object itself and moved by aesthetic and anthropological interests I had regarding it – I arrived at the Funk Ball.

The Funk Balls are events that take place in the sports grounds of the *favelas*, a kind of shanty town, or at disused sports clubs outside the main communities. Those festivals, although mostly attended by young *favela* inhabitants, are also a tradition of Rio de Janeiro nightlife. Every youngster living in the city will have attended one of them or at least danced along to its music, *Funk Carioca*. The term *Carioca* refers to Rio de Janeiro, the city of origin of the rhythm that emerges from a re-signifying process, with roots in North American Soul and Miami Bass. By the end of the 1980s, it was accompanied by Brazilian lyrics, and it was in the Rio de Janeiro's *favelas* that it acquired its final shape, producing a genuinely made-in-Brazil contemporary electronic music.[2]

As soon as I arrived at the party some preconceptions had to be undone. The first and quite significant one was that the style of trousers that I had recognized by the term '*Calça da* Gang'/'Brazilian Jeans' and which is the subject of this chapter, is actually designated by a different local category. The trousers at the Ball are called '*Moletom* Stretch Trousers' ('*Calça de Moletom* Stretch'), a terminology built upon the name of the fabric, *moletom,* and its stretching capacities. Until then I had considered the trousers as a regular pair of jeans, which is how they were described in the media and by their most famous producers, the Gang brand. So, unlike the terminology employed by the Brazilian media, which drew attention to one of the producers of this style, the grass-roots category led me to direct my attention to the materiality of the object – that it is made of a fabric that is not denim but simulates its appearance. The terminology at the Ball was also an encompassing one, emphasizing a wider style defined by the materiality of the fabric and referring to its larger cultural context. The Gang brand, as seen at the Ball, is merely one of the producers of this style. There, it was the style itself that mattered and not who was the creator of the style. I, in accordance with my interlocutors, also started to care less about finding out who was its first producer, even if we can say that there was in fact one.

My main aim in this phase of investigation into *Funk Aesthetics* was to examine in closer detail what became the key context of production of the taste that has given birth to the '*Calça da* Gang', known in international contexts as 'Brazilian Jeans'. The terminology employed by global media[3] refers to the distinctiveness of a style created in Brazilian lands rather than to jeans actually produced by Brazilian hands. The latter are the focus of Pinheiro-Machado's chapter in this volume. Her work focuses upon the consequences for producers and retailers and the implications of particular brands.[4] The present chapter, by contrast, deals with the native category '*Calça de Moletom* Stretch', which implies a decentring of the centrality of the brand and an orientation instead to issues of creativity and style.[5]

This chapter attempts to show that it is from the materiality of the objects (Miller 1987) and their qualities of agency (Gell 1998) that one can access the logics governing their uses and related taste. By focusing on a specific piece of clothing that, in my understanding, epitomizes some of the main features of the way women, and also men, deal with clothes and body in the Funk universe, I do not intend to deny the importance of the classificatory systems of goods (Lévi-Strauss 1966; Sahlins 1976). On the contrary, events in my fieldwork urged me to build an overall and systemic whole formed by the clothing used at these parties. Yet, the data made it evident that the relation between the objects, their symbolic qualities, would not suffice as a way of explaining the meanings attached to these 'Trousers'. Rather, the ethnographic account requires the reconciliation of several theoretical approaches more than taking them as exclusive.

Having, as an underlying conceptual point, the notion that all meaning is assigned locally (Geertz 1983), the clothing will be placed here in dialogue with other aesthetic events in the festival, such as professional performances, music, song lyrics and dance. This approach allowed me to establish a triangle within which my argument is constructed: an ethnography of clothes, the body and dance, where each of these does more than merely overlap with the others – in the end they fully merge together (Latour 1994, 2005).[6]

The Ball

For reasons concerning the politics of power governing the site I had chosen to do my fieldwork on, I was told by the party's manager that I should not talk to the dancers at the events. If I wanted to do my research there I should carry it out in a discreet and silent way. Not daring to question this, I went to the top of the stand facing the dance floor and started to watch the festivities from there. My project of considering the objects through their materiality and agency had to be postponed, at least for a little while. However, what seemed to me a rather menacing instruction produced a good position from which to grasp the dynamics ruling the party and gave me the map of the context of production of the taste and the aesthetics I was to investigate. In order to satisfy the classificatory eagerness that had hit me, the product of the pure observation, I built a system of oppositions, resulting from the contrasts observed at the party. This systematization of the aesthetics that I had observed produced the beginning of my own clarification of the logic governing both the taste and the social relations at the Ball.

My initial perspective focused upon the notions of attire and spectacle as a means to apprehend the aesthetics of the party. The clothing is taken as forming a wardrobe, as in a play: a set of clothes made for a specific presentation, with characters differing from each other according to their different social roles and the contrasts between these. The *Funk Wardrobe* is approached as a set formed by relations of opposition, established by the various elements that constitute the group of clothing and body ornamentation. The object, from this point of view, is not considered as an independent entity but as an element belonging to a relational system and therefore must derive its meaning from the chain of oppositions established between the other elements of the grouping (Lévi-Strauss 1963). The temporal and spatial divisions of the Ball allow one to say that this is also experienced as a spectacle by the dancers, with moments of climax, formations that make us think of a pas-de-deux, separation between audience and artist and intervals.[7]

The party starts at midnight and the songs played are the 'Funk *Clássico*', a category designating older *Funk Carioca* songs with more naïve lyrics, and the romantic 'funk *melody*'. The groups of dancers are divided by gender and, occasionally, we see large mixed groups. We can also see some pregnant women, often with their tummies uncovered and exposed, sometimes dancing and *rebolando*, swaying their hips from side to side. In addition, we can see contrasting pairs of girls dancing together. Around one o'clock in the morning the Funk songs played are contemporary and dominated by dance rhythms. Their lyrics revolve around two main themes: the frequently violent daily life at the *favelas* and the relationship between men and women. At this point, the sports ground is already crowded, and the spectacle we are watching comes to its peak. The *trenzinhos* (little trains), which are moving queues formed by dancers mainly of the same sex, start to move. They sinuously cut the mass of youngsters dancing on the floor, allowing the viewer to enjoy the show as they snake past. A song called 'One o'clock'[8] celebrates this moment of zenith. Soon, groups of professional singers and dancers will present themselves and their choreography and style of clothes offer a synthesis of the qualities of the aesthetic forms observed among those present at the party.

The venue has two environments. The main one is at the sports ground and is host to the Funk ambience. At the very beginning of the night, and in the middle of it, soft hip-hop music is played in the same sports ground. In a different smaller and warmer environment the romantic and a slow variation of the Samba rhythm called Swing or Pagode Romântico is played and danced. This second space is sought by youngsters mainly at two times: as soon as they arrive at the club, when the sports ground is still empty and the hip-hop is being played, and in the middle of the night, when funk again gives space to hip-hop and a sort of interval is produced. This allows a short break during the party: go to restrooms, check on the appearance of one's hair, buy candies, drinks, cigarettes and food, and relax in the romantic area.

The female Funk dance is predominantly composed of sensual movements. The girls *rebolam*, swing their hips in circular and side-to-side movements, also driving them backwards. They may also move their hips forward, according to the songs lyrics. The boys, in turn, are more parsimonious in relation to the erotic content of their dances. Some of them may swing their hips, trying to catch the girls' attention. Usually those boys wear no shirts, leaving their bodies to be watched. But they also mock the girls, mimicking the way they dance by throwing their hips backwards. But if sensuality in male dancing is not an exception, it is also not a norm nor is it its distinctive feature. What predominates in the boys' dancing are strong and straight movements, made with their arms and legs, the opposite of the sinuosity of the female body when dancing.

Encounters in the *trenzinhos* produce a proper opportunity to observe this contrast between bodies, dances and aesthetics. While the girls exaggerate the sinuous movements, the boys emphasize angular movements. They push their shoulders forward at the same time as they move their hips in diagonal and opposite directions. The female *trenzinho* is softer. The girls swing their hips, while they stroll. Sometimes they stop and push their hips backwards. They also perform a movement that goes through their whole bodies in the vertical. A sinuous line, like a snake, invades them, winding from the top of the head down to their stomach and hips. At times, this sinuous vertical line is accompanied by a horizontal one, made by one of the arms that waves in the air, beginning with the hand.

The typical male style of dancing corresponds to the clothing that the boys wear: global brand sneakers, like Nike, Adidas and Puma, long polyester shorts, and mesh cotton t-shirts, both of them baggy, that is, away from the body. They also might

Figure 5.1

wear caps, again conspicuously showing the brand logo, or leave their heads uncovered to show their hair, adorned with amazing abstract and figurative motifs. These designs are produced by dyeing the hair or by shaving it with razor blades. This is the typically *funkeiro* way of dressing and adornment at the party, inspired by the surfwear style.

A second style to be distinguished within male attire corresponds to the guys wearing very wide jeans trousers and often remaining at the party without their shirts, which can be mesh cotton t-shirts, as used by the *funkeiros*, although distinctively featured by the fact that they are fitted to the body. These two singular styles of clothing are related to equally different body looks. The *funkeiro* style is used by the *magrim*, the 'skinny ones'. The second style is used by the *bombados*, the muscular boys, referring to the idea that they acquire their well-shaped bodies not only by exercising but also by taking *bomba* (bomb), meaning anabolic drugs. They work out the 'whole week' to be able to display their bodies at the party, as they told me. Hence the preference for tight shirts, that highlight the muscles of their torso, by contrast to the wide trousers concealing their legs, which are, as they say, 'as thin as the legs of a *sabiá*', a species of bird.[9]

Eric and Emanuel are two representatives of the styles described above and each of them has a group of friends. Following their daily lives, I could note how the body and clothing aesthetics also related to different 'lifestyles'. However, a similar division cannot be made for women's clothing. The girls' attire is difficult to synthesize. Contrary to what was observed among the boys, I did not note amongst the girls a

Figure 5.2

relationship of continuity between the forms of dance and dress nor an aesthetic homogeneity in a grouping of friends.

Take, for example, the clothes of a group of friends. Lívia wears a short, strapless dress, in white polyamide and Lycra mesh, printed with a pattern of large red and green flowers. Sofia wears a version of the '*Moletom* Stretch Trousers': a clingy, knee-length black piece, with big stars formed by the small perforations made on the surface of the fabric. As a top she wears a white bodice, a corset, also very tight and made of a polyamide and Lycra blend. Irene's outfit is red, and she wears a short sleeveless top and short *godet* skirt, made of the same material as Sofia's bodice. Her friend wears a mini-skirt of dark regular blue denim, without elasticity or adornments, accompanied by a tight black top, again in polyamide and Lycra

Figure 5.3

mesh. Another girl wears a version of *'Moletom* Stretch Trousers' without any detail, and a loose top made of pink silk fabric, with no elasticity or ornamentation.

Regarding the analysis of the boys' attire, the classificatory approach proved to be productive. It was possible to identify in their taste a logic that was likely to produce a communication system in which the goods act as 'bridges' and 'fences' (Douglas and Isherwood 1979). In other words, I noticed a strong correlation between the clothing styles, the appearance of the body, the dance movement and 'lifestyle'. However, I could not observe the same homogeneity when approaching the girls. Besides that, the extensive repertoire formed by the girls' garments made it evident that any systematization alone would not be enough to elicit the logic governing the set of clothes. It was time to leave the top of the stand and go down to the dance floor, and register the girls' discourses regarding the uses of clothes and body adornments. To understand the significance of their clothing I had to look more closely at individual choices and materiality. To grasp the meaning of this aesthetics I also had to experience the party producing it.

Figure 5.4

The Stylistic Trademark of the Female Attire

This second part of my analysis leads through a complementary theoretical perspective that arose as my fieldwork developed. A temporary transfer of the party to an adjacent sports club was accompanied by the disappearance of the restrictive and intimidating figure who had initially been my host. More importantly, at the new location the funk ambience was created on a roofless terrace, which, unlike the sports ground, was not divided into different planes. As a result, I was thrown into the midst of the party and began to be ordered by the new architectural form. The absence of physical boundaries put me in proximity with the people and made me see that pure observation and simple classification was not sufficient to account for the richness of the stylistic universe that I was following. When looking at a girl I could not tell anymore what was guiding my eyes: her body, her clothes or her dance. I could not tell because the whole thing, the 'actant' (Latour 1994, 2005), resulting

 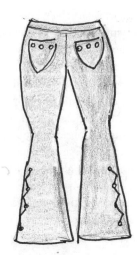

Figure 5.5

from the interaction of person, thing and movement, captured my mind. So if I had the intention to consider how the objects silently order our steps in the world, the world of the objects made me answer the call of materiality and follow the conceptual turn promoted by Miller (1987, 1994a) and Gell (1998).

This is where the '*Moletom* Stretch Trousers' reappear. The 'Trousers' actually look like a regular pair of jeans and their fabric is made out of a blend of cotton and Lycra, having, therefore, a composition identical to regular stretch denim. Nevertheless, the threads of the fabric are spun as a jersey, allowing the fabric to stretch in both vertical and horizontal ways, while the regular denim-Lycra blend can only stretch horizontally. There are here two main points to be retained, both of them following from the materiality of the object. One is the choice of simulating blue jeans because the fabric can acquire any desired colour, although the great preference has always been placed on those appearing to be jeans. The other point concerns the malleability of the trousers. I will focus first on this latter aspect.

The fabric '*moletom* stretch' produces a pair of jeans extremely comfortable for dancing and their elasticity, according to what the girls say, is strongly connected to the freedom of movement the 'Trousers' allow. In addition, the reduced thickness of the fabric allied to its clinginess enhances the round Funk body that is by itself emphasized by the sinuosity of the dance. The garment has to be thin in order to produce little volume over the body, working as a second skin and revealing the body's curves. This blending with the body is also achieved through the design of the garment that, no matter what the version of the style, never has back pockets, highlighting the bum even more. The pockets, when present, are in fact only represented by stitches, being yet another source of simulation. The 'Trousers', rather than producing forms, enhance a body that is in itself curvilinear. As the girls at the

Figure 5.6

party said, the 'Trousers' do not 'give a bum', but you must have one in order for it to be beautified. Thanks to their stretching capacities, the 'Trousers' can be used in sizes smaller than usual, promoting in this way a tensor effect.[10] For these reasons, thin and slim bodies do not benefit from the 'Trousers' effects, becoming even more straight and curveless when covered by this garment.

Besides that, the fabric, as it is thicker than most regular jerseys, is able to support baroque craft elements – such as rhinestones, tacks, embroideries, lace fragments and other materials – and be elaborated by the 'holes' (*buracos*), produced by the insertion of eyelets, fishnet material, incisions, rips, shreds, and through perforations forming abstract or figurative motives, such as stars, hearts or butterflies, also possibly adorned by rhinestones, allowing the flesh to be exposed. These embellishing resources produce a garment well suited for the extraordinary sphere, both for the richness of its aesthetic elaborations and the sexiness of its looks. Finally, the 'Trousers' can have a flare or boot cut, can be knee-length, like tight Bermuda shorts, or mid-calf. Despite all those variations, they all remain authentic '*Moletom* Stretch Trousers', a style the particularities of which is intrinsically associated with the

Figure 5.7

materiality of the fabric. Here, jeans have never been 'blindingly obvious' (Miller and Woodward 2007).

According to Gell (1998), by referring to a style we are also referring to an object, because a particular style is formed in the interconnection of the artifacts and any unity of a stylistic whole refers to the corpus of artworks. The objects and motifs are all transformations of each other. As a holographic image, which has the information, albeit attenuated, of the totality of the hologram, any unity allows for the reconstruction of the corpus of artifacts defining the style. A collection of artworks, from this perspective, is 'not a collection of separate objects, but just *one* object with many parts distributed in many different places' (Gell 1998: 167). Gell's perspective is quite attuned to that of the Funk girls. As I have already mentioned, at the Ball, more relevant than the creator is a whole style defined by the internal relations among its different versions. What limits the '*Moletom* Stretch Trousers' is the fabric and the designs made upon its surface. Those are 'the limited dimensions upon which the variability of a domain is expressed' (Miller 1987: 128) and by which this particular style is defined.

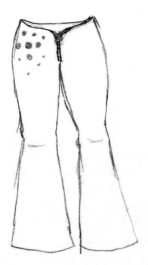

Figure 5.8

If we compare the 'Trousers' with alternative pieces of clothing worn by the girls, we see that they can be once again more appropriate for dancing. This is clear from the girls oral and body discourses. The girls might wear skirts that are basically of two types: loose or tight, but always short. One corresponds to those known as 'Darlene', made from thin and light mesh, with a tight band surrounding the area of the hips, from which a loose and *godet* flounce hangs.[11] The other style of skirt used is the regular and tight miniskirt, usually having the appearance of jeans, possibly made of denim, stretch denim or '*moletom* stretch'.

Flávia and her friend Marcinha do not like to use loose skirts for dancing because, they say, there is always a 'stray hand' trying to touch their bodies. For instance, Irene, on the same night she was wearing the red outfit I described above, consisting of a 'Darlene' skirt and a short sleeveless top, became upset because some boys stopped behind her and insisted on watching her dancing. For this same reason Vera justifies her taste: 'I, myself, do not like [to use skirts to dance]. I like to enjoy myself [*me esbaldar*] while dancing. You know, we put a hand on our knee, then the person behind us ends up seeing our backside [*fundilhos*].'

The skirts, in general, leave the girls excessively exposed, although some may not care about it or may even enjoy it, as we will see later on. They may use tiny Lycra shorts to protect themselves, as Lívia did on the night she wore her white strapless dress. The 'Darlene' skirt has the advantage of not clinging to the body like the tight mini-skirt does, physically limiting the movement of the body when dancing. On the other hand, the 'Darlene' skirt makes its user more vulnerable because it goes up and down with the dance movements. The '*Moletom* Stretch Trousers', in turn, protect the girls from the boys' approaches. Furthermore, the tight mini-skirt, like the regular denim trousers, constrains the movements of the legs. The former restrains the thighs and the latter does the same to the knees. Finally, the *shortinho*, tiny shorts made of denim, which was once quite representative of the Balls and the girls' taste and aesthetics, is today out of fashion.

The '*Moletom* Stretch Trousers' also have to be considered in relation to the male universe in order to expand our understanding of their meaning. The basic tight/loose opposition, or the distinction observed from the proximity or remoteness of clothing to the body, unfolds at different levels: the high-heeled sandals and clogs used by the girls compared to the boys' flat sneakers; the synthetic fibre predominating in women's clothing, synthesized by elastic Lycra yarn, as opposed to the 'natural' cotton t-shirts for men; and the long and 'natural' girls' hairstyles versus the short and arteactual boys' style. There are also contrasts in the type of movement performed, and another important difference concerns the state of mind expressed at the party. While the boys have the habit of mocking the girls, the girls, even when performing more energetic movements, have a concentrated and disdaining expression.

Boys and girls seek to achieve comfort through their clothes but they do it through local values and ideas about beauty and gender, and the pair of opposites tight/wide must be understood from the perspective of the body. The elastic female attire attends the needs of the female body in motion, enhancing a certain valued type of body, while giving comfort to it. A reverse logic governs the male clothing. The boys also seek comfort but as owners of slim and angular bodies they achieve it by, at the same time, filling the outline of their silhouettes with broad and non-elastic clothing. Ironically, it is rather the male clothes that produce a body upon their users' silhouettes, not the other way round, as the media discourse assumes.

The second and minority style among men, the one of the 'pumped boys' ('*bombados*'), with muscular torsos and thin legs, has a logic that is at a half-way point

Figure 5.9   Figure 5.10

Figure 5.11

between the ones governing the girls and the attire of the 'skinny' boys, and helps to illustrate both of them. We saw that these boys wear extremely tight t-shirts on their torsos, so that even the smallest movement of their arms, as Emanuel told me, 'already shows the muscle', meaning that it reveals the round forms of the body. In this way, the *bombado's* taste presents a dynamic similar to that which governs the female one. On the other hand, the extremely wide jeans trousers also worn by them conceal their skinny legs while drawing a new silhouette, being in this way close to the reasoning guiding the clothing choices of *funkeiros*.

The Seduction that Makes the Ball

The Funk Balls in Rio are parties divided by gender and ruled by seduction. Girls and boys mutually provoke each other, often in a ritualistic manner, in such a way that the atmosphere of attraction ends up generating an environment sometimes similar to an arena where two antagonistic groups face each other. Seduction at the party brings the genders closer by opposing them, letting us elaborate on same-sex and cross-sex gender relations (Strathern 2001).

Friday, the girls say, are 'full bag days', for they leave home and to go to work carrying hair conditioners, body lotion, deodorant, perfumes and make up. In the evening they leave their offices and go straightaway to meet their boyfriends, lovers or 'stayers' (*ficantes*), the latter being a transitory position that might or might not evolve into the status of a boyfriend. On the other hand, Saturday nights are occasions for leaving home carrying as few things as possible. When dressed up for a Funk Ball the girls' clothes frequently do not have pockets, as we have already seen in the depiction of the '*Moletom* Stretch Trousers'. As a result, they may carry

Figure 5.12

mobile phones, lipstick and some money tucked in their necklaces or bras, or in the purse of the anthropologist accompanying them. At the ball it is important to have one's hands free in order to dance unconstrained. As a boyfriend may also constrain a girl's enjoyment at the party, someone's boyfriend may be called *mala*, a 'suitcase', an annoying and heavy object that does not leave your hands free. The boys express a similar idea. Eric told me that at the Ball one cannot stand still: you cannot 'stop' (*parar*) but have to spend the whole night 'spinning' (*rodando*), meaning that he has to circulate all the time, making it impossible to be attentive to only one girl.

Saturday nights are meant for going out with same-sex friends, without having the opposite gender as company. The chance of going to the Funk Ball and express- ing the distinction between the genders can turn the sports ground into what appears to be an arena where a clash between rival groups will take place. And the main weapon of the conflict is, in the case of the girls, the body aesthetics through which they exercise seduction and test the power they might have over the other sex. And the more girls gather together, the greater the effect on the boys.[12]

In one night, Lívia, my main interlocutor during fieldwork at the ball, and her friends, formed a group of eight girls. On several occasions a group of boys gath- ered around them, ostensibly watching them. They, as expected, pretended not to see them, and kept concentrating on the performance of their steps. They formed a circle, and for a while kept crouching down and moving their hips back and forth, vigorously and frantically, almost touching the dance floor and always in accordance with the song's lyrics. On nights like these, they leave the party pleased for having 'drawn attention' to themselves (*chamado atenção*). A girl can also seduce individually, but again with the pure and simple objective of exercising seduction, and in this way feel that she has power over the boys. One night at the party, Sofia was wearing a loose white 'Darlene' skirt, and was warned by Lívia about the boy who had already been dancing behind her for a few minutes, trying to touch her bum with his genitals, playing with her skirt as it moved up and down. Sofia seemed not to worry about it. She let the boy become tired of his game, which was also hers. Another interesting situation had as a protagonist a girl dancing with friends on one of the steps of the stands facing the dance floor. She sees a boy approaching from the floor to watch her and this makes her enhance even more the sensuality of her dance. The boy, still on the ground, stops in front of her, while the girl, being above him, stares at horizon, pretending not to see him. A friend of the boy also arrives and he lays his forehead on his friend's shoulders, as if weeping. The girl keeps dancing, caring even more about the provocative portion of her dance. The situation is then undone by the approximation of the girl's friend, as if he was her boyfriend. The boy on the floor leaves and the girl goes on dancing with her groups of friends.

Once again, the encounter between female and male *trenzinhos* gives a good measure of the sociality (Strathern 1991) constituting the party, involving both conflict and connectivity. I have watched and enjoyed this while I was experiencing the Ball with the girls. The situation created was likely to be classified as a performance,

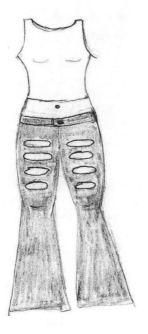

Figure 5.13

giving a good measure of the relations established between men and women, both involving seduction, provocation, jocularity and contempt.

Two guys lead a male *trenzinho*. They choose a girl and stop in front of her, making strange movements with their bodies, as if wanting to scare her, while it is clear that their intention is to play. The expressions on their faces tell us that it is certainly a joke. Both of the boys flex one of their arms, placing their hands on their own shoulders. In this position they bring their arms close to their eyes, as if they were an instrument by which it is possible to look at a specific point of the girl's body: a telescope or a gun, the sight of which is the elbow. And in this way they 'film' the girl. A little further on, they stand face to face with a *trenzinho* of girls. They stop in front of it, preventing its passage, with their legs wide open and extending their arms up and down. They form a single and allegedly fearful creature with four arms and four legs. The girls, in turn, dance without even looking at them. They perform their circular movements, gently rolling their hips and ignoring the provocative boys. They stare at the horizon, without outlining any expression, either of discomfort or delight. The female composition goes on. It stops in front of a group of *bombados* who dance with sensuality and conspicuously display their bodies. The girls release a unison 'uuuuu', admiring them, and continue to move. They see another cluster of boys and by pretending not to see them they pass through them. The girls have their

Figure 5.14

hair, arms and waists touched by the boys, who do this most of the time in delicate ways. This is the time to be flirting or gently declining invitations for a date.

The strong contrast formed by male and female aesthetics materializes the rivalry and the seduction embodied in Funk sociality. The 'Trousers', by summarizing the features valued in women's attire, relate aspects of corporeality and are also enmeshed in notions of personhood. They present the relation between the genders and the atmosphere of seduction governing the party, for at a Funk Dance one is either a man or a woman from the perspective of the body.

Conclusion

By way of conclusion, I would like to elaborate upon some aspects of the ethnographic account I have just made. I will start by returning to a female piece of clothing that I mentioned briefly. The *shortinho*, once quite fashionable at the Balls, became representative of an era when the girls had a narrow range of alternative aesthetic choices. In the 1990s there was even what was once called *Baile do Shortinho*, an evening when, as the name of the party denotes, the girls were invited to wear such garments. The arrival of the 'Trousers' at the Funk Balls was concomitant to an enlargement of the material culture choices available for consumption by Brazilian popular classes. From a different perspective, the market started to recognize the weight and impact that popular classes' demand and consumption could have on their global revenues. The '*Moletom* Stretch Trousers' represent an era of self-assertion by working classes, a feature that can be better understood by focusing once more on the female Funk attire.

The composition of the girls' outfits reveals a central concern with their formal aspect. As Paola, Lívia's cousin, said: 'there must always be something matching.' This internal coherence of the set, of its formal elements, which Modern Art has tried to turn into its distinctive trace, as Geertz (1983) has shown, is also present in this 'popular taste'.

On the night I first met Shirley, a very pretty eighteen-year-old *mulata*, she was wearing a version of '*Moletom* Stretch Trousers' dyed and washed in order to imitate the blue jeans fabric. Her trousers were adorned by flowers spread all over their surface, produced by small perforations made in the fabric, 'holes' that were sparsely adorned by rhinestones. Shirley's shoulder top was tight and made of Lycra and polyamide mesh, in an acid hue of green, printed with small white dots that decorated the areas close to the necklace and the top's lower portion. She was also wearing a white belt, with a heart-shaped buckle made of silver metal, painted by white and green. On her feet she wore a pair of white wedge sandals, and on one of her hands she had a ring and few bracelets in the same shade of green seen on the other garments. The green and the white colours were also present on the cap covering her black hair, enlarged by braid-like extensions. As a finishing touch, her eyes were highlighted with green eyeshade.

I could go on giving many more examples describing this same pattern governing the assembly of a Funk outfit. But the point I would like to make is that both the baroqueness of the '*Moletom* Stretch Trousers' and the formal aspect present in the overall looks speak against a 'Taste of Necessity' (Bourdieu 1984) that supposedly inclines the working-class choices to build a 'pragmatic, functionalist "aesthetic"' (Bourdieu 1984: 376). According to Bourdieu, taste is 'a virtue made out of necessity' (Bourdieu 1984: 177), and the members of the lower classes are condemned to an aesthetic of absence (Bourdieu 1984: 178) as their taste is limited both by budget restrictions and by their incapacity to be autonomous in their aesthetical choices, following the trends dictated by high classes and in a constant process of imitation.

The production of taste at Rio de Janeiro's Funk parties, on the other hand, denotes a different tendency from that deployed by Bourdieu. Both their formal aspect and the locality of the production speak for a relative autonomy from any hegemonic taste in the conformation of *Funk Aesthetics*. Similar reasoning can be made when relating the way corporeality is conceptualized at Funk parties comparative to some other Rio de Janeiro contexts.

Following Mauss's (1979) notion of 'body techniques', an extensive bibliography has been created dealing with corporeality in Rio's elite, claiming that both a homogenization of body appearances (Malysse 2002) or a 'civilizing process' (Elias 1978) govern the spread of a 'corporeal fashion' (Goldenberg and Silva Ramos 2002). At Funk Balls the emergence of the female attire as a 'second skin' then seems to correspond well with a broader Rio de Janeiro's and even Brazilian taste. However, the presence of fat, thin or very fat girls, always wearing tight clothes, seems to indicate a nexus between body and person quite different to those observed among Rio's elites.

The aesthetic choices at the Ball obey a structuring taste that has been guiding both clothing and corporeality at Funk Balls since their origins. Although having a restricted supply of material culture, the girls at the Ball always prized tight clothes and the exposure of their tummies and bums, as related to me by Veronica, a woman who frequented the parties in the 1990s, or as previous records attest (Goldenberg 1994; Vianna 1988).

The appropriation of the style here under concern, as I have shown before (Mizrahi 2003), is compatible with the dynamics of Brazilian culture, which, rather than corresponding to a trickle-down effect (Simmel 1957), subverts this logic into an upwards direction. There is a bubble-up trajectory that converts Brazilian popular culture expressions into symbols of national identity (Fry 1982; Vianna, 1999). Besides that, through their neo-baroque aesthetics the girls state visually that they don't want to be situated in a reified place of poverty associated with lack and absence. On the contrary, the visual potency of the 'Trousers' and their aesthetics assert that if they want to be recognized, this should be in accordance with their own taste. The 'Trousers', in this way, can be seen as a representation of the new status acquired by Brazilian popular classes in the overall Brazilian economy.[13]

But the 'Trousers' do not only represent the Funk party girls, or the atmosphere of seduction and desire present at the Ball. They effectively carry this power: the power of eroticism, seduction and provocation. They are the 'Trousers' that 'attract attention' (*chama atenção*) and 'no matter where we pass everyone looks', as the girls say. Those expressions are used by them to deploy the effects they cause while wearing the 'Trousers', or when generally speaking about something that instigates the eye and awakens interest. It is the whole thing, body, clothing and dance, which causes the beautiful effect while it is in motion.

As is evident from comparison with other contributions to this volume, the nexus between materiality, corporeality and personhood is constructed locally. The male Berliners discussed by Ege adopt the same 'carrot-cut' jeans, no matter whether they have muscular or skinny bodies, which implies that in his case the body is less relevant and that there is a non-dialogical relation between materiality and corporeality. By contrast in the case of the female Italian consumers analysed by Sassatelli (this volume) perfect jeans are those that can 'hide some [...] curves and downplay the hips'. In the case of Funk, boys choose styles in accordance with their particular bodily features, while girls seek garments that externalize and enhance the voluptuousness of their bodies. Which is why this chapter focuses on issues of both corporeality and personhood that synthesizes the materiality of the clothing and that of the body. In modern Brazilian contexts, as Lagrou (1998, 2007, 2009) has shown for the Cashinahua people, Amazonia, you cannot avoid the nexus between object, body and personhood while dealing with art and aesthetics.

Before concluding this chapter, I would like to stress one last aspect. At the beginning of the section headed 'The Stylistic Trademark of the Feminine Attire' I isolated two aspects related to the materiality of the style as being relevant for its meaning. At that point I mainly elaborated on the malleability of the fabric. Now, I want to dwell on a second aspect, that of the possibility of simulating the appearance of denim and playing with the meaning of its symbolism. The fact that the most valued versions of the style are those in which the fabric copies the look of jeans speaks for the centrality that fashion has for these youngsters and shows that appearance deeply marks their identities, as Miller has shown for Trinidadians (Miller 1994b). The style we have been analysing stems from a dialogue between the local and the global, producing an aesthetic that could only have emerged in Rio de Janeiro. The materiality of the '*Moletom* Stretch Trousers' is tied to a particular context of production, making it exemplary of the notion that the intrinsic values of the objects are used within a cultural logic (McCracken 1988). It is a mark of locality of the Funk context (Appadurai 1996), given by the Funk corporeality in its encounter with a global taste, expressed by the omnipresence of jeans in different world cultures, as the chapters throughout this volume assert. It is precisely the materiality of the fabric that allows the merging of local and global logics.

If the media discourses, expressing the ambiguities involved in the style's appropriation by high and middle classes and celebrities, simplify and explain the success of these 'Trousers' merely by reference to their effect upon the body – giving them a bum, the grass-roots discourses reveal by contrast that the object in itself does not have any such meaning. Different confluences have produced the '*Moletom* Stretch Trousers' and the girls at Rio Funk Dances should be considered as its most authentic creators. If it were not for their appropriation and the consumption of the style, the invention would never have been echoed or reproduced. If the girls are inspired by the hegemonic taste, as suggested by the idea that this is the simulation of denim, they also demonstrate the possibility of consolidating identity through *mimesis* and producing difference by the act of copying (Taussig 1993). The incorporation of the jeans as an element in their particular aesthetics is one more expression of the encompassing way Funk culture is invented and the ability their creators have to manipulate representations, as I have argued (Mizrahi, 2009). And this desire for the new and the change gives assurance that new trends will always be incorporated and created by young '*funkeiros*'.

Figure 5.15

Notes

1. All the pictures and the drawings used in this chapter are my own.
2. The rhythm has achieved a wide circulation, becoming one of the more loquacious symbols of Rio de Janeiro. You can dance funk all over Brazil – at popular classes venues, at expensive nightclubs, at middle class concert houses – and in Europe.
3. See, among others, *Elle America,* February 2002.
4. In fact the funk ball is not necessarily relevant to the kind of participants who are the subject of Pinheiro-Machado's chapter.
5. The native category '*Calça de Moletom* Stretch' is compatible with a hierarchy of jeans brands at the Funk ball, something I have discussed elsewhere (Mizrahi 2006a). For the present chapter I consider the three categories 'Brazilian Jeans', '*Calça da* Gang' and '*Moletom* Stretch Trousers' as analytically equivalent, their usage reflecting differences in social contexts. They also express a process of re-signifying the object in its circulation, as its meaning becomes modified along the trajectory, reflecting differences in manufacture, consumption and ambiguities within and outside of the Funk Ball (Mizrahi, in preparation).
6. In the present account I elaborate mainly on the results of my Masters thesis (Mizrahi, 2006b), through which I established a discussion on the meaning of feminine and masculine clothing. The fieldwork was carried out in a specific Funk Ball, between July 2004 and November 2005. I have accompanied a group of girls and boys, by going with them from home to the party, visiting them in their work offices and when shopping for clothes and body adornments. They lived in different *favelas*, although they worked and went clubbing together. On the other hand, my PhD thesis is built upon the deconstruction, made possible by the fluidity of Rio de Janeiro's social boundaries, of reified categories such as individual and society, and relates this same aesthetics of the body to music creativity and the connective dimension of art, in order to deploy *Funk Carioca* as a product of a wider cultural context, given by different social groups and geographical areas of the city. This second fieldwork was accomplished through the network of relations of a *Funk Carioca* artist, Mr Catra, during May 2007 and December 2008.
7. Cavalcanti (2006), while elaborating on Rio de Janeiro's Carnival, argues that the spectacle differs from the festival in that in the former there is a separation between the viewer and the artist, while in the latter there is a blending of both aspects. Actually, at the party I have studied, a fusion of these two concepts is produced, since the tenuous line between professional and amateur dancers is often dissolved. In my Masters thesis I show in detail the aspects that allow me to talk of the party as a spectacle as well as those that can be analysed from the perspective of the festival.
8. *Uma Hora*, by M.C. Frank.

9. For a thorough analysis of the boys' tastes and their own strategy of relating to the other sex see Mizrahi (2007).

10. This feature was used by media discourses to describe the trousers as a *Wondrebra* for the 'bum'.

11. The native category 'Darlene' was created based on the name of a female character of a famous Brazilian soap opera at that time.

12. The boys, on the other hand, state their power in a more literal way, mainly by the use of brands, that relate them both to the girl as to their main rival, the 'playboy', the middle-class educated young male. Brands are used by male 'funkeiros' in this double confrontation of alterity (Mizrahi, 2007).

13. This change of status and weight was accompanied by studies investigating the weight and role played by popular classes in the consumption sphere of the Brazilian economy (Barros, 2007; Almeida, 2003).

References

Almeida, H.B. de. (2003), *Telenovela, consumo e gênero: 'muitas mais coisas'*, São Paulo: Edusc.

Appadurai, A. (1996), 'The Production of Locality', in Appardurai, A. (ed.), *Modernity at Large: Cultural Dimensions of Globalization*, Minneapolis, MN: University of Minnesota Press, pp. 178–99.

Barros, C. (2007), *Trocas, hierarquias e mediação: as dimensões culturais do consumo em um grupo de empregadas domésticas*. Tese de Doutorado apresentada ao Programa do Instituto de Pós-Graduação e Pesquisa em Administração, COPPEAD, da Universidade Federal do Rio de Janeiro.

Bourdieu, P. (1984), *Distinction*, London: Routledge & Kegan Paul.

Cavalcanti, M.L. Viveiros de Castro (2006) [1994], *Carnaval carioca: dos bastidores ao desfile*, Rio de Janeiro: Editora UFRJ.

Douglas, M. and Isherwood, B. (1979), *The World of Goods*, London: Routledge.

Ege, M. 'Picaldi Jeans and the Figuration of Working-class Male Youth Identities in Berlin: An Ethnographic Account', in D. Miller and S. Woodward, *The Global Denim Project Book*, London: Berg.

Elias, N. (1978), *The Civilizing Process*, Translated from the German by Edmund Jephcott (Vol. 1): 'The History of Manners', Oxford: Blackwell.

Fry, P. (1982), *Para Inglês Ver: Identidade e Politica na Cultura Brasileira*, Rio de Janeiro. Zahar.

Geertz, C. (1983), 'Art as Cultural System', in C. Geertz (ed.), *Local Knowledge: Further Essays in Interpretive Anthropology*, New York: Basic Books.

Gell, A. (1998), *Art and Agency*, Oxford: Oxford University Press.

Goldenberg, M. and Ramos, M.S. (2002), 'A civilização das formas: O corpo como valor', in Goldenberg, M. (ed.), *Nu e vestido*, Rio de Janeiro: Record.

Lagrou, E. (1998), 'Caminhos, duplos e corpos: uma abordagem perspectiva da identidade e alteridade entre os Kaxinauá', PhD dissertation, University of St Andrews, St Andrews, Scotland.

Lagrou, E. (2007), A fluidez da forma: arte, alteridade e agência em uma sociedade amazônica, Rio de Janeiro: Topbooks.

Lagrou, E. (2009), 'Lines, Doubles and Skin: Mediations between the Visible and the Invisible among the Cachinahua', in C. Alès and M. Harris (eds), Image, Performance and Representation in South American Shamanic Societies, Oxford: Berghahn Books.

Latour, B. (1994), Jamais fomos modernos, São Paulo: Editora 34.

Latour, B. (2005), Reassembling the Social, Oxford: Oxford University Press.

Lévi-Strauss, C. (1963), Structural Anthropology, New York: Basic Books.

Lévi-Strauss, C. (1966), The Savage Mind, London: Weidenfeld & Nicolson.

Malysse, S. (2002), 'Em busca dos (H)alteres-ego: Olhares franceses nos bastidores da corpolatria carioca', in M. Goldenberg, M. (ed.), Nu e vestido. Rio de Janeiro: Record.

Mauss, M. (1979), 'Body Techniques Essay', in Mauss, M., Sociology and Psychology, translated by Ben Brewster, London: Routledge & Kegan Paul.

McCracken, G. (1988), Culture and Consumption, Bloomington, IN: Indiana University Press.

Miller, D. (1987), Material Culture and Mass Consumption, Oxford: Basil Blackwell.

Miller, D. (1994a), 'Artifacts and the Meaning of Things', in T. Ingold (ed.), Companion Encyclopedia of Anthropology, London: Routledge, pp. 396–419.

Miller, D. (1994b), Modernity: An Ethnographic Approach, Oxford: Berg.

Miller, D. and Woodward, S. (2007), 'Manifesto for a Study of Denim', in Social Anthropology, 15(3): 335–51.

Mizrahi, M. (2003), A influência dos subúrbios na moda da Zona Sul [The influence of the outskirts on the southern area], monograph (Pesquisa coordenada para a Universidade Estácio de Sá), Rio de Janeiro.

Mizrahi, M. (2006a), 'Figurino Funk: uma etnografia dos elementos estéticos de uma festa carioca', in D. Leitão, D. Lima and R. Pinheiro-Machado, Antropologia e Consumo: diálogos entre Brasil e Argentina, Porto Alegre: AGE.

Mizrahi, M. (2006b), 'Figurino funk: uma etnografia sobre roupa, corpo e dança em uma festa carioca', Rio de Janeiro: Dissertação de Mestrado em Antropologia Cultural, PPGSA/IFCS/UFRJ.

Mizrahi, M. (2007), 'Indumentária funk: a confrontação da alteridade colocando em diálogo o local e o cosmopolita', Horizontes Antropológicos, Porto Alegre, ano 13, n. 28. http://www.scielo.br/scielo.php?script=sci_arttext&pid=S0104-71832007000200010&lng=en&nrm=iso (accessed 9 June 2010).

Mizrahi, M. (2009), 'De agora em diante é só cultura: Mr Catra e as desestabilizadoras imagens e contra-imagens Funk', in M.A. Gonçalves and S. Head. (eds), Devires imagéticos: a etnografia, o outro e suas imagens, Rio de Janeiro: 7 Letras.

Mizrahi, M. (in press), Revision of 'A influência dos subúrbios na moda da Zona Sul' [The influence of the outskirts on the southern area], Monograph, Universidade Estácio de Sá.

Sahlins, M. (1976), *Culture and practical reason.* Chicago, London: University of Chicago Press.

Simmel, G. (1957) [1904], 'Fashion', *American Journal of Sociology,* 5 lxii (6): 541–58.

Strathern, M. (1991), *Partial Connections,* Lanham: Altamira Press.

Strathern, M. (2001), 'Same-sex and Cross-sex Relations', in T. Gregor and D. Tuzin (eds), *Gender in Amazonia and Melanesia: An Exploration of the Comparative Method,* Berkeley: University of California Press.

Taussig, M. (1993), *Mymesis and Alterity: A Particular History of the Senses,* London: Routledge.

Vianna, H. (1988), *O mundo* funk *carioca.* Rio de Janeiro: Jorge Zahar Editor.

Vianna, H. (1999), *The Mystery of Samba: Popular Music and National Identity in Brazil,* Chapel Hill, NC: University of North Carolina Press.

–6–

Indigo Bodies: Fashion, Mirror Work and Sexual Identity in Milan

Roberta Sassatelli

Sexuality is the domain of intimate embodied relations where particularly strong emotional bonds are forged. Sexual matters have to be dealt with in all cultures but they are characteristically managed in different ways. Bodies may be sexualized via a number of social practices, including beauty treatments, exercise, body decoration and clothing (see, for example, Entwistle 2000; Guillaumin 2006; Waquant 1995). Such sexualization always occurs against the backdrop of a much more general cultural imagery with which an individual may or may not conform. In contemporary Western societies, many have noticed not only the growing presence of sexualized spaces (bars, clubs, gyms, etc.) (Green 2008) but also of sexualized body images in everyday life, mainly due to, among other things, commercial imagery (Bordo 1993; Wernick 1991) and popular media, including fashion magazines for both women and men (Frith et al. 2005; Gauntlet 2002). These increasingly play with fantasies of seduction and eroticism, with clothing as a potent signifier of sexualized subjectivity. Sexualized clothing includes not only obvious items such as corset-like underwear, laces, stilettos, furs or leather, which have obviously been the apex of fashion and fetish (Steele 1996), but also quite mundane, everyday items such as denim jeans. Of all mundane clothing in Italy, denim jeans have been the most overtly sexualized – especially as their marketing was extended to women. Since the early 1970s the Italian fashion industry has made the link between women, jeans and sexuality quite explicit, with a particular emphasis on very tight jeans 'enhancing' the female shape in a series of images taken from behind (Fiorentini 2005; Volli 1991). Oliviero Toscani's campaign for Jesus Jeans (1973) epitomized by a photo of a woman's bottom in Denim shorts – coded by the provocative claim 'who loves me, follows me' – showed potently how fetish elements, projecting reference to genital sex onto the whole embodied self, have been associated with both denim fabric and denim jeans. Since then, the image of a sinuous, curvy female in tight jeans and high heels has become the archetype of female seduction: nothing is more sexy than a woman's bottom 'filling up those Jeans', sings Vasco Rossi in a popular recent rock song characteristically titled 'Play with Me' (2007): 'How long do you spend inside that pair of Jeans/You wear them not, you possess them/and when I see the movements you make/You know I cannot resist.' The song's video is an apotheosis of fetishism, in which the woman's bottom in denim stands for her fashioned, sexy self.

In this chapter, I explore how, in practice, denim jeans contribute to the everyday sexualization of the body. Despite their codification as potentially sexy, jeans remain mundane, almost ubiquitous items, perceived as remarkably versatile for all practical purposes in ordinary life. They are subject to fashion dynamics, and indeed represent an important segment in the fashion industry. They thus provide an excellent spot for the exploration of sexualization as an ordinary practice that emerges from – and aside to – normal daily rounds, as much as it is performed in specialized places or choreographed in a myriad of glamorized symbolic forms. I will introduce my discussion by initially considering how Denim's relationship to fashion illuminates its relation to embodied subjectivity and individuality more generally. As argued by Steele (1996: 4) fashion is a 'symbolic system linked to the expression of sexuality – both sexual behaviour (including erotic attraction) and gender identity.' However, rather than developing a semiotic approach, considering how the fashion system plunders fetishism or sexual subcultures for inspiration, I explore how the expression of sexuality (attraction and gender) is mediated by a particular clothing, denim jeans, which enjoys a particular status within the actualization of fashion in everyday life. In other words, I start naturalistically from reported practices of meaningful ordinary use of an ordinary item such as jeans, interrogating the chains of meanings that link identity, embodiment and sexuality. The mediating role of denim is revealed as subjects perform what I define as 'mirror work' to negotiate their own body perception in relation to normative ideals of beauty and sexuality. As I shall show, denim jeans afford a perception of 'fitness' that articulates comfort with compliance as well as authenticity with adaptability. Feeling fit is crucial to feeling sexy: something that is articulated via gendered notions of seduction. The evidence is drawn from ethnographic interviews[1] conducted with youths from Milan in their homes, and in particular in their bedrooms, allowing access to their wardrobes and easier discussion of embodied and visual matters.

Jeans as Super-fashion and Personal Patina

Pondering over her wardrobe, Francesca, a stylish, freshly graduated woman in her mid-twenties, says that, whilst they are 'vital' to her, 'Denim jeans just sit with the rest [of her clothes]: they are just in the middle of the mess, but I take them out much more often, so always know where they are' (Interview 15). These few words allude to the particular position that jeans – normal and yet special – occupy in young people dressing practices. This partly reflects what youth from Milan participating in the study has considered the almost unique relation that occurs between denim jeans and fashion. Jeans are perceived as being in a dialectical tension with fashion:

they are both fashion and anti-fashion, and to some degree also transcend it. As one of the interviewees has claimed: 'Denim is always on fashion, and at the same time, jeans follow fashion, because according to fads, they change their shape and model' (Interview 7).

Most interviewees were quick to recognize that jeans are shaped by fashion dynamics. In recent times close-fitting jeans have become fashionable: the 'latest trend' is perceived as 'very tight, on the ankle', 'slightly low waist and tight', 'no funny colours, but fitting down the whole leg', 'a very tight-fitting shape that seals legs, bottom, calves and goes down very tight to the ankle.' Jeans thereby defined as 'fashionable' are suitable for special occasions, such as parties or dining out. Despite this conformity around current fashions, most interviewees were also clear how difficult it is to pin down jeans as fashion. They 'change, but they are always fashionable' was a general response. The transformative sameness of Jeans was highlighted by the minutiae of their variations, and the simultaneous presence of different fashionable finishing or cuts. As maintained by Flavia (Interview 23), a medical technician in her mid-twenties living with her boyfriend in a small but central flat; 'in my opinion jeans fashions change very fast, so in my wardrobe there are bell-bottom jeans and tight ones, both kinds were once trendy and perhaps they still are'; on his part, Ivan (Interview 29), a 26-year-old radio journalist, says 'to be considered fashionable jeans have to be always different, new, but there are no fixed rules: some details change but in the end they are always jeans.'

Denim jeans thereby occupy a particular position in what I call the *clothing-identity symbolic space* (Figure 6.1): coinciding with a heightened sense of individuality as against both fashion and anti-fashion on the one hand, and normality and eccentricity on the other.

Let's explore this a bit further. 'Following fashion' in Denim has always been juxtaposed to and qualified by reference to 'personal style' or 'individual taste', with the suggestion that whatever the specific trend followed, this also matched by what one has 'really' or 'always liked'. We could, of course, write this off as yet another pseudo-individualization typical of all commodity semantics (Baudrillard 1998). Still interviewees have qualified jeans *as against* other clothing precisely

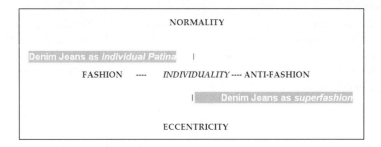

Figure 6.1. The clothing-identity symbolic space.

by reference to individuality, stressing embodiment and the sedimentation of memory on the garment as a specific quality of jeans. Jeans – thus we hear – must be personal, a sign of one's individuality – or as said by Chris (Interview 36), a twenty-five-years-old student, they need to facilitate a sense of the 'I' in a dialectical relation with fashion: 'I imagine myself as an individual, who distinguishes himself by using fashion in his own way.' To stress this, in quite a few cases, the compliance of a pair of jeans with the latest trend may even become a reason not to buy them. Jeans 'fully express a transgression desire', precisely because the more they are consumed the more they become yours: 'they are fast as life, they are rebellious, you can sit everywhere, on the floor or anything, throw them anywhere, you don't have to bother, they can only become more part of you'(Interview 15, 26-year-old graduate female clerk). Yet, transgression is not articulated as eccentricity, namely the desire to be different for difference's sake. Blue as freedom and reminiscent of the 1968 counterculture (Volli 1991), they embody informal relaxation, articulating one's own peculiar enactment of normality, itself conceived as 'easiness' and 'versatility'. Males especially considered that they desired jeans to remain 'against the tide', even though they were positively perceived as ubiquitous and affordable for all. Thus a few suggested that they preferred more 'normal' jeans, which last irrespective of fancy fads, and stressed that their preferred jeans were all but 'eccentric' in a way that heightens individuality. Favourite jeans quite often 'do not simply pass unobserved, but they are not too conspicuous either [...] they are no fuss, simple but not just banal' (Interview 11). Indeed, here are some broader excerpts from the field:

> Fads or brands do not affect my choice very much. Now, the jeans I wear, yes being themselves a not very flashy pair of jeans they express my desire for transgression so they are describing a bit my relation with fashion. I see them more as jeans just for me, not necessarily for people looking at me, [they are] jeans expressing the will of getting out from the fashion logic, according to which we have to be in a certain way for the others.
>
> (Interview 23, clerical worker in her mid-twenties)

> Considering where I bought them and how many pairs there were, I think those were fashionable jeans, you could tell that their line was well-thought. As I said I was listening to seventies music and, in theory, seventies clothing is not fashionable. But you could tell that those jeans were a modern version of a seventies model and, despite the fact that I really liked them, this fact [that they were fashionable] has even reduced a bit my preference for those jeans ... [Jeans] in their essence need to remain a bit like personal, against the tide.
>
> (Interview 32, student in his late twenties)

Overall then denim jeans are viewed as timeless rather than merely a reflection of the latest style:

Jeans are always fashionable, I don't think that jeans will never go out of style, you know, jeans are eternal, as long as they are a basic classic model, because in the moment I have a bell-bottom jeans, a pair of narrow jeans, faded jeans or jeans with cuts.. maybe they really correspond to particular periods: Seventies, 'paninari' [a posh northern Italy youth culture of the 1980s] ... So yes, these jeans are peculiar, but they will surely be in fashion again sooner or later, so we shouldn't throw them away, but the more a pair of jeans is classic, the more they fit with every situation and period. (Interview 20, university student in her mid-twenties)

It appears that jeans are implicated in the dynamics of fashion, but ultimately transcend, such dynamics.[2] Jeans may therefore be said to be conceived as *superfashion.* Youths from Milan are quite conscious of fashionable cuts, finishing, colouring and discolouring, as much as they are well aware of brands. Unbranded Jeans, or less heavily promoted brands, are generally recognized as more prone to personalization, while heavily promoted 'posh' brands come with a more precise bag of meanings, which may or may not become vernacularized.[3] Most recognize a certain cut, colour or finish helps them to relate to a group, to feel part of an imagined community of taste, something that is said to characterize all clothing. Someone who has to a hang out with 'punk-style people' feels better 'wearing a baggy pair of jeans', another states that if 'I have to go out with my boyfriend for dinner, I would wear more posh, jeans', or even that 'more sexy, low-waist jeans are perfect for a party night.' But once again this is tempered by an insistence upon their individual nature and relation to one's own perceived body shape.

In most cases, a person's favourite jeans were those that better 'represent' or 'fit' oneself. Not just the body but also one's own life experiences. What really matters – says a male electrician in his mid-twenties (Interview 28) – is that 'they suit my style, they fit me well, that's all'; and this is because, specifies a male university student in his early twenties (Interview 35), 'nothing really makes me feel at ease as my jeans, they are like telling people who I am, but not that blatantly, as everyone wears jeans [...] they just fit me, and I feel more self-confident.' As they are used for many seasons, and rarely thrown away, denim jeans become, with time, an index of one's individual peculiarity: the patina of time is not so much deposited on their surface as a sign of belonging (to a family, a group or a clan see McCraken 1988; Sassatelli 2007); an *individual patina* effect develops around the imprint in the Denim fabric of one's own embodied peculiarity, which tells of one's own personal life experiences and relations, both quite often described with reference to the intimate sphere of friendship or love rather than more public social belonging.

Individual patina is central to that part of our interviews when we asked to see people favourite jeans, to recall where and when they acquired them as well as occasions of wearing by showing us old and recent photographs. All interviewees identified a favourite pair of jeans, which were often bought hastily, but then gave rise to quite a vivid realization that they were 'just 100 per cent perfect', 'the jeans for me!' All these favourites were highly individualized in their minds: with a past, a present and a future. The occasion of purchase was specifically recalled and the bodily sensation felt during the try-out was often reported in some detail. Favourite jeans endure the passing of time, going through a set of transformations and modification due to wearing and tearing. In most cases, favourites had been worn till they were 'literally wasted', with numerous mending and patching, prolonging use and delaying disposal:

> I used them so much that, at a certain point, they had cuts on the back, but I made my mother sew them and I used those pair of jeans again, maybe with skirts, so you couldn't see the sewing ... but I kept using them, because I liked those jeans so much ... they were perfect and, in the end, when they were falling apart, I was forced to throw them away.

> (Interview 22, female student in her mid-twenties)

> They were over used, I wore that pair of jeans so many times. I tried to use them again, despite the fact that they were cut, well, first I used them with cuts, then I tried the classic remedy of my grandmother, patch, but the result was a bit ugly and eventually they got cut in some other part and I had to throw them away.

> (Interview 29, male shop assistant in his mid-twenties)

Time had effectively helped in establishing a deep emotional relation with one's own favourite pair, expressed as 'loving' or 'being fond of my jeans'. Thus, even when they can no longer be worn, the idea of throwing them away is unthinkable. Anyway, anytime, they are imagined as a memento to be kept: 'if they were just destroyed' – says Giovanni a technician in his mid-twenties (Interview 16) – 'I would be very sorry to throw them away because I've been wearing them for ages. If I will not be able to wear them again for any reason, for sure I would never throw them away. No! I would feel too sad about it.' Likewise, the idea of losing one's own favourite jeans is typically described as painful, to the point that one interviewee declared that he 'would miss a piece of my life, really!'

While we may like an old pair of slippers, refuse to throw them away and yet not have the courage to wear them publicly, worn-out jeans are publicly acknowledged. Unlike other clothing, time congealed in the discolouring marks and the imprint of repeated usage on the jeans surface is considered as added value. Our respondents agreed that jeans are made to 'age well', recognizing a feature that has been vastly exploited by the clothing industry, to the point of mechanical distressing, the standardizing mimicking of personal usage and even the commercial glorification of personalization (something made explicit by the Swedish company Nudie in their Web site which is a gallery of worn jeans and the tales they tell about the wearer) (see Miller and Woodward 2007). When used for a while, a pair of jeans may become 'nicer' and more 'aesthetically pleasing', suggests most of our interviewees.[4] It 'fits' better, because it blends with one's own body visibly and yet subtly:

I have many pair of jeans with cuts, to be honest I would probably use them till they were falling a part except if the cut was one of those that shows everything underneath … I like the pair of jeans with some cuts, they even tell a bit who I am.

(Interview 21, female student in her early twenties)

… a used pair of jeans has more 'flavour', they taste more like you do, and moreover, jeans are not as some classic male trousers, [but] something that when used are also more beautiful.

(Interview 30, designer in his late twenties)

There are two aspects to this personalization, which may be summarized as *comfort* and *display*: the former works at the level of embodied experience, the latter at the level of performed embodied identity A favourite pair of jeans gets better with use as it affords physical sensations of ease. The fabric gets softer, and bending and moving is more natural: they soften but retain something of their 'strong texture' as denim, which one interviewee said 'offers some resistance to your body.' A worn-out pair also 'tells a story' about the wearer. It carries along the many experiences of the wearer, enriching his or her present identity by adding some kind of temporal, biographical depth – something that appears to be particularly appreciated by young people: they represented 'a part of me', 'a period of my life', a 'step in my life', 'my adolescence'; they have 'followed' one's own 'growth', going through all the 'self-revolutions' in tastes and dressing style. As Marina (Interview 10), a clerk in her early twenties has mentioned, 'I have made no voluntary modification, but it has aged: I had to mend it as it got shredded on the back below as I stepped on it, it is very light blue, you see, but it has really become my favourite […] I prefer them now.' Claudio, also in his early twenties (Interview 17), suggests that his favourite, worn-out jeans 'makes me feel I have had a life.'

Fitting and Making Fit: Mirror Work and Beyond

To illustrate principles of choice and use, and to characterize denim jeans, youth from Milan have all stressed that they, more than any other item of clothing, work like a 'second skin' – something that is comfortable and protective and yet enhances the body. Their favourite pair of jeans is perceived as both 'fitting' uniquely one's own embodied self and 'making' one 'fit' better the world around, stressing the best of oneself on the backdrop of perceived body ideals.

How is this sense of jeans as second skin achieved? It entails both covering certain body parts and revealing others. Jeans appear quite 'special' in their capacity to 'hide imperfections' while, simultaneously, 'underlining' body shape, enhancing it. Purchase decisions are typically made after trying out a few pairs, with such *covering/revealing* rationale being identified as the master principle of choice. This was universally recognized by females, and repeatedly articulated in their descriptions of jeans shopping, all of which portray vivid scenes of encounters with mirrors and body reflections:

> well, I said, 'wow, these fits me nicely', finally as I want, my hips look lees wide, my bump is rounder' ... I looked slender like I wanna be, they made an impression on me, just like a click in my head.
>
> (Interview 4, female promoter in her mid-twenties)

> ... I said to myself, well they squeeze my love handles, so I will wear on the top something hiding this problem, something large but short ... because anyway thighs look thinner , so I can avoid putting on a jumper tied to the waist in order to hide the bottom, as I usually do with my other trousers!
>
> (Interview 21, female student in her mid-twenties)

Facing the mirror with the 'right pair' of jeans on may elicit quite strong feelings of ease and self-confidence – something that is typically described with words such as 'suddenly recognizing myself in a better shape' or 'finally looking as I want to be.'[5] The best jeans, we heard, make you feel you look your very best from the very first try-out, and subsequently gain value as they add a form of personal patina over time. Accounting for such sentiment one interviewee, a twenty-something student with a plump figure (Interview 20), remarked: 'it's difficult to explain, but if I have to imagine myself at the top of my shape, self-confident and happy, I see myself wearing that particular pair of jeans.' This very first impression left by a favourite pair of jeans when looking at oneself in the mirror may leave such a deep impression as to orientate one's own use of, and emotional engagement with, the mirror in the time to come.

To look at oneself in the mirror is a practice full of meanings. The mirror does not simply reflect the self – it reflects it through a particular view, which is informed by expectations as to subjectivity and body ideals as well as by broader cultural notions on how we must look at ourselves, when and for what purposes. The mirror has somehow to be activated through what I call 'mirror work' (see also Sassatelli 2010). By mirror work I mean the work that a subject has to undertake to use the mirror in ways that are appropriate to the scene, fit his or her notions of self, and negotiate with received body ideals in a game of revelation and concealment of body details. Looking at oneself in the mirror can be daunting even in the solitude of one's own bedroom, and quite demanding on self-esteem. It is certainly crucial for clothing practices both at home, and at the point of purchase during shopping. Now, as one of our interviewees has said, one's own favourite pairs of jeans provide an *anchor for self-confidence* during mirror work: 'if I'm in a wrong mood I say "my God that's ugly!"', but also in those cases if I'm at least wearing those particular jeans I feel a bit better' (Interview 29). Jeans are perceived as all-matching and all-purpose, and favourite jeans often condense such qualities: as one interviewee said of his favourite jeans, 'they represents me, as I am very easy, I feel fine in all situations and that jeans is like me, if I want to sit on the ground no problem, if I am in front of Scala [the Opera theatre in Milan] and I want a coffee where it costs 8 euros, I do not feel ashamed to get in with such a pair' (Interview 1).

What such stories imply is that one's own favourite jeans are versatile and resourceful. They work as an instrument through which a tension between elitism and equality is played out (Davis 1989) and their status as 'slang' in the fashion language (Lurie 1981) may be read as purposeful informality. However, they are versatile also because, many of our interviewees insist, they are felt as enhancing one's own body shape: 'I look good in them, which makes me feel good and self-confident, which is as much as you can ask from any clothing for whatever occasion, even if it may not be the absolutely most adequate choice' (Interview 1).[6] We should not dismiss similar, apparently banal, statements, but explore them as evidence of the role that embodiment plays in clothing practices. As Flavia, a working girl in her mid-twenties, maintained (Interview 6), 'I already know those jeans fit me perfectly, maybe I look at myself in the mirror to see how I look combining them with something else.' Jeans are thus not only used to reduce the complexity of choice in a clothing market that is allegedly more vast and varied; they somehow help face the mirror paradox, which is that you may avoid looking in the mirror if you anticipate an image that is too far from your ideal embodied self, and yet you won't achieve a proper sense of your style as a negotiation of such ideal if you do not look at yourself in the mirror. As such jeans function as a 'coping mechanism' (Goffman 1967), helping to keep one's own anxieties about the body (excesses, softness, flabbiness, etc.) at bay, consequently performing adequate clothing practices.

Ironically, in some cases, jeans become so objectified as the basis of mirror work that the actual use of the mirror may become secondary. As Davide, a clerk in his mid-twenties (Interview 3) says, 'it happens that I look at my self in the mirror, but after a while it's habit, anyway you know for sure that those jeans are fitting you well, so you are confident'; or in Lucrezia's words (Interview 12):

> with those jeans I can do without a mirror, which is good, you may be short of time and you never know really how you will feel facing it, [but with these] I can concentrate on details, like a belt or something, taking for granted the rest is in shape.

In such cases, rather than a coping device to meet up with fashion and style demands, denim jeans may become 'a cognitive shortcut': 'I can stop asking me if I am fine, if I will look fat, I know they are comfortable and make me look good ... they make my life easier' (Interview 15).

Narrations of mirror work also reveal a contrast between ideals of male and female embodiment. Females tend to stress a universe of meaning that is rooted in *negative* notions such as 'protection' or 'safety'. Trousers are usually mentioned as providing for a sense of security. Denim jeans in particular, for all their getting softer with time, are perceived as relative 'hard' in terms of keeping one safe, something rooted in the very materiality of the garment: strong, tough, enduring, thick, impenetrable. As mentioned with a touch of humour, 'let's just say that wearing a pair of jeans is not like wearing a bikini, it's a form of safety, I would say that jeans are first of all a protection' (Interview 20). This negative element, keeping danger and fear at bay, is thereby developed in aesthetic terms: the element that best accounts for the preference for jeans as against other clothes is their capacity of hiding those body curves perceived as 'excess'. With the ideal body being recognized as slender and curvaceous at the same time, impressions of thinness are at premium. This may be pursued both by containment – with tight-fitting models that 'contain', 'enclose', 'press a little' or even 'squeeze a bit' those female body parts, such as the bottom and the upper tights, which are often perceived as too big – or by envelopment – with baggy pairs that help adjusting body proportions, adding volume at the bottom of the legs. In both cases, the desired impression 'to look thinner than I really am', to 'hide some of my curves and downplay the hips' is achieved.

Males, for their part, tend to stress a universe of meaning that is qualified by *positive* terms: the choice of jeans depends not so much on their capacity to hide imperfections or reduce size, on the contrary, they are qualified more forcefully as stressing one's own body and augment an impression of strength, force and bulk. Thus, Matteo, a designer in his later twenties (Interview 30), says that he does not 'think that my pair of jeans can hide any imperfection: I didn't chose a large model, but very tight [one] that is marking the body curves instead of hiding them.' By and large, whilst females reported to prefer 'slimming-down' jeans, males were concerned precisely with the opposite, conceptualizing a good pair of jeans as one which adds body, rather than diminishing or squeezing it. Yet, slenderness is, to a degree, a myth shared by all. Fat is surely not appreciated by males either, who likewise fell the cultural pressure towards slimness, and may themselves undergo severe diets in order to comply with such ideals, resulting on occasion, in a heightened pleasure in wearing skinny jeans that show-off one's own achieved physique. Such as in the case of Daniele, an artist in his mid-twenties (Interview 27), who likes jeans that stress the 'slenderness of the legs': 'in the past I was fat and now, being thin, I want to underline the goal I reached with so many sacrifices.' Typically, though, a strong and muscular body – 'big but not fat' – is a source of masculine pride, as Franco, a university student in his late twenties (Interview 32), admits: 'I am quite happy having big thighs, large and with strong muscles, I like when you can notice my legs and this fact affected even 70 per cent my decision [to buy this model of jeans].' Typically, for heterosexual males, well-fitting jeans, not too skinny ('otherwise they are embarrassing'), hard but comfortable, are considered ideal: their strength against the body allows for an heightened perception of one's own body prowess and potency, their enveloping but not squeezing fit underlines figure in a way which is recognized as appropriately masculine.[7]

Females' rhetorical emphasis on 'hiding imperfections' bears witness to the heavier burden of normative aesthetic ideals on women's bodies; compared to those of males, women's bodies are felt to be much more under scrutiny, a potential source of criticism, and of value judgements quite consequential in terms of social acceptance and recognition. Young women were more aware of the aesthetic demand on their bodies, emphasizing thinness, in combination with sexual attraction represented by the idea of 'curves' – some body parts, essentially the bottom, the hips, the thighs, were indicated as a major concern. Aesthetic demands in choices of jeans for women were more obviously related to eroticism and sexual attraction. Rather than using denim jeans to feel less conspicuous as females, deploying masculine codes to disguise femininity, women mainly appear to translate and selectively adopt these codes to stress femininity. The performance of a 'feminine figure' in jeans happens mainly via a *seduction* frame. To this end, feminine curves have to be mastered, both stressed and controlled, in a dialectic between *expression* and *repression* of sexuality, which has been associated with contemporary rules of seduction, shaping the sexualization of the body within fashion and consumer culture (Baudrillard 1997; Steele 1996). Thus, although the female body may effectively be squeezed into a tight-fitting pair, even with the help of a lower than recommended size, the generally reported feeling is one of 'comfort'. Comfort, in this case, is explicitly related to making one's body fit aesthetic body ideals, rather than comfortable freedom of movement, which is more the notion of comfort indicated by males as complying with their masculine embodied self ideals. Heterosexual males indeed appeared to achieve a masculine look by downplaying seduction: their main concern was to look good *without* looking gay, thus rather than a seduction frame they more typically activated a (traditional) *masculinity* frame, stressing activity, movement, potency – as opposed to the more passive 'gazed on' position that females seemed to opt for, even with jeans.

Feeling Sexy in Unisex Clothes: Sexualizing Jeans

It is partly the particular role jeans play in mirror work that leads the striking majority of the participants in the study to consider jeans as a 'second skin', whose attributes are characterizations of an explicit sexual nature. Jeans are something that is either tight to the figure or produces a frisson on the naked skin – in both cases stressing one's own perception of one's own body as something sexualized. Jeans appear as heavily sexualized items, especially among youth. This indeed seems to contradict their otherwise mundane, unisex nature. Let's explore.

Denim jeans were a staple of our interviewees' wardrobes, both male and female and they were considered a remarkably 'unisex' item 'fitting perfectly every body' in terms of gender. Yet, males, and especially females, tended to express their liking of jeans as sported by others in explicitly gendered terms, which quite often adumbrated heavily gendered notions of attractiveness. So we hear young women saying that '*a man* in jeans is always more attractive', that they 'like a lot *men* wearing jeans' or the idea that 'any man, even my father, looks better in jeans', or that 'on men, jeans that are a bit tight on the bum and then large on legs ... those make me crazy.' They also, quite often, mentioned other women 'looking good in jeans', highlighting more stringent aesthetic demands and stressing that 'especially if she [the exemplified woman] has the right figure, if she is a beautiful girl, with jeans it's just perfect!' Young Milanese men differed in their remarks according to their sexuality. While homosexual males tended to mirror women in their liking of close-fitting, bottom-showing models on themselves, heterosexual males concentrated their remarks on women. They considered women very attractive in jeans, stressing the sexual imaginary that is associated with certain models and styles of wearing – and in particular they appreciated the emphasis on 'the hips' that jeans are said to afford the female figure: 'I like a woman with tight and low rise jeans because a woman deserves to have tight jeans.' Quite often heterosexual males also mentioned their liking of 'dresses', 'skirts', 'anything which lets a bit of skin on view ...'

Heterosexual males' and females' reference to body shapes or parts that are portrayed as erotic adumbrates the gendering of jeans and their latent power as a sexual tool. However, sexualization of jeans occurs mainly as a practical accomplishment and with the help of a number of material and symbolic qualifiers besides body parts or characteristics, including style of wearing, accessories and places:

> In my opinion jeans are a very sexy garment, always in relation to what kind of person is wearing them, because jeans are sexy if the person wearing them have naturally the right figure, I'm not among these people but if I have to think about the usual 'super model', I always imagine her wearing a very tight pair of jeans and high heels. I never think about a 'hot girl' not wearing jeans, also when I go to clubs I see all them wearing jeans, so I always put together 'hot girl' and jeans'
>
> (Interview 8, clerical worker in her early twenties)

> That particular kind, with the low crotch and lower pockets, was improving my behind. Maybe it was lacking a bit on the legs, making them look shorter, but it was sexy in my opinion. Well I was seeing myself as sexier with those jeans than in classic jeans.
>
> (Interview 29, musician in his late twenties)

Sexualization is aided by specific body features that denim jeans at the same time enhance *and* produce. A 'right figure', for females, is essentially captured by the formula 'slender and curvy' often quoted by our interviewees. The specifications for a male figure appear less normative and precise, but, as suggested, slenderness, together with muscularity and tallness are often mentioned. These body characteristics facilitate sexualization, but in combination with specific models. Low-rise jeans have often been mentioned as particularly sexy, and so are very tight ones, especially for women (and gay men). Prevalent both among males and females is the image of close-fitting jeans that blend with 'body curves' and 'mark the female figure', its femaleness as indicated by the inaccessible accessibility of a heavily sexualized bottom. The reference to the fact that 'in women jeans mark the bum' is ubiquitous. Males are quite explicit in linking this to sexual imaginary, extending the reference to genitals, and applying it to both men and women: 'tight jeans mark the private parts of men and also of women, you can see everything beneath so the result is very sexy [...] even though a great part is left to the imagination' (Interview 28). Still, close-fitting or skin-showing jeans become particularly sexy if worn in combination with certain accessories: 'It always depends on which item you combine them with, if you wear just jeans alone they are not sexy, but if you wear them with a particular t-shirt and a certain pair of shoes they can absolutely be sexy' (Interview 22). High heels or a special top can make even 'baggy rapper jeans' sexy. Images of sexy jeans are also, quite commonly, accompanied by the visualization of special places and occasions, such as, prominently, a party or a disco dance.

Jeans are often reported as being a 'perfect choice for dancing', both by males and females. On such occasions, youth from Milan appear to use denim jeans in an overtly sexualized manner, taking on different meanings depending on gender and sexual identity: heterosexual males in the study have generally stressed denim jeans' 'comfort', downplaying its seduction potential; females in general, and homosexual men in particular, referred more directly to their seduction potential. All stress that denim jeans are a 'passport for any situation', which allows them to face any contingency, thus providing security and attraction. Young females often use jeans for a first date, even with a 'stylish guy' who may be difficult to please, as it's a 'safe option'. As one of the female participants said:

> it is the item I wear more often to go dancing, especially if I am unsure which kind of place is it. I wear these and I know I will feel comfortable. [...] Like recently to go to Plastic [an alternative Milanese disco pub] I had to meet up with a guy whom I knew little, and the place is full of weird people, so, I choose my favourite jeans, a black top with naked back, and very high heels boots, nothing special, but a very sexy combination after all.

> (Interview 15, hostess in her mid-twenties)

Jeans are not only unisex items – they are also perceived as potentially very sexy. They fit both male and female bodies, but, as a second skin, they draw attention to the sexual potential of male and female bodies, thus stressing their aesthetic compliance with heavily sexualized body ideals. The cultural imaginary that surrounds denim is deployed to this end (Botterill 2007; Volli 1991). Several participants in the study stressed that jeans are very sexy because 'they have this wild and jaunty element', and despite their mass diffusion, they 'still have this way of being a bit wild and cowboy's', they bring to mind memories of the 'American West', the 'frontier', an 'untamed', 'natural', past where life was more real, strong and free. As previously noted, jeans may also express transgression and in this case sexualized transgression, mainly as a way to convey an image of erotic openness. This is particularly evident among females, who often refer to seduction as a course of action through which they interpret jeans on special occasions:

> sometimes I wear those jeans having the idea of provoking a bit, of being a bit more open, let's say that if I stand in a certain posture wearing those jeans, I can have a glance more from my boyfriend, so it is a transgression in the way of me being sexier than usual.
>
> (Interview 7, clerical worker in her early twenties)

> I'm wearing those jeans because I want to show up more, if I weren't aiming this as result I would wear a bell-bottom jeans with a jumper, instead I decide to wear tight jeans with high heels shoes and a top: that makes an impression, it says something like I am a bit more into a seduction game
>
> (Interview 13, male in his mid-twenties)

All in all, in what appears as an appropriation of the sexual imagery that surrounds the advertising campaigns of well known brands such as Dolce and Gabbana or Diesel (see Sullivan 2006; Volli 1991), the gendering of jeans is predicated on uneven sexualization and eroticization: just as heterosexual males felt fit – and that they were fitting their social personae – with jeans that helped perform a masculine look, downplaying seduction, heterosexual women tended to feel this way when their jeans could also be easily translated into a seduction tool. They all agreed that their favourite jeans are a safe bet for seduction, and that they are often deployed, with accessories and demeanour, to get sexual attention or simply be 'appreciated by boys'. Often conceptualized as a matter of insinuation and imagination, seduction in jeans relates to how the body is framed by jeans (especially 'curvy slenderness') and construed as anticipation of what is out of sight. Denim jeans seem to provide the seduction game with some normalizing anchoring. In contrast with a miniskirt, for example, jeans are 'less explicit', they work 'subtly, without giving off too much'. They are still somehow perceived as an originally male item that is appropriated by women as a symbol of explicit 'liberated' sexuality that can, nevertheless, be inoffensive: they do not open the female body to the male gaze uncompromisingly, they have to be activated by women (with a pose, a laugh, a word, an accessory, a hole in the fabric that allows a little skin to be seen, etc.). It is thus left to a woman to play with her own sexualization. In a duality which is characteristic of fashion more generally (see Simmel 1904; see also Davis 1989), such sexualization is itself at once highly individualized and normalized, as shown by the 'ordinary' nature of denim jeans as against explicitly 'sexy' clothing that would do without individual activation. Rather than being objectified once and for all in an outfit that petrifies sexual meanings beyond their wearer's intentions, seduction in jeans requires the wearer's continuous keying of his or her own body as sexually charged, stressing, yet again individuality and agency.

Concluding Remarks

In this chapter I have explored denim jeans as a culturally thick item of material culture, which is deployed, more or less willingly, to perform identity, sexuality and seduction. Just as sexuality is predicated on personal identity, and indeed conceived as its most intimate aspect, the sexualization of jeans cannot be seen in isolation. It builds upon a foundation that is constructed in jeans' much wider relation to fashion. Within the clothing-identity space, denim jeans are perceived as a particularly strong index of individuality. Each washing turns a new page, time imprints its memory on an increasingly uneven and paler background which follows the movements and the shapes of the user's body just like the washing's discolorations adumbrate embodied experience. As such, jeans appear as a 'second skin': as one voice from the field explained, 'they have a story written in the fabric which is your story.' But they do not just reflect one's one story, or one's one body. They reflect a continuously activated and carefully preformed authenticity, foreshadowing the possibility of neutralizing fashion while playing with it (*superfashion* and *personal patina*), as well as the opportunity to enhance one's own sexual attractiveness by providing a sense of fitness, with culturally sexualized clothing that both *fit oneself* and *make oneself fit* broader beauty ideals.

Favourite jeans are heavily implicated in the visualization of a better, easier, and sexier, embodied self – a fit self. We shouldn't be surprised of this slippage of meaning, fitness after all having been originally defined as the capacity to survive by reproduction, presumably attracting partners. They are both an everyday item (charged with meanings such as 'natural', 'simple', 'relaxing', 'normal', 'modest', 'casual') and a heavily sexualized item, often deemed the 'sexiest of all', especially for women. This duality is intrinsic to their sexual potential: it takes away pressure from the erotic investment of the body, stressing a nonchalant seduction that promises to remain free and playful, always in the hands of the seducer. Of course, these dynamics are quite heavily gendered: jeans minimize defects and stress appreciated body parts or characteristics, but men are more concerned with expressing bulk and strength, whereas women are more concerned with concealment and containment. Such negative terms are turned into positive ones once a woman feels her favourite jeans have helped her to achieve the appropriate curvy slenderness, and she is willing to deploy them as a seduction device. In its turn, the successful deployment of seduction is the ultimate guarantee that an appropriately sexy feminine figure in jeans has been achieved. The ability to create a sexualized image that draws the gaze to one's own body comes from all the previous mirror work in which a certain degree of confidence has been negotiated through jeans, precisely as they are felt as increasingly personal and fitting one's own expected social persona. Just as they express people's ability to both pay respect to fashion and remain transcendent of it by commanding personal patina and superfashion qualities. Denim jeans are thus deployed to perform what is perceived as individualized sexualization in the prescribed forms of dichotomic gendered codes.

Notes

1. This chapter draws on material collected as part of a larger research initiative that is being pursued by the author with a number of her final year MA students using ethnography, ethnographic interviews and visual methodologies. Among these students, I especially thank Simona Ettori, Federica Galeazzi, Niccolò Motta and Michele Pilloni for their passion and precious help in collecting the empirical material here analysed. This paper, in particular, relies on 40 in-depth interviews with youths from middle-class neighbourhoods in Milan. The interviewees were aged 20 to 29, twenty males and twenty females, predominantly heterosexual, although a number (nine) of male homosexuals have also been included. The interviews took place between the winter 2007 and the spring 2009, lasted between 1 and 2 hours, with quite a few being furthered by a shorter follow-up to pursue some of the more intimate issues. I wish to thank all participants in this study for their willingness to share with us their experiences. A resounding thank to Daniel Miller for his unfailing support and helpful editorial advice, and much gratitude to Rossella Ghigi and Nicoletta Giusti for their careful reading and comments.

2. These arguments are reinforced by the reported practices. Describing their shopping for jeans or their picking up a pair from the wardrobe to wear, our youth from Milan is willing to appear fashion-conscious, but likewise mentions 'taste' or 'what fits me best' as the ultimate motivation. Particular makes of jeans may be 'the last arrivals in the shops', may 'feature everywhere in fashion magazines', but these circumstances are described as just providing the chance to realize one's own taste and aspirations. For these reasons, even old jeans may be still be used, and quite frequently, 'even though they are not so fashionable anymore'.

3. A verbalization of one's own relation to brands was also specifically pursued in the research. Many of our interviewees referred to specific brands, even though they tended to stress other factors as major determinants – and in particular 'the cut' for identity representation and 'price' for purchase decision. The symbolic universe recalled by the brand is recognized as largely managed by the manufacturer and its promotional techniques, whereas the cut is said to allow individual bodies to speak for themselves. Body shape itself makes it difficult for brands to construct an imagined community of alike users, all identified with the brand image. Brands can also be misleading if considered as a mark of identity, as they only signify identity in conjunction with body demeanour and self-presentation. In many cases, even when the brand was considered important, verbalizations have

stressed personalization. So branding is articulated less in terms of imagined communities, brand values, quality guarantee and more in terms of a dialectic of appropriation.

4. In a few cases, the wearing and tearing of one's own favourite denim jeans implies a diminishment of value, because 'newness' appears as a value, and general wear-ability may deteriorate greatly with time. 'Even if is true that the fact that they are damaged means that a pair of jeans went trough many experiences with you and this fact is nice – says a female student in her mid-twenties – once they are really old, and damaged, it is not like you can wear them everywhere like when they were new' (Interview 20).

5. Comfort as the feeling that one is able to meet, to a degree, one's own body ideals is prevalent in the (female) description of wearing a lower size than usual: 'I had a wonderful feeling, really wonderful, because after a tough diet, during which I suffered a lot, wearing a light colour pair of jeans, tight and size 40, fitting me so well, it was a great satisfaction' (Interview 21). Of course a double-exploitation game can be initiated around this, with fashion companies playing with sizes to provide easy satisfactions, and costumers deliberately orienting themselves towards brands that allow them to feel slimmer by generous sizing.

6. To notice the fact that the vast majority of our interviewees considered that denim jeans were the most versatile clothing, but likewise felt that versatility stopped short of very formal occasions, which were heavily gendered: mainly graduation ceremonies, job interviews and marriages for women, only marriages for men. Denim fabric partake this destiny to a large degree: for females, a fashion accessory in denim (such as a bag) may indeed be used in a job interview to provide a touch of 'easiness' or 'originality'.

7. Gay respondents differed markedly in both their strong liking of tight jeans, their generally greater attention to fashion and their willingness to play with a seduction frame in the sexualization of their clothed bodies. On the other hand, heterosexual males were characterized by concerns such as those expressed by Matteo (Interview 30) who declared: 'I have a pair of jeans in the closet that are surely rule-breaking, but that I think are hard to wear just because they are extreme. Instead my favourite jeans are classic, showing leg, calf and bum but they are not so tight. These ones that instead are in my closet. I still didn't dare to wear them as they are really tight and much more rule breaking.'

References

Baudrillard, J. (1997), *Della seduzione,* Milan: Se.

Baudrillard, J. (1998), *The Consumer Society*, London: Sage.

Bordo, S. (1993), *Unbearable Weight. Feminism, Western Culture and the Body*, Berkeley, CA: University of California Press.

Botterill, J. (2007), 'Cowboys, Outlaws and Artists: The Rhetoric of Authenticity and Contemporary Jeans and Sneaker Advertisements' *Journal of Consumer Culture*, 7(1): 105–126.

Davis, F. (1989), 'Of Maids' Uniforms and Blue Jeans. The Drama of Status Ambivalence in Clothing and Fashion', *Qualitative Sociology*, 12(4): 337–55.

Entwistle, J. (2000), *The Fashioned Body*, Cambridge: Polity.

Fiorentini, A. (2005), 'Considerazioni sulla recente storia del 'Blue de Genes' In Italia', in *Jeans! Le origini, il mito americano, il made in Italy,* Firenze: Maschietto.

Frith, K.; Shaw, P. and Cheng, H. (2005), 'The Construction of Beauty: A Cross-cultural Analysis of Women's Magazines Advertising', *Journal of Communication*, 55(1): 56–70.

Gauntlet, D. (2002), *Media, Gender and Identity*, London: Routledge.

Goffman, E. (1967), *Stigma: Notes on the Management of Spoiled Identity*, Englewood Cliffs, NJ: Prentice-Hall.

Green, A. I. (2008), 'The Social Organization of Desire. The Sexual Fields Approach', *Sociological Theory*, 26(1): 25–54.

Guillaumin, C. (2006), 'Il corpo costruito', *Studi Culturali*, 2: 307–42.

Lurie, A. (1981), *The Language of Clothes*, New York: Random House.

McCraken, G. (1988), *Culture and Consumption*, Bloomington: Indiana University Press.

Miller, D., and Woodward, S. (2007), 'Manifesto For a Study of Denim', *Social Anthropology/Anthropologie Sociale,* 15(3): 335–51.

Sassatelli, R. (2007), *Consumer Culture. History, Theory and Politics*, London: Sage.

Sassatelli, R. (2010), *Fitness Culture. The Gym and the Commercialization of Fun and Discipline*, Basingstoke: Palgrave.

Simmel, G. (1904), 'Fashion', *The American Journal of Sociology*, 62(6): 541–58.

Steele, V. (1996), *Fetish: Fashion, Sex and Power*, Oxford: Oxford University Press.

Sullivan, J. (2006), *Jeans. A Cultural History of an American Icon,* New York: Gotham Books.

Veblen, T. (1898), 'The Beginnings of Ownership', *The American Journal of Sociology*, 4(3): 352–65.

Volli, U. (1991), *Jeans,* Milan: Lupetti.

Wernick, A. (1991), *Promotional Culture. Advertising, Ideology and Symbolic Expression*, London: Sage.

Waquant, L. (1995), 'Why men desire muscles?', *Body and Society*, 1(1): 163–79.

–7–

Jeanealogies: Materiality and the (Im)permanence of Relationships and Intimacy

Sophie Woodward

I wear his jeans when I'm on my own in my flat ... I don't know why ... I guess it makes me feel like I'm still close to him, kind of comforted ...

Georgia, a woman in her early twenties living in London, is wearing the jeans of a man she is in an ambiguous on-off relationship with when she utters these words to me. After spending the night with him at his flat, she borrowed them the next morning to keep warm on the journey home and continues to wear them when she is back in her own flat. Wearing the jeans, she feels he continues to be, in some part, present with her and makes her more able to deal with the ambiguity of her relationship to him. During ethnographic fieldwork that I conducted into women's wardrobes in the UK, several women I worked with wore their boyfriend's jeans, and 'boyfriend' jeans themselves are currently a well established category of jeans in the UK. Georgia's example raises the ways in which clothing is used to negotiate women's relationships to others. The very appearance of cloth and clothing is one that lends itself to associations with connectedness, with rich metaphorical potential in terms of the weaving together of people, and the fabric of their relationships. The connectedness of woven cloth is extended both to metaphor and also to anthropological attempts to see the process of weaving and exchange of cloth as symbolizing kinship relationships (Weiner and Schneider 1989). The embeddedness of clothing in people's relationships is, however, not given the same attention by Weiner and Schneider (1989) for clothing in the West and the wider context of fashion. Instead, clothing in the contemporary UK is subsumed under fashion, and concomitant associations of image, appearance and individualism. It is the contention of this chapter that, in the context of the UK, the relationships people have to clothing are not reducible to wider contexts and values of individualism. This chapter will focus upon the material acts of wearing, donating and borrowing denim jeans, as a means through which relationships to others are negotiated.

One of the predominant relationships in the provisioning and gifting of clothing in countries such as the UK and US is that between mother and daughter (Clarke

2000; Corrigan 1995; DeVault 1991) as particular taste patterns are inculcated, and as an act of love, although this relationship may become more contested as the daughter moves to adulthood (Miller 1997). In my initial ethnography on women's wardrobes there was a clear contrast between the long-term gifting of clothing over time between mothers and daughters and the lending of clothing between relatives or long-term friendships and more short-term clothing exchanges (Woodward 2007). The type of clothing lent and the expectations of whether it will be returned immediately or not served to create and reinforce the relationship. In this chapter, I focus in the main on a particular kind of relationship, between women and their boyfriends. In light of this focus, it may appear somewhat unexpected to use the trope of the genealogy, which seems to imply a structured family history. When this structured formalized set of relationships is mapped onto the passage of clothing, it would imply that clothing, or jeans, would be similarly rigidly structured as they are used to define relationships between generations. Alternatively, at the level of broader cultural histories, to talk of a genealogy of jeans, a 'jean-ealogy', conjures up associations of the lineage of denim jeans as descending from Levi-Strauss in the late nineteenth century and the well established histories and stories of denim jeans. The jeanealogy suggested in this paper is somewhat different from either of these, as it forms part of my broader orientation to clothing in the context of the UK, which is to focus upon the everyday and ordinary practices of selection, wearing and choice of clothing. The meanings that arise from the jeans do not originate from the creativity and authorship of the designer but instead through the ways in which denim is worn and exchanged and as it comes to enable and materialize everyday relationships. Therefore, the jeanealogy is understood in a much more fluid, less formalized sense than conventional notions of the genealogy would allow for.

The notion of fluidity in personal relationships is emphasized by writers on intimacy within contemporary British society. Giddens (1991, 1992) suggests that the changes in the labour market amongst other social changes – for example sex is no longer wed to procreation – means that there is a shift in the structuring of relationships and a transformation of intimacy. In his account, this leads to a greater diversity in relationships, and the 'pure relationship' that is 'entered into for its own sake' (Giddens 1992: 58). At the core of Giddens' idea is what Jamieson has termed 'disclosing intimacy' (Giddens 1998: 1), where the relationship is negotiated and maintained through the verbalization of feelings and desires. Whilst there are many critiques of Giddens' ideas, in relation to the emphasis upon choice and ignoring persisting gendered inequalities, the primacy given to the verbal and spoken is of particular concern in this article. I opened this chapter with the spoken words of a woman I worked with ethnographically; however, these words carry meaning when situated in the context of much wider observations of her practices. These words are not ones she would ever articulate to the man she is seeing. As material culture, the jeans do not reflect the relationship, but her wearing of his jeans are a medium through which she is able to articulate that which she is unable to verbalize to him. In her critique of Giddens, Jamieson (1998) discusses the multiple layers of intimacy, as verbalizing feelings are only one expression or aspect of intimacy. The jeans may therefore externalize contradictory aspects of a relationship, for example in terms of dependency and independency. A similar contradiction is exemplified in the pure relationship, expounded and idealized by Giddens, which is not bound by tradition and entered into freely, yet simultaneously carries within it the possibility for this union to breakdown. In this chapter, I will suggest that clothing effectively externalizes the fragility of a relationship, which dovetails with Weiner's claims, albeit in a very different context, where she suggests that the 'softness and ultimate fragility of these materials capture the vulnerability of humans, whose every relationship is transient' (Weiner 1989: 2).

Personalization through Wearing

The material upon which this paper is based comes from ethnography carried out in London and Nottingham over a fifteen-month period of women's wardrobes (see Woodward 2007 for full details of the methodology and research findings). There were twenty-seven women in total in the research sample, recruited through snow-ball sampling. Over half of the women were connected to each other through kin-ship, work, or friendship groups (three networks in total). To suggest that denim jeans offer the possibility of connections to others seems to pose something of a paradox, given that they are cited by many women I worked with as being an item of clothing to which they have a very personal relationship, a point we have elaborated on in the introduction to this volume. There are pairs of jeans that women would not let anyone else wear – for example, when women have found the elusive 'perfect jeans' or a pair that they have worn over such a long period of time because the intimate personal relationship that they have to the jeans would be disrupted by someone else wearing them. However, several of these same women also wore the jeans of their boyfriends or partners. In many cases this is due to the larger body size of their boyfriends, as women are easily able to fit them. By virtue of the denim carrying the former wearer, women are able to negotiate a relationship to someone else, and in some instances use it to expand upon their own personal aesthetic.

Authenticity and Masculinity

Steph, the first case study, is a woman in her early twenties who is originally from Ireland and wears her boyfriend's jeans regularly. Although he is still living in Ireland, and as such is not present with her all the time, Steph is not wearing the jeans as a sentimental reminder of him but primarily to expand upon her own ward-robe. This is part of a wider tendency that emerged from the main ethnography, where women do not necessarily treat items gifted or passed on to them as cherished heirlooms or items that reify a particular person or relationship. Although the act of wearing serves to establish a connection to others, as the relationships to others are externalized in items of clothing, women are able to use these same relationships to expand the possibilities of who you can be through clothing (see previous discussions of this in Woodward 2007). Women may be able to expand their usually personal aesthetic through the taste of a friend or their mother. This strategy, at the micro level of the wardrobe, is mirrored in the wider practices of wearing vintage or second-hand clothing (see Clark and Palmer 2004; Gregson and Crewe 2003), where it is possible to imagine the narratives behind the garments. It is an affordable way to expand upon the possibilities of what can be worn and it allows a perceived stepping outside of mainstream fashion.

Wearing her boyfriend's jeans, for Steph, is part of her wider attitude to clothing as she states on numerous occasions that she loathes the high street (despite buying items such as her skinny jeans from there). Over two years, she gradually made her boyfriend's jeans a part of her wardrobe, first wearing them when he left them in her flat as he stayed over, and now, she owns two pairs that he has had to relinquish to her, it would seem, permanently. She wears her jeans almost every day alternating between wearing her boyfriend's jeans, and her other skinny drainpipe jeans (which were the fashion at the time when I was working with her), which she wears with trainers and her 'rocker' t-shirts. Different types of jeans are the basis for her to create very different daily looks. Steph's boyfriend is around four inches taller than her; he is narrow hipped, but wears the jeans loose on him. On her they are low slung, and she has to hold them up by wearing a chunky belt. They are straight-legged jeans, and are so loose fitting that they do not cling to any part of her body; the legs are too long that she has to turn them up on the outside. She wears the oversized jeans with fitted pink or cream silk camisole tops, and soft silk-mix, angora or cashmere cardigans. Although the jeans are unmistakably men's jeans, as the crotch starts half way down her thighs, the combination with the pink camisole, and the soft angora cardigan in pale colours means that the overall look is far from masculinized. In many other cases, jeans are valued through the personalized way in which a pair of jeans adapt to the wearer's body. For Steph, these particular jeans, through their voluminousness, serve to emphasize the smallness of her body. The only place that the denim has started to wear down and soften is at the base, where she trips over the edges of the turn-ups. In adopting a masculinized style of jeans, and rejecting a conventional femininity that jeans might allow, she serves to emphasize her vulnerability and delicateness as she constructs an alternative mode of femininity (such as in Holland 2004). The femininity that is articulated through the jeans serves as a repudiation of the hypersexualized, semi-clad masquerade of femininity that is present in many mainstream representations of young women (Levy 2006).

Steph exemplifies a core contradiction many young women embody between the desire to be fashionable through participating in fast fashion and simultaneously wanting to reject and repudiate the fashion mainstream and the femininity it embodies. Her verbalized dislike of high-street fashion becomes practice through shopping in charity shops, and also in wearing her boyfriend's jeans. She is able to thus deal with the potentially alienating features of mass fashion in terms of both the rapidly changing temporal cycles and its perceived inauthenticity. Although authenticity is a highly contested term, it was used by many women I worked with in discussing their relationships to clothing. It is a term through which they articulated their own practices; the authentic is often perceived as being in opposition to commercially produced styles. This opposition is problematic when seen in the light of the ways in which commerce appropriates and represents everyday consumption patterns. In the case of denim jeans, this happens through processes such as distressing, where the abrasion of the fabric through wearing is replicated through commercial design processes. It also happens through the selling of 'boyfriend jeans' in various high street stores, as they tap into the borrowing practices that women partake in. Boyfriend jeans are both a commercially produced style, and are also, in Steph's case, based upon borrowing her actual boyfriends jeans, as she tells me they are the 'real thing', as they come to seem more authentic by virtue of once being worn by her boyfriend. In wearing men's jeans she is also drawing upon the original narratives of denim jeans, which, in its origins, is a masculinized trajectory. The jeans she borrows are pure cotton (with no elastane fibres, as is the practice with the majority of current women's jeans), which serves to accentuate the authentic connotations of the masculinized, pure cotton, blue denim. She has worn the jeans on and off for two years now, and the jeans have become more personalized through both her boyfriend and Steph wearing them. This process over time allows her to step outside of the constantly changing temporal cycles of fast fashion. They can be seen to form a rejection of the alleged speed of fast fashion, as they acquire their meaning through a slow process of abrading and being worn down. The jeans become personalized not by directly taking on her body shape (as is the case when women wear more fitted jeans over a period of time). Instead as the jeans are worn down at the base as they drag on the floor and so the relationship between her body and the jeans is different to that which her boyfriend had (as the worn-down area of the knees falls below her actual knee).

Multiple Wearers

In the preceding example, the jeans are seen as authentic because they were not bought by Steph as the commercial women's wear category of 'boyfriend jeans' but belonged to her boyfriend. In other examples in my fieldwork, authenticity is evidenced in the histories of wear that are apparent in the fabric. It derives from the patina of age, which is present in denim where the fabric has abraded and become softened as the soft white cotton fibres show through. This wearing can be either a personalized process, as they are worn habitually over a long period of time, or, in the example to be discussed here, of someone who not only wears the jeans of a former partner but jeans that have been worn by several members of her extended family. Vivienne, a former political campaigner and researcher in her fifties living in north London, has one pair of jeans that used to be black denim but are now worn down to a faded grey colour, with soft white patches, where the soft cotton fibres have worn through. These jeans are fourth hand and were given to her by her daughter's boyfriend (formerly worn by her daughter, and her boyfriend's father). In the previous example of Steph the jeans externalize the relationship between two individuals and in a broader sense this is what boyfriend jeans encapsulate. This example serves to highlight the ways in which multiple relationships, and also forms of intimacy, may be present within one item of clothing. Jamieson (1998) has argued that the intimate relationship between two people, as exemplified by Giddens' pure relationship (1992), has been idealized in contemporary society. This idealization has served to obscure, in Jamieson's account, the multiple forms of intimacy – such as practical caring, dependency, sharing – within any one relationship and within many different forms of relationships. So too here, the journey of the jeans does not reify one relationship, but has incorporated several family members. The jeans do not carry any one person's body, but are gradually altered by each wearer in turn. The jeans have passed between more than one family, making a connection between both.

Although, in the previous example, Steph is not treating the jeans as something to be preserved as they are – she still refers to them as her boyfriend's jeans (even though they have been longer in her possession). They are strongly associated with the former wearer and, as they are loose and baggy, they have not taken on Steph's body even through repeated acts of wearing. In the case of Vivienne's jeans, they are not used to remember a specific person, but rather by being worn by a series of people, each person leaves their traces on the garment as it materializes the network of connections between them. The vestigial traces of the wearers are present within the worn down nature of the jeans, yet as the jeans have been passed between people, these traces overlap and it is hard to identify any individual pattern of wear. The jeans come to materialize the passage of time and the construction of the family. The connections between people that are being discussed here are very different from formalized notions of a genealogy. Weiner and Schneider (1989) cite Gitting's research into funerals and the transition in the seventeenth century to people having to provide their own black drapes for funerals. They discuss this as a point of transition for clothing in the context of the West as it 'no longer expressed the continuity of the groups with ancestral authority and their reproduction through time' (Weiner and Schneider 1989: 11). What this does not account for is the informal passing on of clothing or gifting of items, which establishes a connection between generations or between family members. Even in a climate with dominant values of individualism, this always exists in relationship to wider social relations in which it is embedded from which it arises. The individual is always constituted relationally, seen through clothing practices in the wearing of borrowed and gifted clothing. As these relationships develop and change throughout the life course, Stanley (1992) has questioned and challenged the conventional way that biography is understood as the story of an isolated individual. Instead she argues that significant others cannot be reduced to the position of 'shadowing figures' as the biographical self is constructing through relationships to others. This is seen as much within the wardrobe a woman owns, as women draw in their relationships to others in their clothing choices. This is reflected within an individual item like Vivienne's jeans, which carry many different wearers. Each individual personalizes the item and the one pair of jeans interconnects many different people.

In both the cases of Vivienne and Steph, the wearing of the jeans of others allows a stepping outside of fashion, borrowing clothes from others is an alternative sourcing strategy to the high street. This is part of Vivienne's wider strategies towards clothing, as she owns very few new items of clothing, with many being so old and worn that they are falling apart, as her daughters often pass items up to her. Although this distancing of themselves from fashion can be linked to buying and sourcing from second-hand shops there is a point of difference as bought second hand involve an imagined, anonymous narrative. For Steph, she is wearing jeans that connect her to one other person, and for Vivienne, the jeans allow her to become part of a woven network of the narratives of a series of people. It allows her to define herself through her connectedness to others; it is jeans that allow her to do this most effectively as it carries the personalized traces of the wearers, yet the jeans have now softened so much in places that they are threatening to disintegrate all together.

The Impermanence and Fragility of Relationships

Vivienne's jeans have lasted long enough to carry the imprint of several wearers, but they will not last forever. The simultaneous durability and fragility of denim will be explored through this final example of Georgia, a woman in her early twenties. The jeans in questions cannot be called her 'boyfriend' jeans, as she has an ambiguous relationship with a man whom she has been 'seeing' for over six months. He refuses to use the word 'boyfriend' and she is unsure whether he is seeing other girls; they meet up regularly, yet the lack of definition of their relationship means she feels uncertain as to when he will come and see her next.

This example highlights the problems with Giddens' (1992) pure relationship, which is based upon the freedom of choice of two individuals, who are self-reflexive over their feelings and desires, which leads to a relationship between equals. Numerous critiques of Giddens, such as Jackson (1996), suggest that this fails to account for the persistence of inequalities. As Duncombe and Marsden (1999: 103) note, what contemporary relationships characterize more widely is not the equality that Giddens so optimistically touts, but that sexual differences persist. Georgia exemplifies this, as she confides on occasion that she wishes he was her boyfriend. Although she harbours this wish at the moment, while he thwarts her desire for a steady relationship, this situation may well change were he to capitulate. For Georgia, a key part of her social relationships are friendships with other women, a key topic being the hopelessness of men. This highlights a problematic and complex relationship between public narratives, personal narratives and everyday practice.

There are public stories about gendered expectations of relationships – for instance that 'all women want commitment' and 'men want to sleep around' (Hollway 1984), another one being 'all men are bastards', which Georgia at times highlights. The narrative she adopts does not negate the fact that she simultaneously expresses a desire to be connected to this particular man, and how these public narratives of 'wanting a good boyfriend' seep into her own expectations. This also highlights a paradox between a possible desire for independence, being single and bonding with her female friends, and also the desire for connection. Dependency and connection to others start to raise questions about the 'pure relationship'. This example also problematizes an understanding of relationships based merely upon the verbal, as is assumed in notions of 'disclosure' taking a central place in a relationship, which does not allow for contradiction. This is similarly true for the notion of reflexivity: wearing his jeans may also signify an absence of reflexivity and a desire, on occasion, to allow a material connection to this man, without verbalizing her contradictory experiences and feelings. These may be too complex to articulate. This reflexivity is also not gender neutral; Hochschild (cited in Heaphy 2007: 142) develops the idea of emotional labour in particular workplaces that some women have to master as part of their jobs. Heaphy (2007) has argued that this is as true at the level of relationships, where the expectation is for women to be more reflexive.

Even when Georgia's man is not in her flat, he is still present by virtue of the items he has left there. Some are left deliberately, such as a toothbrush and a warm winter jumper, and others are items she has bought back to her flat when she goes to see him. If they go out one evening, and she goes back to his house, so as not to look like a 'dirty stop out' (her words) the next day, she borrows a pair of jeans or a shirt. For days after, she may carry on wearing the jeans, but only around the house, until he reclaims them on his next visit. He is over six inches taller than her, and so, as in the first case study, when the jeans are worn they hang loose from her hip bones, and drag over her feet unless she rolls them over at the top. When she first puts them on, they still carry his scent, and are softened by him wearing them. The jeans are still animated by the last time he wore them as they have loosened around his knees, carrying the smell of his sweat and aftershave, as if they are a living garment making him seem present in her flat still. The size and looseness of the jeans emphasize her vulnerability as the jeans carry her absent lover's ghostly presence. She is able to feel comforted by wearing the jeans in the face of the uncertainty of whether she will see him again. She wears them when she feels her most vulnerable, and as she can still remember the feel of his body and arms around her, the jeans wrap around her body too as they mediate his presence and his absence. When she feels her most vulnerable, she is only able to partially verbalize this, as instead it is materialized: her simultaneous vulnerability and connectedness to him, as the jeans act as a form of security and stability that the relationship itself may not offer. The jeans have taken on his body shape and his scent and in wearing them it is as if she is able to inhabit the second skin of his jeans.

She only wears the jeans in the house and, even then, it is only on occasion and as such wearing his jeans is in many ways very different to her usual relationship with her clothing. Wearing the jeans helps her to negotiate the uncertainty of this particular relationship. There is a strong assumption that clothing in the contemporary UK is about 'expressing yourself', or is linked to individuality (see Woodward 2005 for a critique of this). In this instance, Georgia is adopting a completely opposite strategy: she is relinquishing her claims to be an individual in this moment, and instead wants to attach herself to her absent lover. When she is alone, after he has left her – this is when she feels vulnerable. Wearing clothing owned by others (or in other occasions gifted) enmeshes the individual back into social relationships: in this case her relationship to him when they are apart. As I have already discussed, the self is always constituted through multiple relationships, yet on this occasion it is only one relationship that she can conceive of herself through, and the clothing allows her to continue the connections to him. Wearing his jeans allows a simultaneous acknowledgment that she feels comforted and also her sense of vulnerability.

She is also implicitly acknowledging that the relationship itself is not permanent. The connections between clothing, social relations and permanence have been explored, albeit in very different contexts, by Weiner (1989). In two examples, in the Trobriand Islands and Western Samoa, she explores how cloth is used to symbolize kinship relationships and groups and how these same kinship identities are 'translated into political authority' through clothing, (Weiner 1989: 33). Her discussion is useful in highlighting how the properties of cloth are such that, in each case, they effectively manage to materialize kinship relationships and their connections to authority. The cloths she refers to in the Trobriand Islands are bundles of banana leaves (which involve extensive labour) and women's fibrous skirts (which are distributed after someone's death). Women's cloth wealth 'serves as the anchoring matrilineal force, demonstrating the success of regeneration in the face of death' (Weiner 1989: 40). In the case of Western Samoa, where chiefs' rankings are also associated with certain descent groups yet are not given by birth, the cloths she refers to are fine mats made from pandanus fibres, which are delicately plaited and soft as fine linen (and are more demanding to make than Trobriand bundles). The question Weiner (1989: 62) addresses through both of these examples is why cloth, which she terms 'soft wealth' is utilized as a symbol of authority and kinship identities, and not 'hard wealth', which would serve as a more permanent record. Weiner argues that it is precisely the impermanence of cloth that makes it effective as it captures the vulnerability of power. The cloths utilized in each case have some permanence, when they outlast an individual life-span, yet the characteristics of cloth are such that 'as it rots and disintegrates, bring to the histories of persons and lineages the reality of life's ultimate incompleteness' (Weiner 1989: 63).

Although this is a very different context from the one I outlined earlier in this chapter, the ideas about how cloth effectively materializes permanence and imperma-nence can be applied to the issue of the way in which denim mediates relationships to others. Denim carries the former wearer on numerous different levels; the most fleeting way being the traces of the living body directly after wearing, as the fabric is still warm from the body and carries its scents, which disappear as the jeans are washed. The fabric itself also carries the wearer in a more permanent way through continued wearing, the moving body leads to body- and usage-specific patterns of wearing and the fabric wears down. The more fleeting traces of the living body and the slightly more permanent traces of bodily movements co-exist. In Georgia's case she wears the jeans to feel connected to her absent lover, yet at the same time, as his living traces do not remain, and she has to give back the jeans, she simultaneously recognizes that the relationship itself is fleeting. Denim very effectively mediates this ambivalence, due to the ambivalences that inhere to the fabric – it is both rigid and it softens; it lasts but it does not last for ever. This sense of the impermanent traces of others is present in all of the examples discussed, as the wearing of the jeans of others allows for informality in the connections between people. For example, Vivienne's jeans have taken on several wearers and are able to incorporate different branches and members of the family. Weiner's primary focus is upon the making and the exchange of cloths, yet in my ethnography, although items are passed on, the emphasis is upon the wearing and the relationship between body and garment. Through this dynamic relationship, the form and texture of denim changes, as it is mutable and shifting in its interplay between toughness and relative durability, with a process of change and ageing as the fragile soft threads are revealed.

Conclusion

This chapter has used the idea of a 'jeanealogy' as a tool to think about how denim externalizes and helps negotiate a particular kind of relationship. A genealogy in its most widely applied incarnation involves tracing a family tree right back to the orig-inal ancestors. This is understood in an evolutionary sense, or even in the popular meanings as tracing a family's previous generations in an attempt to plot the family's ancestors. The jeanealogy proposed in this article is somewhat different. Weiner and Schneider can be seen to embody the classic anthropological sense of a genealogy when they note that in the West clothing does not express a groups continuity 'ances-tral authority and their reproduction through time' (Weiner and Schneider 1989: 11). However, the relationships that I am considering here are more fluid and informal.

Taking the example of Vivienne as a case in point, the daughter has now separated from the boyfriend from whom she received the jeans, and the jeans have disintegrated. In many instances there is not such a convenient correlation between the biography of the clothing and that of the relationship, as a desire to remember someone might outlive the clothing that disintegrates and dies too soon. This example does, however, highlight the impermanence of relationships that are absented from a formal genealogy. The jeanealogies I have traced here are informal, intransient, and partial as they may include fragments of incomplete relationships. This is particularly apt in the case of boyfriend jeans, given that these are predominantly worn by younger women and such relationships are particularly vulnerable to terminating.

The three examples all show different ways in which women may negotiate their relationships through clothing. For Steph this is about a relationship to a specific individual, her boyfriend, yet the jeans are a means through which she can expand upon the possibilities of her own wardrobe. Relationships are instead a means through which to expand upon the possibilities of the self (Osteen 2002), as clothing is a material means through which this can be negotiated. The individual and relationships to others are not mutually exclusive but relations to others may be the medium through which women may construct a personal aesthetic. What Steph's example has in common with that of Vivienne is that both use jeans that were originally someone else's in order to step outside of mainstream fashion and use the slower life cycle of a pair of jeans in order to do this. Even if commerce attempts to appropriate the slow process of ageing of a pair of jeans through processes such as distressing, for many women I worked with this carries connotations of inauthenticity, as fast fashion attempts to pick up the personalization and the gradual changes of a pair of jeans. In Miller and Woodward (2007) we discussed how the generic-ness of a pair of jeans is something that people could use to reattach them to the world when they feel the most vulnerable and separated from social relations. This was discussed in relation to an ethnographic example of someone who was paralysed with indecisions over what to wear to a party and ended up wearing a pair of new jeans. In this chapter, I have instead discussed how denim jeans are used to reconnect the individual to a very specific relationship; by drawing upon denim's capacity to carry the former wearer. Whilst on some occasions the wearing of jeans may be about the creation of an individual look, at other times it is very clearly about mitigating against the problems of feeling adrift from connections to others, as jeans are able to articulate this feeling of vulnerability and reconnect the individual. In a wider sense, it has been argued by many that there are fewer norms, traditions and guidelines for relationships, seen in the decline in traditional institutions like marriage, and also in the shifting meanings of these institutions. At the same time, I would contend that alongside a decline in such clearly defined traditions, there are also persistent normative expectations, in some of the examples discussed here, of how a relationship should be. There is paradoxically less security as many traditional expectations have been eroded, yet normative ideas persist alongside inequalities. Despite shifts in intimacy and ways of relating, the relationship is far from the freedom of choice that Giddens supposes. In the examples discussed here, jeans are able to mediate multiple contradictions between dependency and independence, the burden of love and the comfort of support (as expounded by Beck and Beck-Gernsheim 1995), and vulnerability and connectedness.

References

Beck, U. and Beck-Gernsheim, E. (1995), *The Normal Chaos of Love,* Cambridge: Polity.

Clark, H. and Palmer, A. (eds) (2004), *Old Clothes, New Looks. Second Hand Fashion,* Oxford: Berg.

Clarke, A. (2000), '"Mother swapping": the Trafficking of Nearly New Children's Wear', in P. Jackson, M. Lowe, D. Miller and F. Mort (eds), *Commercial Cultures,* Oxford: Berg.

Corbman, B. (1985), *Textiles: Fiber to Fabrics,* New York: McGraw-Hill.

Corrigan, P. (1995), 'Gender and the Gift: The Case of the Family Clothing Economy', in S. Jackson and S. Moores, *The Politics of Domestic Consumption,* London: Prentice Hall.

DeVault, M. (1991), *Feeding the Family: The Social Organization of Caring as Gendered Work,* Chicago: University of Chicago Press.

Duncombe, J. and Marsden, D. (1999), 'Love and Intimacy: The Gendered Division of Emotion and "Emotion Work"', in G. Allan (ed.), *The Sociology of Family Life,* Oxford: Blackwell.

Giddens, A. (1991), *Modernity and Self-Identity,* Cambridge: Polity.

Giddens, A. (1992), *The Transformation of Intimacy: Sexuality, Love and Eroticism in Modern Societies.* Cambridge: Polity.

Gregson, N. and Crewe, L. (2003), *Second-Hand Cultures,* Oxford: Berg.

Hatch, K. (1993), *Textile Science,* Minneapolis, MN: West Publishing.

Heaphy, B. (2007), *Late Modernity and Social Change: Reconstructing Social and Personal Life,* London: Routledge.

Holland, S. (2004), *Alternative Femininities,* Oxford: Berg.

Hollway, W. (1984), 'Gender Difference and the Production of Subjectivity', in S. Jackson and S. Scott (eds), *Feminism and Sexuality: A Reader,* Edinburgh: Edinburgh University Press.

Jackson, S (1996), 'Heterosexuality as a Problem for Feminist Theory', in L. Adkins and V. Merchant (eds), *Sexualizing the Social: Power and the Organization of Sexuality,* London: Macmillan.

Jamieson, L. (1998), *Intimacy: Personal Relationships in Modern Society,* Cambridge: Polity.

Levy, A. (2006), *Female Chauvinist Pigs: Women and the Rise of Raunch Culture,* New York: Free Press.

Miller, D. (1997), 'How Infants Grow Mothers in North London', *Theory, Culture and Society* 14(4): 67–88, London: Sage.

Miller, D. and Woodward, S. (2007), 'A Manifesto for the Study of Denim', *Social Anthropology,* 15 (3 December): 1–10.

Osteen, M. (ed.) (2002), *The Question of the Gift,* London: Routledge.

Stanley, L. (1992), *The Auto-biographical I,* Manchester: Manchester University Press.

Sullivan, J. (2008), *Jeans: A Cultural History of an American Icon,* New York: Gotham Books.

Weiner, A. (1989), 'Why Cloth? Wealth Gender, and Power in Oceania' in A. Weiner and J. Schneider (eds), *Cloth and the Human Experience,* London: Smithsonain Institute Press.

Weiner, A and Schneider, J. (eds) (1989), *Cloth and the Human Experience,* London: Smithsonain Institute Press.

Woodward, S. (2005), 'Looking Good, Feeling Right: Aesthetics of the Self', in S. Kuechler and D. Miller (eds), *Clothing as Material Culture,* Oxford: Berg.

Woodward, S. (2007), *Why Women Wear What They Wear,* Oxford: Berg.

–8–

Carrot-cut Jeans: An Ethnographic Account of Assertiveness, Embarrassment and Ambiguity in the Figuration of Working-class Male Youth Identities in Berlin

Moritz Ege

Introduction

Adapting Georg Simmel's classic reflections on fashion, Daniel Miller and Sophie Woodward (2007: 341–2) have suggested that the near-global ubiquity of jeans offers people different ways of negotiating the conflicting socio-cultural forces of conformity and individuality. In Woodward's British study, for instance, using a familiar and hardly spectacular example, jeans provided a 'relief from the burden of mistaken choice and anxious self-composition' that women continuously felt (Miller and Woodward 2007: 343). In terms of experience, the authors argue, such conflicting forces manifest in locally differentiated 'genres of anxiety'. With an anthropological sensibility both for the grain of experience and for local-global dynamics, they call for inquiries into specific versions of such genres, from the vantage point of this particular type of clothing, denim, and for compiling 'the responses that populations forge for themselves in dealing with certain contradictions of modernity' (Miller and Woodward 2007: 348). This chapter is a contribution toward this end. It engages ethnographically with one such situation, the popularity of a specific type of denim, the carrot-cut (a high-waist pant that fits comparatively tightly around the behind and the crotch, widens a bit toward the knee, and narrows again toward the hem – loosely resembling the shape of the vegetable) and a specific brand, Picaldi Jeans, among a large number of boys and young men in Berlin (and in Germany more widely), first as an ethnic youth practice, and then increasingly in connection with German 'gangsta rap'.

In depicting the practices and distinctions within this context, I also take up the notion of 'anxiety' and widen it into the social field, taking into account other people's responses to and judgments of the style represented by those jeans. These responses become quite heated, as this subcultural style involves issues of assertiveness, deviance, racism, and class contempt or even disgust.[1] While this brief analysis provides no more than a snapshot of this phenomenon, the overall project is undertaken in order to contribute to an understanding of the cultural processes which co-constitute post-working-class identities and figures (see below) within an increasingly diverse European society in which socioeconomic forces and an activating, neoliberalizing welfare state have made the fault lines of social inequalities – both in terms of class and ethnicity – increasingly visible.[2] In the language of public discourse, this concerns the joint problematic of 'immigrant integration' (*Integration von Ausländern*) and the emergence and consequent social management of a 'new underclass' (cf. the policy debate pushed forward by, for instance, Nolte 2004) in post-fordist times through increasingly disciplinary-paternalistic types of citizenship.

In the first section of this chapter, I briefly lay out the situation in which these local 'genres of anxiety' arise. This involves some aspects of local migrant youth cultural history and aesthetics, developments within the genre of rap music internationally, and the transnational history of a small business. For the sake of concreteness, I also thickly describe some of the ways in which people wear those jeans and their differential relations with other options. The second section takes the form of a case study in which I portray one individual person, in order to represent some of the complexities and life-world relevancies. On the level of experience, I highlight the motive of *ambiguity* with regard to toughness and deviance which this person communicates and reflects and which, in my analysis, plays a large role in the overall cultural dynamics surrounding the 'Picaldi style'.[3] The third section takes up some of the ways in which other, more middle-class or respectability-oriented people view the jeans and the style – and I use this term broadly – they have come to stand for. This touches on the politics of labelling and *embarrassment* more broadly, as they relate to contemporary constellations of culture, class, ethnicity, and gender – seen through an analytical lens of classificatory cultural dynamics (Bourdieu 1984; Neckel 2003) and figuration: I take the concepts of cultural figures and figuration, which obviously have an extensive intellectual history, mainly from the American anthropologist John Hartigan who states that 'figures call attention to the way people come to consider their identities in relation to potent images that circulate within a culture.' In Germany, one crucial ascription in this context is the term 'Proll', which has been in use since the 1970s. Connotationally, the word retains its etymology (the proletariat, the working-class), but its denotational meaning is primarily behavioural and performative. Dictionaries list 'Prolet' as a 'person who lacks manners' and 'Proll' as a 'coarse, uneducated, vulgar person' (Duden 1999: 3024). These terms are being used in shifting and imprecise ways, which indicate, as I will argue, a number of uncertainties or anxieties. While the Berlin case is in some respects unique even within Germany, similar sociocultural processes of 'figuration' are taking place in many European countries, the most well-known being the case of the 'chav' figure in the UK, which emerged around 2004 (Tyler 2008).

Carrot-cut Jeans: From 'Saddle' to 'Zicco', from Diesel to Picaldi

As so often, the narrative is a part of the phenomenon. Picaldi's story is a part of local lore, transmitted by word-of-mouth and through a few journalistic accounts. Picaldi's carrot-cut jeans[4] are based on a denim model by Diesel Jeans ('Saddle'), which has been in continuous demand from, among others, youth and young adults with Turkish, Arab and other migrant backgrounds, since at least the mid-1980s, but has been considered outdated at best by many other style-conscious young people, and the press and the fashion world more generally, for a long time. In the late 1990s, before Diesel stopped selling this model, it was copied and re-branded by a small-scale local retailer, Unplugged, who ordered a batch of this design from an Istanbul-based manufacturer, named Picaldi, which had been founded in 1988, but hadn't been producing that type of jean. Since then, the retailer's store in Berlin-Kreuzberg has grown into a small retail chain with twelve stores, an online dealership, and a handful of franchises in other cities. Moreover, Picaldi has been transformed, in Germany, from an obscure manufacturer's name, which was typeset to resemble a famous brand, into a relatively well-known brand of its own, albeit a controversial one.[5]

In many arenas of urban social interaction, the type of jeans in general, the carrot-cut ('Karottenschnitt', see below), and the brand in particular acquired the status of a marker of both ethnic and lifestyle identity among boys and young men with Turkish, Arab and other immigrant backgrounds, most of whom come from working-class, relatively low-income families.[6] It plays a significant part in creating identities within adverse circumstances. Many customers describe their own outfits as 'gangster style' or 'gangsta style', referring to imagined or real connections to organized crime, the shadow economy, and gangsta/gangster figures in various registers of international popular culture. Another term that is frequently used is 'Kanakenstyle', which takes up a partly re-signified, but still offensive, racist insult. In its initial advertising and store decoration, Picaldi built on gangster references, putting up 'Scarface' screenshots, and stressed their cheap prices, comparing themselves, tongue-in-cheek, to a discount supermarket chain ('Nix Aldi, Picaldi!'). Picaldi's jeans were sold much cheaper than Diesel's 'Saddle', at about 35 euros or half the price.

Picaldi found a second major group of dedicated customers, largely working-class, white German young men in the former East (of the city and the country), many of whom live in areas with a small presence of immigrants, relatively low average incomes, a high unemployment rate. The spread or diffusion of this specific style from an immigrant, lower or working-class setting to an autochtonous lower or working-class group can be described as transversal in character in that it crosses the social field, bypassing the symbolic centre. One the face of it, this combination of niche markets seems surprising, given the prevalence of anti-immigrant and racist sentiments among the latter group. In the case of Picaldi's original customer base, this *type* of outfit was in fashion long before the company picked them up. The stylistic practice and inventiveness seems thus relatively autonomous from commercial strategies. In the East German case, there exists a specific continuity regarding milieu-specific taste preferences, tied to masculine body images, movement sequences, and overall style in the presentation of self. This partly explains the popularity of this type of denim, and the brand that has come to stand for it, across an ethnic line that is otherwise much harder to traverse.

In socioeconomic and occupational terms, Picaldi's customer base is somewhat diverse, but it is predominantly – though certainly not exclusively – recruited from the working class and lower middle class, and, in terms of the education system, from the vocationally oriented middle and high schools (*Hauptschulen, Realschulen, Berufsschulen*). Both the views of many Picaldi employees I interviewed and a small customer survey (with about 100 respondents) I completed in late 2007 confirm this assumption. Much to the chagrin of many among the company's leaders and employees, in the view of outsiders and in various media outlets, 'Picaldi' has come to stand much more narrowly for an 'underclass' of welfare recipients and violent offenders; the *Frankfurter Allgemeine Zeitung*, for instance, illustrated a reporting piece on living conditions of unemployment/welfare-recipients (*Hartz IV*) with the high price of a pair of Picaldi jeans, and various other articles in the press reiterated such associations.[7]

A Type of Jeans: Shapes and Distinctions

None of this is independent of the object in question itself – its form, the aesthetics of the male body it shapes, and the relational position of this type of jeans among other available option that are intentionally *not* chosen. This type of jeans, which Picaldi markets under the name 'Zicco' (and many other names for individual models), is often called 'carrot-cut' (*Karottenschnitt*).[8] It is a high-waist pant, which

Figure 8.1. Abbildung 2: Picaldi advertisements from 2004/2005.

makes for a higher fit than other denim cuts. It fits relatively tightly around the behind and the crotch, it widens toward the knee, and it narrows again toward the hem.[9]
Compared to other men's carrot-cut jeans, these features are especially pronounced
in the Zicco. Over time, Picaldi also introduced a wide variety of colours, dyes, ap-
pliqués and prints, as well as some other fabrics such as beige or light blue corduroy.

Most salespeople agree that the Zicco is made to be worn rather high, on the
waist. Depending on the wearer's physique and the combination with other clothing
items, this can make for different looks; many 'big guys' wear the jeans 'high', as
originally intended by the designers, and they wear knit sweaters or sweatshirts with
a waistband, maybe even tucked into the jeans, and/or a bomber or college/baseball
jacket. Doing so supports the V-effect on the upper body, the stress upon narrow
waistline and broad shoulders. This 'pumps up', as people say (*es pumpt auf*), the
trousers seem sportive (*sportlich*), masculine (*männlich*) and figure-accentuating
(*figurbetont*), as most salespeople and customers put it in in-store conversations. The
men's appearance is one of being 'broadly built' (*breit gebaut*), 'like Michelin men',
as a designer calls it, laughingly. (I will return to the character of such laughs.) The
overall look is somewhat related to that of a sweat pant or the type of lighter pant
that bodybuilders often wear. With their skinnier legs and narrower shoulders, many
customers, especially the younger ones, lack the muscular physique needed to fill
out the trousers, as it were, but they nonetheless wear them high-waist. The fabric,
which isn't very heavy in most models, dangles a bit and is, for instance, blown
back by the wind. The jeans seem wider. This results in a different body appearance
which, however, remains tied to the scheme mentioned above. As a Picaldi spokesperson put it in an interview: 'In those jeans, one automatically has an imposing appearance: muscular thighs, good behind, stately pace. That highlights the masculine
aspect.'[10] Many, however, wear t-shirts that aren't tucked in, or sweaters and jackets
without a waistband, which results in a less obvious look.[11]

Figure 8.2. Zicco, worn rather low; Picaldi catalogue Spring/Summer 2008, S. 6.

The second option for wearing the Zicco jeans is to buy them in a larger size. This, of course, makes the fit looser, and one can wear the jeans lower, on the hip. Worn in that low-rise way, they are almost reminiscent of baggy pants, without being quite as wide and long.

The aforementioned taste-predispositions in different groups are remarkable in themselves, as they fundamentally contradict many accounts of tendencies toward postmodern classlessness in youth culture. However, these traditions might not have been relevant to this extent had they not been reinforced by other, converging developments within hip hop/rap music, which played a crucial role in the process of figuration. This markedly verbal-discursive genre, by now the dominant idiom for large parts of youth culture and split up into a variety of subscenes, has been crucial to Picaldi's unexpected expansion. Picaldi jeans became discursively entwined with a few commercially successful local rap artists, most of them in the gangsta rap mould. In this process, the brand has not only been popularized, it became tied up with a distinction integral to these rappers' confrontational mode of self-fashioning.

I cannot do justice to this scene, its aesthetics or its politics here. In the early years of the decade, the focus of national attention shifted to the Berlin scene. To put it somewhat crudely, a widely adopted stance there was that the previously dominant scenes in German rap were doing hip hop in an ultimately inauthentic[12] way ('All MCs are gay in Germany', 'Alle MCs sind schwul in Deutschland', as Kool Savas put it),[13] whereas Berlin rappers had both fewer politically correct inhibitions and better rap skills and also, in many cases, an authenticating 'street' background. One version of this self-positioning motive, put forth by Bushido most prominently, concerned clothing: in this view, just like others lacked the experiential background that would qualify them for 'authentic' rap, they put on American-style baggy jeans, 'fake' costumes, whereas 'real' street-savvy gangsters and hustlers wore brands such as Cordon and Picaldi. This distinction also plays out on the level of shape and physique. Straight-cut baggy pants are famously worn 'low' on the hip or, more often, further down, so that the behind can hardly be made out. From shoes to shoulders, the silhouette has the shape of an A (as in the shape of the classic graffiti character type with shoes larger than the head) rather than a 'carrot' below the belt and a V above it, as with the carrot-cut: Wearing a carrot-cut, one still has 'an ass in one's pants' (*einen Arsch in der Hose*), as a German idiom, referring to courage and self-assertion, goes.[14] In this context, then, there is something like an antagonistic relationship between the carrot-cut and baggy jeans – however serious or playful this antagonism is imagined. The differential relation between the carrot-cut and straight-cut jeans, in contrast, derives primarily from a sequence, not an antagonism; here, biographical phases and status passages come into play. Many of Picaldi's customers, by an age between sixteen and twenty-two, choose to give up their Ziccos and pick 'straight cuts', which may signal an overall change in style and attitude. This distinction reflects emic categories rather than the overall classification language in the denim industry.

Tarek's Case

Given this background, what does the life-world relevance of these jeans consist of? Which distinctions and what forms of togetherness are being created, upheld, challenged or broken down in this process? What, specifically, characterizes the predominant 'local genre(s) of anxiety'? In order to approach these questions and chart out some answers on the level of experience, I choose a narrative case-study approach. The person I want to focus on is a young man I met in the course of field research, Tarek M., who is twenty years old. While he should not be considered an all-round 'typical representative' of a social group or a habitus, but rather a case of complexity, a *homme pluriel* (cf. Lahire 2001), I argue that his case does indeed exemplify some intersubjective dynamics that in part constitute the overall context.

Tarek M. was born and raised in a relatively 'quiet' district on the south-west side of Berlin to a Lebanese father and a German mother, both of whom run a small grocery store in the neighbourhood. He is the youngest of four siblings. In the year in which Tarek and I have been meeting every once in a while, he has been in a difficult overall situation in terms of the transition from school to work. He mostly lives with his parents and he helps out in his parents' store, for which he receives no monetary pay, but he has not been able to secure the car salesman apprenticeship he wishes to take up, and he failed the entry exam at the Mercedez-Benz factory, where only a few applicants succeed every year.

Symbolic Boundaries and Social Relations

With regard to the style-identity-place-nexus, Tarek recalls the big change that occurs at the transition from primary to secondary school. In seventh grade, students enter a secondary school, an *Oberschule*, and they become tracked into different schools according to their grades and the teachers' verdict on their abilities, which brought him to a *Hauptschule*, the lowest-achieving option out of the three school types. There one inevitably meets people from other areas and begins to make spontaneous classifications, affinities and alliances based on style, among other things, he says. At that point, in Tarek's class, there was a clear break, socially and spatially, between those who were considered 'Germans' and those who were informally designated as 'foreigners' (i.e. descendants of recent immigrants, many of whom do not have German citizenship), which registered in different ways, for instance in seating arrangements. The 'Germans' made up about two-thirds of this class. Simultaneously, the distinction between the cool ones and the others became important. First of all, in his view, the emerging patterns of clothing among boys were very much an ethnic issue. 'You could recognize it by the clothing immediately. We were basically always dressed dark. Dark, casual (*lässig*).' This distinction between two groups of students appears to be saturated with discourses, images, and affects from a variety of media, including film, music, and local narrative lore. The local discourse of Berlin rap at the time offered a particularly meaningful and attractive way of making sense of one's immediate surroundings. Furthermore, the primary-secondary school transition and the following years coincided with the rise of the Picaldi style and its increasing semanticization in the context of the hip-hop world. As I have shown above, Picaldi's carrot-cut jeans, as opposed to baggy jeans, became one crucially important marker of difference in that context. In this particular instance, then, subcultural and ethnic distinctions played themselves out very much in accordance with the playbook I outlined: 'The ones up front there [he points to the other group on a sketch], they had [somewhat disgustedly] skater-pants, skate sweaters and things like that', as Tarek says.

The classroom situation he recollects highlights emotional and affective undercurrents of such symbolic boundaries, which would suggest that there was some awareness of being in a socially low-status environment, and on a problematic track. The basic facts of discrimination were hard to ignore, from racist violence to small-scale resonances of structural exclusion such as, for instance, when he was the only one among his 'immigrant' peer group whose citizenship status allowed him to join a school trip abroad. On the other hand, on the experiential level, Tarek also speaks of a sense of privilege, prestige, aesthetics and power among 'the foreigners', *diese Macht bei den Ausländern*, echoing other ethnographic accounts. Even though he and his friends were a minority in terms of numbers, in his account, for a variety of reasons, they held interactional power (as opposed to institutional power), even dominance within the classroom, because of their assertiveness (*Durchsetzungsfähigkeit*) and cohesion. Furthermore, they possessed what can be called cultural attractiveness, which amounts to another form of symbolic power. It becomes confirmed, for instance, by the discursive framing in which Germans who took up style patterns (language, dress) of youth with migrant backgrounds were considered 'wannabe-Turks', and it is confirmed through a variety of folklore and representations. The notion of male 'swagger', which recently underwent a revival in US popular culture language, captures the homologies that pertain between the quality of assertiveness, the shape of a 'masculine' physique, and the Picaldi carrot-cut (cf. Skeggs 2004). Many other aspects of this experiential world could be considered, such as the discursive motive of 'foreigners' cohesion versus Germans' individualization and dissociality (cf. Sutterlüty/Walter 2005, 194f), and one could attempt to trace back their causes. This, however, is not the place to do so. Here, I have touched on these experiences of simultaneous exclusion and assertiveness in order to specify the generic fact that cultural meanings of specific pieces of clothing, such as a pair of carrot-cut jeans, rely on emotions and affects that underlie symbolic boundaries. Furthermore, the cultural semiotics of identity and alterity, as they manifest in clothing codes, are enmeshed not only with symbolic and imaginary (subcultural, ethnic) communities, affinities, and figures, but also with 'real' groups, with interpersonal, interaction-based networks. The classroom is one important setting, as are scene-like forms of urban sociality, and of course family relations, friendships, and partner-ships. The importance of family and friendship networks in this regard becomes apparent when we consider that for Tarek, as for most people in his social world, shopping represents a touchy subject because of his financial situation. Not having a significant source of income, he mostly depends on other people to spend money for him, and he has been doing so for a longer time than is generally thought proper. Hence, it is no longer his parents who supply his clothing, but his sister who buys both basics such as jeans and, when money is flush, more expensive brand-name items, such as much sought-after knit wool sweaters. In any case, this gift-giving is part of a both practised and idealized sense of family reciprocity: She wants his brother to look good; he is concerned with her well-being as well and, for instance, frequently serves as her driver. This is not to suggest that there are no or few family conflicts, but it shows some of the ways in which individual pieces of clothing carry not only sentimental value, but also materialize interpersonal relations of love, care, and control. Such relationships go beyond the family; in Tarek's case, as with many other people, clothes, such as jackets, sweatshirts, pants, watches, jewellery, are ex-changed within an inner circle of friends. All of these aspects contribute to an under-standing of the fact that the symbolic borderlines, despite their superficial and con-tingent nature can *matter* deeply and why, in this context, identity is easily harmed.

Embodiment, Figuration, and Ethics

Another highly charged issue concerns the normative side of *relating to cultural types* more generally: imitation, mimesis, replication, emulation, or figuration. In a process that is discursive and physical, people construct their identities and shape their bodies in relation to the individuals, including stars and cultural heroes, they positively relate to: visually, aurally, affectively. While doing so comes – as we all know – with practical challenges, it also leads straight into the normative or even ethical dilemmas of conformity and individuality that pervade teenage life. Tarek, for instance, speaks animatedly about the relationship between the image that rap music projects, the reality that people live, and the role of such representations. In this respect, the last few years were a tumultuous time, given the fast rise of German gangsta rap. When it comes to rappers like Azad, Bushido and Massiv, many critical observers wonder whose commercial calculations are at play, who benefits, what are the representational costs (in terms of prejudices and stereotypes) and who bears these costs? Tarek, too, is concerned with the stereotypes that cir-culate about *Ausländer*. Almost whispering, he tells me he's been listening more closely, and critically, to rap lyrics and what they say. When it comes to the ways in which people embody the cultural figures that circulate through popular culture, he thinks, many people – young, male, youth with a migrant background, mostly, he means here – exaggerate in 'reflecting' (*widerspiegeln*) the music. The question –

'Pseudo-Gangstertum' – is much-debated within the wider circles of rap music, as is evident to anyone who has ever looked at a rap discussion forum or online video comment section (cf. Androutsopoulos 2005: 172). People say, Tarek continues, that Bushido 'reflects' the street. But really, it's the other way around: people follow Bushido's every move, they copy him in whatever he does. It makes him angry because people do stupid and violent things they wouldn't otherwise do, because they get into a sort of arms race in which people show how crazy, how *krass* they are, and furthermore (and this is a different, but important point), because in doing so, they are like sheep.

This practice of 'reflection', in Tarek's understanding, manifests both in that people increasingly carry knives and in specific forms of demeanour and clothing. 'Before there was this kind of rap, it wasn't like this: one in three wears an Alpha jacket, one in two wears an Alpha-Jacket. Back then, it was only the adults. The big ones. The bodybuilders and the like, bouncers and so forth, they had Alpha jackets. Now, suddenly, everyone has one.'[15] This streetwear arms race, as it were, indicates people's questionable, presumptuous, sheepish, and ultimately destructive imitations and identifications. He believes that in contrast to many others, he observes that music's malicious influence without distortion, and his stylistic practices are of a different nature. I challenge Tarek who, as I have come to notice in an earlier session, wears an Alpha Industries jacket himself, and I ask him in what sense exactly the people he talks about, the classic 'cultural dupes', are so different from himself. In reference to other people not being able to keep reality and fiction apart, I object that he and his friends seem able to do so, and from what I can tell, they also like to come across as tough, in some way or another. 'Oh, I know that difference. [It's a matter of upbringing, he says later.] But, you know, in order to scare people off (*abschrecken*), I do what they talk about in music. You can scare people away. That's really the way it is.'

I ask him what situations he means, and he talks about meeting people from outside the city who, he believes, suppose that Berlin is really tough, *krass*, and are scared. He likes 'confirming' that stereotype. Then, automatically I act tough (*ich mache einen auf hart*). When they ... why should I make myself smaller than I am, you know?' He then goes on to talk about people from distant neighbourhoods in the East, which are, as he points out elsewhere, known for the street dominance of white German working-class 'toughs' and anti-immigrant violence.

> You know, I don't know, or maybe from Marzahn or so ... Then I say, then I don't present myself ... We're no chicks (*Küken*)! Then I act tough (*ich mache einen auf hart*). 'I'm from Tempelhof', you know... That's normal. But I'm not flicking my knife or anything like that.

Obviously, some verbal posturing is going on here. At the same time, this going back and forth between rhetorical escalation and de-escalation points to an ambiguity that is not merely rhetorical. Significantly, he stresses the *performative* level when he uses phrases such as *einen auf hart machen*.[16] In youth language, there are many such metaphors that, in one way or another, differentiate between an intentional subject, on the one hand, and his or her performances, on the other hand. In those metaphors, the degree to which the subject controls or is controlled by that which is performed, or by the immersive quality of an imagination, varies.[17] Clothing is among a number of practices within this problematic. In a context of discrimination, racism, class disgust or negative classification, the question of embodying cultural figures is highly charged and relevant both practically and normatively. I will explicate this relation in the remaining section of this paper.

Ambiguity

'Is he a good boy? Isn't he a good boy? No one should know, that's how I want it to be', Tarek says, smiling shyly. He's referring to a cliché (*guter Junge*), which has been used in rap quite a bit, and, in contracted form (*Ersguterjunge*) figures as the name of Bushido's rap label. Tarek's girlfriend Steffi uses a female adaption as a login on her laptop: *Siesgutesmädchen*. I had asked him about things and values that really matter to him. The context of this utterance is 'saving face' and maintaining a clean slate.

T: That's the most important thing. But some people don't do that. Save face, I mean, and … For instance, in my case, it's like – nothing bad can be said about me. [M. Mhm.] About me … Maybe I'm doing bad stuff, but nobody knows. [M. laughs softly] You know? That's normal! As long as you don't know anything about me, you can't gossip. You can guess what I do. But you don't know, you don't know what I do. You know? [M: Okay.] That's always the question. Is he doing things? Is he not? Is he a good boy, is he not a good boy? [M. laughs softly] When it comes to me, this remains an open question. Nobody knows.

M: You remain a riddle?

T: For many, I do.

M: And for you, it's important that it is that way?

T: Yes. That's how it should remain.

There is an obvious situational irony at play: in this interview I, a researcher and outsider through age, ethnicity and various aspects of cultural background, try to find out various details about Tarek's life, and I am very much in the same position as the clueless anonymous 'you' (*du*, sometimes, agrammatically, 'he', *er*) that Tarek talks about. In that sense, his statements figure as commentary to our relationship as well as to his relationship to other people that surround him.

In both instances, this ambiguity is a question of the 'presentation of self' and 'impression management' (Goffman 1959) through figuration. Despite its obvious undertones of adolescent fantasy, there are at least two reasons why the ambiguity he produces through this form of impression management should not be trivialized: first, because there is some seriousness to the pole of toughness and violence within Tarek's life-world, not only in that people, including himself, do fight from time to time, but also in that there is some proximity to crime. Tarek's sister's boyfriend, for instance, was spending time in prison for violent assault as we were speaking, and through the wider network of friends and cousins, he knows a few people involved with 'Lebanese mafia' groups, which make up a significant segment of organized crime in the city, especially the drug trade. Secondly, and relatedly, ambiguity should be taken seriously as a cultural form because despite its obvious social costs, it has an *empowering* quality, which helps us understand what these jeans – as one element of a larger package – *are* on a subjective, experiential level.

Power, Spinoza famously posited, consists in the power to act, to affect and be affected (cf. Hardt 2007). The ambiguity Tarek intends to communicate, then, can be experienced as a small-scale, interaction-based form of power in both of these ways: in burdening alter with the question as to ego's violent or at least particularly assertive potential, ego 'affects' alter – scares him or her, for instance – and is himself affected, in that he gains options that arise from alter's confusion or passivity. For instance (and this happens quite frequently), ego gains the option of de-escalating – 'I'm just playing with you' – while seeming to never have made an effort to intimidate anyone in the first place. Such dramas are enacted on an everyday basis. They often take spatial form, such as when individuals or small groups of people demonstratively take up a disproportionate section of space and make others yield. Very abstractly speaking, ambiguity of this kind can be considered a form of interactional advantage.

Such poses and the concomitant experiences are not new, but their shape and significance depend on the specific cultural 'moments' of which they are elements.[18] What matters (and varies) greatly, for instance, is the extent to which such poses are supported by the logics and imaginaries of contemporary global popular culture, their specific shape and politics, and their resonance with more local forms. In the case at hand, this ambiguity on the level of impression management, I argue, seems analogous to the ambiguous structure of the 'real' in gangsta rap, as it has been analysed by various critics. In the context of gangsta rap, for instance, the question almost automatically arises in what sense conflicts between rappers ('beef') are 'real'. Despite the fact that the social contexts of US and German gangsta rap are enormously different, much the same can be said for the 'real' and 'beef' in German gangsta-rap. Were the shots fired in late 2007 (just before an album release) on Massiv 'real' or were they staged? To what degree of violence will 'beef' between rappers such as Kool Savas and Eko Fresh, or between Sido and Bushido, or between Fler and Bushido, lead? On the one hand, there certainly are 'literalist' interpretations of the genre, especially from young teenagers. On the other hand, many appreciate the model of a successful cynic. For many more people, however, this ambiguity (which, of course, isn't necessarily exactly seen as such) is in itself a large part of the *pleasure* of the genre. It can become appropriated as an attitude. Tarek's practices of impression management, which leave the question of whether he is a 'good boy' or 'not a good boy' intentionally open, provide a good example for such analogies. These two forms of ambiguity seem to be mutually reinforcing, inspiring and legitimating. Having that sort of resonance can be a powerful experience. A theoretical account is given by Brian Massumi who theorizes figures in an abstract but nonetheless evocative way, describing them, among other formulations, as 'a point of subjectification' and 'a gravitational pull around which competing orbits of affect and thought are organized' (Massumi 1998: 54).

Projected Embarrassment

Focusing on the 'inside' view, the experience of wearing the type of style that Picaldi is the most prominent part of, then, often involves such ambiguities, which hold an empowering quality for many. Specific projections of self-confidence are involved, as is a degree of aggressive assertiveness. For a causal *explanation* of these attitudes, one would have to consider the interplay of cultural dynamics and broader, structural social forces, and complete this account with other aspects of experience, which is an important task that I cannot accomplish here. Instead, in a provisional step of cultural analysis, I wish to further characterize the 'local genre of anxiety' by taking into account other, equally partial, but in some ways more socially powerful perspectives.

Picaldi is, as its press spokesperson puts it euphemistically, an 'emotional brand'. Many people actively dislike it; moreover, they despise it. One rap-aficionado I interviewed said he'd 'rather cut [his] balls off' than wear Picaldi. Another, who owns an urban/streetwear store, immediately started talking about 'Stone-Age people' and said that since he's been selling to people like that he avoids his own store's sales floor and basically hides away in his office. People regularly roll their eyes or laugh uncomfortably when the brand name is mentioned. There are nightclubs with 'No Picaldi' signs on their door. A sales clerk told me of a school in which Picaldi clothing was not allowed (though I have not been able to verify this). Searching for Picaldi on social networking sites such as Studi-VZ, Myspace or Facebook, one finds fan-page groups and groups with titles such as 'Thanks to Picaldi, I am able to immediately spot idiots.'

Such a list of impressions could be expanded and transformed into an entire phenomenology of dislike, contempt and disgust – both in the multiethnic western and in the predominantly 'German' eastern part of the city. Moreover, it indicates a basic fact of contemporary culture: despite undeniable tendencies toward a pluralization of identities that can be 'recognized' and seen as 'legitimate', in youth culture, too, there are basic ethnic and class divides that underpin cultural identities. A crucial concept in the language of disgust and contempt is *peinlich* which translates as 'embarrassing'. In the attitudes that many (basically, but not exclusively, middle- and upper-class) people hold toward Picaldi and its customers – and this concerns different forms of dislike – *projected embarrassment* is an important characteristic. Especially in teenage culture, a person, and not only a situation, can be seen as *peinlich*, 'embarrassing' in that sense. Why, though, would those jeans and the style they belong to be thought of as *embarrassing* in the first place? There certainly are people who feel shame, embarrassment, or humiliation in specific situations, and more widely as well, because they are wearing Picaldi clothing and others disapprove of that. The crucial point here, however, is that some people think, or viscerally sense, that others *should* be embarrassed. Used in that sense, the adjective *peinlich* (embarrassing) refers to an ascription of shame. Of course, the relevance of such 'demands' would be diminished if 'communities' autonomously set their own standards, social relations were experienced as straightforwardly antagonistic, or pluralistic cultural democracy had arrived. Indeed, obviously, most of Picaldi's customers most likely do not feel embarrassed at all. They may not be consciously aware of such dislikes, or they may not care. Lacking an awareness of or regard for other people's judgment is a basic characteristic of the type of assertiveness under consideration here, after all. Popular culture lends discursive frameworks to such sentiments of disregard. In his song 'Sonnenbank Flavour', for instance, Bushido lists various aspects of both 'street' toughness and lifestyle practices, and he describes himself as 'being on the *Proll*-track' (*Proll-Schiene*). In doing so, he articulates a self-confident identification with a much-ridiculed cultural figure. These kinds of value charge reversals and re-significations are, of course, common throughout histories of popular culture, and they play a role in this cultural field as well. In this case, however, the reversal isn't complete or sustainable, as despite such examples, the epithet so far has not turned into an unproblematic term of self-ascription.[19]

Male physicality and sexual attractiveness are crucial to the issue of projected embarrassment as well. With regard to the carrot-cut jean, such questions are alluded to, for instance, in press reports about Picaldi, where customers are referred to as 'macho bodies' or a prototypical *'prole who stages his physicalness without so much as a hint of self-consciousness'*.[20] The most widely circulated text about Picaldi appeared in the major weekly *Der Stern* under the headline 'Auf dicke Hose', which refers to the idiom 'einen auf dicke Hose machen' which has the idiomatic meaning of showing off, playing it big – monetarily, but with sexual undertones. With its high-waist fit and overall body schema, the Diesel/Picaldi carrot-cut, 'figurbetont' (figure-highlighting) as it is, seems like a breech of decorum, a 'flaunted', vulgar, unsophisticated form of male sexual display, which contrasts with bourgeois restraint and modesty, but also with various varieties of alternative masculinities and, importantly, with the 'metrosexual' mode of male sexualization in popular culture of more recent years (cf. Gill 2009; Richard 2005). An article in a city weekly maga- zine about working-class youth, for instance, mentioned 'a fashion that seems to communicate something. Some call it sexual aggressiveness.'[21] Of course, such sources are hardly unproblematic, yet they do seem to make explicit an important subtext: in designating this physicality as embarrassing, I think it is fair to assume that people cannot help but implicitly relate to their *own* physicality, desires, and inhibitions, however important that may or may not be in the individual instance. Furthermore, the notion of embarrassment generally refers to a form of failure, an inability to successfully perform something one sets out (or is set up) to do in the eyes of others. Here, however, people seem to be attacking both *presumption*, such as when they ridicule the apparent strivings of prepubescent boys, who just aren't who they are apparently pretending to be (in all sorts of ways, including sexual), and that which they are striving *toward*. In some ways, such dismissal and ridicule would hardly be socially acceptable among many of its proponents were it not articulated primarily on the class level.

In focusing – in a highly condensed form – on outside views as well as inside views, I have not meant to suggest that the former are what matter most about Picaldi denim. I do suggest, however, that the figurations of inside and outside perspectives elucidate sociocultural dynamics that would otherwise not be visible. Among the many aspects that characterize the experience of wearing these specific jeans as part of an overall style, the embodied attitude of assertiveness – swagger – plays an important role, as I have shown, which is often connected to an empowering sense of ambiguity in self-presentation (with regard to risky behaviour). Is he a good boy? And if so, then in what sense? In the outside view, however, much of that is decoded not in terms of ambiguity but as failure and presumption on the one hand, and a threat on the other. Such an attitude manifests in projected embarrassment, among other sentiments and interaction patterns. These, then, are the 'local genres of anxi- ety' which congeal in emblematic types of denim and its uses.

The Right to Ambiguity

In literary terms, the underlying structure of what I have described and analysed has a *tragic* character in that cultural processes on the experiential level help cement and affectively legitimize social relations and position ascriptions that the actors might not support explicitly. Again, this is not to suggest that these processes are what ulti- mately determines social structures (or even experiences) but they do represent one medium for living through them, and, potentially, challenging them. It is important to also note some fault lines within such processes. Here, the explicitly normative domain is particularly relevant, outside the directly political realm as well. In talk- ing about clothing, perception and stereotypes, many who sport the carrot-cut, and the 'gangsta style' more generally, do not just present themselves ambiguously in regard to toughness. In talking about it (and, I would argue, in practice), they also lay claims to a *right to ambiguity*. The claim can be summed up by a formulaic statement of this kind:

> Yes, I wear stuff that makes me look tough. No, I don't mind that people may take me for a thug. I can see why they would feel intimidated, and I kind of like that. At the same time, these are just clothes. I deserve to be treated like everybody else. Clothes don't tell the story of an individual. No one should be categorized on such superficial terms.

There are many such stories, and they may sound familiar. Often straightforward ethnic discrimination dominates them, but it is rationalized in terms of clothing. 'Everybody' knows, for instance, that getting into a nightclub wearing Picaldi (the jackets and sweater rather than the jeans) and Picaldi-style overall is hard (even though there are exceptions, especially for 'Germans'), and many think that this is unfair. Tayfun, for instance, talks about older people regularly changing the side of the street when they seem him approach. He is genuinely disturbed by their perceptions of him – even though, he says, his 'boxer haircut' is moderate, and he is merely wearing what he likes, just like other young people do, but different rules seem to apply to him. Another such story comes from a young man named Marco, a 'white German' from a middle-class family, who is into the overall Picaldi style. He recalls getting into a long discussion with a girl he found attractive, after he had approached her on the street and she completely ignored his advances. She basically fit the general type of an 'alternative' style. These people, he says (somewhat frustrated after what appear to have been a number of similar rejections), are the most prejudiced of all, because they will dismiss people like him – as a 'Proll' – on the mere basis of clothing.

The critical and reflective mode in which such claims and observations are formulated doesn't seem to square easily with the assertiveness, dominance, and insistence on invulnerability that characterizes the discursive and physical figure that is under consideration here. Indeed, while some talk in that way, many others would not engage in this type of discourse, at least not toward me (and probably not in other situations either). The point is that in claiming something like a right to ambiguity, a rights-granting entity is addressed as a potential interlocutor in a process of recognition. In the context of a stylized, avowedly antagonistic attitude, such recourse is anything but obvious. On the one hand, this fact simply confirms that, in many instances, antagonism is a pose. On the other hand, there also is a profound resonance between such claims and the core structure of the cultural formats that pervade those discourses. This resonance can be illustrated by returning to the similarities between Tarek's practice of impression management and the question of what is 'real' in gangsta rap where, as I showed, the plane of lyrical content contrasts with its being formally framed as aesthetics for which, in our societies, different rules apply. The potential de-escalation of semantic content through discursive recourse to (aesthetic) form or frame is even more apparent in the domain of clothing, where, quite obviously, people are generally willing and able to distinguish between statements made by wearing clothes, and statements in a literal sense. The former can or cannot be taken seriously, and people who do so in a way deemed inappropriate may be ridiculed as lacking an acute enough sense of reality. Furthermore, the physical, affective and social dimensions of clothing, their experiential texture, as it were, do not primarily have a predicative structure, just as the musical texture makes it inappropriate and unfair for rap music to be reduced to its lyrical content – experientially as well as on the level of discursive explication. By wearing, for instance, specific denim, then, one makes statements, in a somewhat conscious manner, but one reserves the right to change frames of meaning: from assertion to ambiguity, from the serious to the playful. Of course, the problematic isn't always explicitly elaborated in terms of such a claim. Its efficacy can only be approximated by comparing it to a rule or to discursive statements. Rather, ambiguity of this type can be felt, performed, lived – it is, in a way, a 'structure of feeling' and its verbal expression is embedded in various practices.

Notes

1. The term 'subculture', as it was refashioned by the Birmingham school of Cultural Studies in the 1970s (cf. Clarke et al. 1976), has come under much criticism since the mid-1990s (cf. Muggleton and Weinzierl 2003), but cases such as this one show its continuing relevance, if only as a pointer toward the articulation of homologies through complex, multi-scale cultural practices, within contexts in which specific social determinants play a significant role. For a view close to my own cf. Hesmondhalgh (2005).
2. In this chapter I remain agnostic toward the important and politically charged debates over analytical terminology, both in regard to processual terms such as exclusion (Bude 2006, 2008a, 2008b; Knecht 1999; Kronauer 2002) and analytical group designations such as working-class (Skeggs 2004), precariat (in the wake of Bourdieu 1998), multitude (Virno 2004), *Unterschicht* in the sense of popular classes (Warneken 2006) or of an 'underclass' (Nolte 2004; cf., for instance, the critique in Lindner and Musner 2007).
3. In this piece, there is little space for theoretical and methodological considerations. My analysis focuses on a 'plane of experience', which incorporates various types of phenomena (or analytical registers), such as sentiments, affects, discourses, structures of interaction and cultural dynamics.
4. And those by some other local brands that have followed this example in recent years, carrying similar faux-Italian brand names, Daggio Romanzo, Blucino and Casa.

5. Through two companies, the owner of Unplugged and his partners import and wholesale the products of the Turkish company Picaldi in Germany (and Austria). Furthermore, much or even most of the design process of the articles sold in Germany takes place here as well, although this has been going back and forth in regard to the 'basics' among the jeans.

6. Such classifications are not only highly problematic, their meanings, borders and their relevance are part of what gets negotiated and 'performed' in such processes. Ethnic classifications with reference to 'migration background', to a category such as whiteness, to nationality and citizenship are only seemingly obvious. All of them, in specific ways, are social constructions and selections that are, however, not random, but rely on a number of persistent institutions and ideologies. The most obvious example is that many 'foreigners' are in fact Germans but not recognized or accepted as such by others, in large part because of ethnic (*völkisch*) understandings of citizenship.

7. As did the album 'Hart(z) IV' by rapper Eko Fresh, in which he was pictured wearing a Picaldi sweater. *Hart* translates as 'tough', Hartz is the last name of a former Volkswagen manager who famously consulted the federal government in the process of social safety net 'reforms' and gave his name to various phases of these reforms, including 'Hartz IV', which largely abolished the distinction between longer term unemployment benefits and welfare (*Arbeitslosengeld II*).

8. The carrot-cut has, for a long time, been much more popular for women's jeans, but that seems to be an entirely different story.

9. On men's jeans as 'adding body' – see Sassatelli's contribution (based on data collected in Milan, Italy) in this volume.

10. In: Spex Nr. 313, 3/4, 2008.

11. The jeans are just one – though especially relevant – element of this style (which can largely be understood as a subcultural style), a basic standard, which people combine with other, sometimes more conspicuous and expensive items.

12. What is 'authentic' is determined by cultural evaluations, not by mere facts in the world (Lindner 2001), and it represents an especially difficult notion within *racialized* contexts.

13. The pejorative use of *schwul* (gay) is common in that scene. While it shouldn't be take as a literal insult, and falling into immediate outrage might just play into the communicative strategy, it certainly remains an objectionable form of homophobia that powerfully reinforces latent forms thereof, and indicates an orientation on specific, unambiguous forms of masculinity and a rejection of what is considered effeminateness. In order to retain some semblance of adequateness to musical differentiations, it should be noted that Kool Savas, for instance, isn't a gangsta rapper but is famous for his lyrical skill in freestyle 'battle' and his vulgar lyrics.

14. 'Keinen Arsch in der Hose haben', not having an ass in one's pants, means lacking courage or assertiveness.

15. 'Alpha-Jacke': pilot jackets by the Texas-based company Alpha Industries.
16. 'Einen auf X machen' basically means to play X, to act as if one was X.
17. Such metaphors include *einen Film schieben* or *in einem Film sein* '(literally 'being in a film'), or composites of *Schiene* 'rail'.
18. It seems plausible to assume that this type of feeling is nothing new at all (cf. Pearson 1983). Furthermore, similar mechanisms of medialization through figures have been at play for at least decades, especially since the 'amplification' of subcultural deviance and violence (think mods versus teds, skins) in the 1950s and 1960s. Cf. the primarily British literature on subcultures, amplification and 'moral panics' (Cohen 1973).
19. Within the context of rap-oriented scene, for instance, people are more likely to adapt terms such as 'Kanake' [sic], 'Gangster' and 'Atze' than 'Proll'. This is reminiscent of what Hartigan (2005) has written about 'white trash' – despite some resignificantion, the term largely remained 'socially uninhabitable'.
20. DeutschlandRadio 'Picaldi und Konsorten – Mode unter Migrantenkids in Berlin', 9 April 2003. It should be noted that, in the radio report, this quote is used critically in summarizing a view that some people (whose prejudices the report is critical of) seem to hold.
21. Zitty 8/2005, S. 21.

References

Androutsopoulos, J. (2005), 'Musiknetzwerke. Identitätsarbeit auf HipHop-Websites', in K. Neumann-Braun and B. Richard (eds), *Coolhunters. Jugendkulturen zwischen Medien und Markt*, Frankfurt am Main: Suhrkamp, pp. 159–72.

Bourdieu, P. (1984), *Distinction. A Social Critique of the Judgement of Taste*, Cambridge, MA: Harvard University Press.

Bourdieu, P. (1998), 'Prekarität ist überall', in P. Bourdieu, *Gegenfeuer. Wortmeldungen im Dienste des Widerstands gegen die neoliberale Invasion*, Konstanz: UVK, pp. 96–102.

Bude, H. (ed.) (2006), *Das Problem der Exklusion. Ausgegrenzte, Entbehrliche, Überflüssige*, Hamburg: Hamburger Edition.

Bude, H. (2008a), *Die Ausgeschlossenen. Das Ende vom Traum einer gerechten Gesellschaft*, München: Hanser.

Bude, H. (ed.) (2008b), *Exklusion. Die Debatte über die 'Überflüssigen'*, Frankfurt am Main: Suhrkamp.

Clarke, J., Hall, S., Jefferson, T. and Roberts, B. (1976), 'Subcultures, Cultures and Class', in S. Hall and T. Jefferson (eds), *Resistance Through Rituals: Youth Subcultures in Post-War Britain*, London: Hutchinson.

Cohen, S. (1973), *Folk Devils and Moral Panics. The Creation of the Mods and Rockers*, St Albans: Paladin.

Duden (1999), *Das große Wörterbuch der deutschen Sprache in zehn,* Bänden. 3, völlig überarbeitete und erweiterte Auflage. Herausgegeben vom wissenschaftlichen Rat der Dudenredaktion. Band 7: Pekt-Schi. Mannheim: Dudenverlag.

Gill, R., Henwood, K., McLean, C. (2005), 'Body Projects and the Regulation of Normative Masculinity', *Body and Society,* 11: 37–62.

Goffman, E. (1959), *The Presentation of Self in Everyday Life*, Garden City: Doubleday.

Hardt, M. (2007), 'Foreword: What Affects Are Good For', in P. Ticineto Clough (with J. Halley) (ed.), *The Affective Turn. Theorizing the Social*, Durham, NC: Duke University Press, 2007, pp. ix–xiii.

Hartigan, J. Jr. (2005), *Odd Tribes. Toward A Cultural Analysis of White People*, Durham, NC: Duke University Press.

Hesmondhalgh, D. (2005), 'Subcultures, Scenes or Tribes? None of the Above', *Journal of Youth Studies,* 8(1): 21–40.

Knecht, M. (ed.) (1999), *Armut und Ausgrenzung in Berlin*, Köln: Böhlau, pp. 7–25.

Kronauer, M. (2002), *Exklusion. Die Gefährdung des Sozialen im hochentwickelten Kapitalismus*, Frankfurt am Main/New York: Campus.

Lahire, B. (2001), *L'homme pluriel. Les ressorts de l'action*, Paris: Hachette.

Lindner, R. (2001), 'The Construction of Authenticity: The Case of Subcultures', in J. Liep (ed.), *Locating Cultural Creativity,* London: Pluto.

Lindner, R. and Musner, L. (eds) (2008), *Unterschicht. Kulturwissenschaftliche Erkundungen der 'Armen' in Geschichte und Gegenwart,* Freiburg: Rombach.

Massumi, B. (1998), 'Requiem for Our Prospective Dead (Toward a Participatory Critique of Capitalist Power)', in E. Kaufman and K. J. Heller (eds) (1998), *Deleuze and Guattari. New Mappings in Politics, Philosophy and Culture*, London/Minneapolis, MN: University of Minnesota Press, pp. 40–64.

Miller, D. and Woodward, S. (2007), 'Manifesto for a Study of Denim', *Social Anthropology/Anthropologie Sociale,* 15(3): 335–51.

Moore, A.E. (2007), *Unmarketable. Brandalism, Copyfighting, Mocketing, and the Erosion of Integrity*, New York: New Press.

Muggleton, D. and Weinzierl, R. (eds) (2003), *The Post-Subcultures Reader,* Oxford: Berg.

Neckel, S. (2003), 'Kampf um Zugehörigkeit. Die Macht der Klassifikation', *Leviathan* 31(2): 159–67.

Nolte, P. (2004), *Generation Reform. Jenseits der blockierten Republik*, München: Beck.

Pearson, G. (1983), *Hooligan. A History of Respectable Fears*, Basingstoke: Macmillan.

Richard, B. (2005), 'Beckham's Style Kicks! Die meterosexuellen Körperbilder der Jugendidole', in K. Neumann-Braun and B. Richard (eds), *Coolhunters.*

Jugendkulturen zwischen Medien und Markt, Frankfurt am Main: Suhrkamp, pp. 244–60.

Sayer, A. (2006), *The Moral Significance of Class*, Cambridge: Cambridge University Press.

Skeggs, B. (2004), *Class, Self, Culture*, London: Routledge.

Tyler, I. (2008), 'Chav Mum Chav Scum', *Feminist Media Studies,* 8(1): 17–34.

Sutterlüty, F. and Walter, I. (2005), 'Übernahmegerüchte. Klassifikationskämpfe zwischen türkischen Aufsteigern und ihren deutschen Nachbarn', *Leviathan,* 33(2): 182–204.

Virno, P. (2004), *A Grammar of the Multitude: For an Analysis of Contemporary Forms of Life*, Los Angeles: Semiotext(e).

Warneken, B.J. (2006), *Die Ethnographie popularer Kulturen. Eine Einführung*, Köln: Böhlau.

–9–

The Jeans that Don't Fit: Marketing Cheap Jeans in Brazil

Rosana Pinheiro-Machado

This article discusses some particularities of the denim trade in Southern Brazil. It shows the emblematic power of cheap blue jeans in the process of the commoditization of social relations in an urban market located in the central area of Porto Alegre,[1] the capital of the state of Rio Grande do Sul in the southernmost part of Brazil.

Following research themes in the field of economic anthropology, I argue that due to the special place denim occupies in Brazilian society, this particular piece of clothing is an important mode of objectification of inequalities and social differences. An analysis of the economic aspects of the jeans supply chain, unveils a series of tensions and broader classifications, which refer to the social construction of limits between the formal and informal economy (see Pinheiro-Machado 2008). A further analysis shows that the position occupied by denim in the market – between the formal and informal sector, and between legality and illegality – is located within a discourse of value regarding authenticity and quality, which are themselves not necessarily based on the material properties of the product.

The perspective adopted in this paper is a contribution to the Denim Manifesto (Miller and Woodward 2007), as well as a challenge to some of its analytical aspects. I aim to foreground the role of the economic dimensions within the Global Denim Project. I also show how the homogenization brought about by the ubiquity of jeans does not necessarily produce equalization but can in fact result in further social differentiation. The power of jeans demonstrated in this chapter reveals both the agency located within an everyday garment and its exceptional nature.

Denim Manifesto and Brazilian Jeans

In the Denim Manifesto anthropologists are challenged to study denim – something that is commonplace in our everyday lives but notably absent from ethnographic analyses. As a manifesto, the authors refute the ontological philosophical logic that an element, such as clothing, that is located on the surface of bodies is intrinsically a superficial problem. Instead they consider the philosophical implications of the use of jeans – a clothing resource that resolves the anxiety and the contradictions of life in the modern world – which recasts it as a clearly anthropological issue. By stating that, at this moment, it is likely that more than 50 per cent of the world's population is wearing jeans, the authors show the importance of understanding the meanings and the local appropriations of this global omnipresence and homogenization.

Thus the emphasis of the Denim Manifesto is on the ubiquity of denim versus the heterogeneity of its cultural uses in particular contexts, from Rio de Janeiro to London. Consequently there is an analytical stress on consumption, even though Miller and Woodward point out the importance of studying the many phases of the denim commodity chain. This problem is compounded in the present volume in that while the chapter by Comstock is concerned with the history of production and distribution, and Wilkinson-Weber with the marketing, most of the chapters are almost entirely concerned with consumption.

This chapter aims to bring back the critical place that commodity chains need to occupy within the Global Denim Project, which includes a reflection on the social consequences of the process of manufacture, retail and distribution of denim. If 50 per cent of the world's population is now probably wearing jeans, it obviously implies that the production and distribution of denim mobilizes a huge work force around the world. Thus, for an anthropological agenda, it is necessary to explain not only how and why people consume denim, but also the consequences of this for how ordinary people find their lives organized around the world of denim.

To understand the role that denim plays in the process of commoditization of societies, we need to turn our attention to several human links created by the capitalist chain in order to 'acknowledge them and understand the responsibilities that arise when we benefit as consumers through low prices at the expense of others' (Miller 2006: 350). It becomes particularly important when we observe developing countries, such as Brazilian society, where social inequalities are still very strong. In this context, both consumption and production are social practices that acquire relevance.

There are currently several core denim production sites in Brazil which distribute jeans throughout Brazil, Latin America, Europe and the US. Jaraguá is such a city in the State of Goiás (in the central area of Brazil). It has 44,000 inhabitants of which 22,000 are working either directly or indirectly in the denim industry. Cianorte, in the State of Santa Catarina (in the south) is called 'the clothing capital', of the region with 50,000 inhabitants of which 15,000 work directly in the textile industry. Half of the gross domestic product of both cities comes from this sector.[2] Such sites mobilize not only their local populations but also hundred of thousands of *sacoleiros* (traders who carry bags) who criss-cross the country on weekly schedules organized by specialist agencies for the purpose of supplying denim to the nation.

My concern in this paper is not so much with the particular version of jeans known as Brazilian jeans or 'Gang pants', which are the subject of Mizrahi's chapter in this volume (see also Mizrahi 2007, Leitão 2007), but the much wider field of everyday denim that is sold and worn in Brazil.

The Context of the Bazaar Economy: Voluntários da Pátria Street

Voluntários da Pátria is a paradigmatic street in Porto Alegre. Although its proper name means 'Volunteers of the Country', there is a colloquial version where 'to go to Voluntários' means to shop in the cheapest sectors and, 'to go to *Volunta*' means to engage in prostitution.

Localized near the city port, the street has had a commercial vocation since the origins of the town. In the nineteenth century, it was the access way for the imperial guard invasions against the separatist movement of the province in a war that went on for ten years (Franco 1998). It is also said that the street has always been a space of prostitution, as well as a place of sexual initiation for men – explaining the stigmatized nickname *volunta*. In the past few decades, the street has been marked by multiple diversities. Religious syncretism is evident through the presence of the church of Our Lady of Navegantes (a Catholic saint, *Iemanjá* in the African-Brazilian religions) who protects the waters and whose procession attracts a million people annually. Commercial development includes stores owned by Palestinians and Jews, which attract consumers from all social classes. It is a bazaar economy based on interpersonal dealings, face-to-face contact, crowds and bargains (Geertz 1979). In recent years, cheap denim has become the main product sold in this market.

There is a also new shopping mall situated in the beginning of the street, which has around 800 stands owned by ex-street vendors. This place is called *camelódromo*. Walking towards one end, we can find a great number of cheap jeans stores, until we reach two factories, which distribute denim merchandise throughout Brazil, but not much to the immediate area, since its products are considered of better quality and of higher price than is usual for this street.

The research reported here was influenced by commodity chain analysis[3] – observing different actors involved in the history of a commodity, as well as perceiving the inequalities created by market practice (see Bestor 2000; Foster 2006; Freidberg 2004; Hughes 2001; Ziegler 2007). I employed these methods within a more micro context, interviewing producers, distributors, vendors and consumers of denim. As part of a bazaar economy, the local narrative on the denim corresponds to local social organization, showing its 'deeply felt rules of etiquette, tradition, and moral expectation' (Geertz 1979: 222).

This particular study forms part of a continuum of ethnographies about informal markets and piracy, which I have carried out since 1999, including the street commerce in downtown Porto Alegre. However, I included more systematic research on denim in 2009 when I noticed its presence in the new *camelódromo*, which suggested a need to capture the narratives surrounding this product.

Extra-ordinary Denim[4]

For many decades, this neighbourhood has had a huge street market where state-regulated and unregulated vendors worked, both situated in the informal economy. That is to say they didn't pay any taxes for the merchandise they purchased from a large commercial region in the neighbouring country of Paraguay. Nor did they provide receipts for their clients. There were around 420 vendors listed by the local government and perhaps thousands of others working illegally. This street market, situated in the heart of the city, was called *camelódromo*, because, in Portuguese, a street vendor is called *camelô*. A great variety of cheap products made in China was sold at the *camelódromo*, especially clothing accessories, clothes, toys and electronic devices. However, the fact that they didn't sell jeans was an intriguing lacuna.

The absence of such a popular product caught my attention because the other commerce around the street market had its stores stuffed to their ceilings with jeans in many varied styles and prices. This fact led me to explore the formal commerce of jeans – situated in the Voluntários da Pátria Street – which sells to all social classes, but especially to the poorest population of the city who lives in the *favelas* in the periphery.

In January 2009, public policy concerning commerce in Porto Alegre stimulated by a combination of local (the downtown 'mess'), national (the struggle against smuggling from Paraguay) and international (intellectual property interests) factors went through an historical moment. The street vendors were taken off the streets and re-located in a 'Popular Shopping Centre'. This site is still referred to as *camelódromo* by the population and the vendors, although the latter no longer consider themselves *camelôs*, but entrepreneurs. This major construction was built over a bus terminal in the heart of the exciting Voluntários da Pátria Street, where the production, commerce and consumption of jeans abounds.

As this chapter will show, this new apparent equality of status acquired through the shift in location of the vendors, still produces quite discrepant discourses, which appear in the form of deligitimization of the vendors as *the other*. Just because their position has been regularized and formalized does not mean that the vendors have been granted any more respect by the rest of the local commercial establishment and surrounding society.

With their new status as an entrepreneurs and businessmen/women, it didn't take long for the former *camelôs*, who used to sell Paraguay products, to start selling jeans in their humble new stores – now with fitting rooms and mirrors. Maria (sixty-one years old), an ex-street vendor who has been working with clothes for thirty years claimed:

> Jeans are very fancy stuff; they come from São Paulo, not from Paraguay. It was impossible to sell jeans on the street. Unlike other pieces of clothing, women don't buy

just any pants. It can make your arse look square and, mostly, it has to disguise the love handles that jump out! Now we have everything right here, so now we can do it.

The total absence of denim among vendors ended the moment the new buildings were dedicated. As they prepared themselves to occupy this new site, blue jeans appeared as a paradigmatic product that symbolized their new status. To them, jeans cannot be sold just anywhere because it is a special commodity, which people need to try on many times. In a conversation with Maria:

Maria: Nobody buys jeans on the dirty streets. We could sell only soft fabrics there because they fit easily. We could not sell hard fabric like jeans. I always say that for one person whose size is 40 we need at least fifteen different pieces of size 40. A girl tries all fifteen pieces and certainly she will like only one. So selling jeans you also need a good stock, many sizes.

Rosana: I have already seen many street markets that sell jeans. Vendors take the clients to shops nearby, and they fit there. Why do not *camelôs* do the same?

Maria: How long do you take when you buy jeans? It needs time ... Sometimes I get angry because girls think that jeans will enact a miracle. The problem is not my jeans, but their body! It is easer to go on a diet than look for jeans which hide their belly!

According to a consumer who was interviewed:

I belong to the type 'little fat'. So my bottom is perfect. I have to show my bottom, but my problem is that in order to have a big bottom we, girls, generally have a big belly as well. It's proportional! So it is hard to find pants that improve bottoms and hide the belly. But jeans can do this, only jeans. [...] My size is 46, but I buy 42. Then my bottom gets a good lift and my love handles get squashed! (Priscilla, a seventeen-year-old girl)

In fact jeans reflect a contradiction between the Brazilian body ideals – big bottom and tiny waist – and Brazilian bodies in reality. In this sense denim became a special product, almost miraculous. Its quality, as noted at the start of Mizrahi's chapter, is that it is credited with the ability to give someone the right bottom. Jeans are not, then, an ordinary slice of daily life. They are something more sophisticated and more subtle. They are an extraordinary product, which has become a special commodity both for consumers and vendors.

Maria considers jeans a fancy commodity for several reasons. From the consumers' point of view, to find proper jeans takes a long time because it needs to fit with their body image. Given this, Maria understands that she needs to sell 'good jeans' – and in her understanding good jeans do not come from Ciudad del Este in Paraguay, since the trade of that region is associated with fake and shoddy goods. Excursions to other Brazilian states are more expensive than to Paraguay. Buying goods from one's own country also means that the product is not going to be smuggled. Besides, there are very fashionable brands made in Brazil today, such as such as *República, Denúncia* e *Osmoze.* Thus, the new entrepreneur status demands a new jeans status. To Maria and others jeans objectify an upgrade to professional status and they feel part of a wider context, a vocation that comes with being part of the formal trade of Voluntários da Pátria Street.

The Struggle for the Established Position

Even though the Voluntários da Pátria Street's universe is generalized as 'cheap commerce', and most of the blue jeans sold in the area are very similar; vendors who trade there notice a great difference between one shop and another. In the sense of the relations between the 'established and the outsider' (Elias 2000), the disputes which break out are manifestations of a wider accusatory system, characterized by gossip. Vendors value price, quality, and authenticity of their products, which are the criteria they see as disqualifying their rivals.

The groups that trade in the street can be divided into three categories of commerce: the *camelódromo* at the beginning of the street, the cheap shops along the whole street, and finally, the factories sited at its end. It is important to note that this social and economic hierarchy extends to the spatial order as well: as one proceeds from the beginning to the end of the street the status of entrepreneurship increases slightly. This spatial hierarchy applies also to the jeans as a parameter from 'good' to 'shoddy' denim.

To exemplify this degree of differentiation, we can take the discourses of the higher end workers with regard to the street where they are sited. These entrepreneurs see their products sold in their own shops within the Voluntários da Pátria. However, they consider that the denim they produce is actually of a high quality, which should not really be identified either with this location nor with its cheap market. They say they are in this area due to an unfortunate coincidence.

One of these factories has only a part of its production in this urban area, having another headquarters in the countryside. The company was established in 1977, and presently has 180 machines and 248 employees. Its 50,000 pieces produced monthly are sold to several Brazilian shops and brands. According to a manager who was interviewed:

> Our product differentiates itself from that ones you can find at *Voluntários* in respect to many factors, but the main one is the outsourcing process. Here everything is made and controlled by ourselves, so the quality control is extremely rigorous. Washing, dyeing, cut, everything ... The product found in these shops around us has been made, in the

first place, from a very thin fabric. Pieces and seams are slack, since what is important in our neighbourhood trade is low price. This kind of consumer is interested in price, only. They do not care whether they take home lopsided jeans.

Despite the fact that their discourse disqualifies the Street where they are located, sometimes we can still find some minimal identification with the locality. As a manager pointed out:

Ok, we are here. This is not our universe, our target public, our goal, our vision … I personally hate this place, and I find it dirty and messy, a bad image for our denim, which is surrounded by shoddiness. Still I recognize the fact that we are sited at this traditional place has also helped us. I feel very comfortable to admit it, because we don't need to prove anything to anybody, we have a respectable brand … We are *what* we are, *where* we are.

However, this was in marked contrast with the situation found during a visit to a second factory. When I said I was researching the denim market in the area, the owner told me that they could not be included in such research, since their presence there was quite arbitrary:

Sorry, although we are at the end of the street we don't belong to *that* commercial universe. Our denim is the opposite to these other's denim. Our marketing is focused on the middle class. Our production is limited and the quality is very high. I do not believe I can contribute to your research.
[Researcher] – So, why do you also have a shop here?
Because is a big space in a cheap area, it's hard to move out …

The producers' discourse on the Voluntários da Pátria market does not make any differentiation between trade from the shops or from the *camelódromo*. The idea of poor quality is generalized to all these as an external world, to which they believe they do not belong. However, when I interviewed the owners of the shops located along the street, I found exactly the same discourse about quality, but this time as self affirmation through opposition to the *camelódromos*.

Comparing the shops with the *camelódromo*, we can find this cast as a relationship between the established and the outsiders. Four decades ago, migrant Palestinian families opened businesses in this area. They acquired a faithful consumer public, by offering them cheap products. By comparison the ex-street vendors are seen as outsiders to the street: a newer source of cheap trade.

The interviews show how a concept of the 'formal' is reflected in a discourse about quality. The more formal trade, the higher the quality of denim. Taking into account the fact that the denim sold in the *camelódromo* and in the shops is bought from the same supplier,[5] the claim to quality here is only a belief, as well as a vicarious statement about formality. In the recent past, street vendors worked without

State regulation, but now they are as regulated as the older shops. In the local narrative, family antiquity becomes formality, and formality in turn becomes the mark of quality.

Amir, thirty-five years old, denim shop owner:

It is funny to see a *camelô* selling blue jeans. It is impossible! They have no money to buy the variety of models and sizes minimally necessary. There are fat and thin women. There are those who love tight, or the opposite ... Everything sold there has poor quality, they don't have know-how. They buy quickly, without any criteria, without knowledge. They also have no structure. Their space is humble, and their businesses do not signify reliability.

Blue jeans pants are clothes that take more time to purchase. Women take twenty minutes trying on one piece, and they check one million times if their bottom is OK. Which woman will spend that kind of time in the *camelódromo*?

Farid, forty years old, denim shop owner:

My public consumer is not only from the C or D social class [the poorest segments]. Many people from the elites come here in order to resell our pants in their classy shops, because we have all the models, all the sizes, for all tastes. From BRL 19.90 to 100.00 [Real Brazilian]. Do you believe that they will be able to sell such variety? Only those who have a significant sized structure can sell denim ... To be clear, they simply haven't the right conditions to sell the same good product that I can sell.

In fact, these informants who discussed their knowledge of denim in this manner are not old traders in the denim field. They belong to families that have old shops there but they started to trade denim only in the last five years. Like the street vendors, they are also new to the local denim market. Looking at the material properties of the jeans, often we find very similar products both in *camelódromo* and in the shops. However, the family's tradition and reputation for trade allows these people to claim a higher status. In many parts of the interview, it was not clear whether they were talking about the quality of the commodity or their financial and spatial foundations. Claims about each of these were mixed with the other.

Reputation and Authenticity in *Camelódromo*

Maria worked in the old *camelódromo* for three decades, selling clothes and caps. She struggled against the expulsion of the vendors from the streets because she believed that consumers bought on impulse. However, following the advice given by marketing experts and fashion specialists contracted by the new shopping mall company, she invested in her new position, renting a large space in the new *camelódromo*, decorated her new space, and installed a new telephone number. Her daring attitude provoked her colleagues' reaction, who said that Maria was now indebted because she had spent too much money in these refurbishments.

She also invited her daughter (Mirian, thirty years old) to work with her in this new entrepreneurship. She believed that her daughter's youth could serve to modernize her shop. In the first week of the business, Mirian was to find a supplier for them in São Paulo. Instead of coming back with their typical large bags full of goods, she brought only two small packs of blue jeans – an attitude that provoked despair in her mother, because Maria realized that her US$1,000 had been invested in a few pairs of jeans. Mirian convinced Maria that the jeans would sell very well because she was bringing genuine, famous, and very fashionable Brazilian jeans brands. These brands of blue jeans cost usually BRL 250, but Maria and Mirian could sell them for BRL 150. It seemed to be a very advantageous transaction.

Mirian considered selling jeans an expression of their new status. For this reason her purchase of authentic branded trousers was intended to give dignity to their new position. However, due do her anxiety to quickly upgrade their status, she did not wait to accumulate enough capital, and therefore she could only afford to buy a total of twenty pieces, in sizes ranging from 38 to 40. The result was three months without selling any jeans. She explains:

> Some girls, who liked the price of our branded products, tried our pants, but they did not fit their bodies. Girls always start their purchase by asking for size 38 but they end up with 44–46. Our problem is that now we have a good place to sell but not enough capital to buy a good range of sizes. Besides, our biggest problem is our consumers are very, very poor, and do not have the money to buy such expensive stuff.

As Maria feared, the new investment was ill stocked, since her jeans, although cheaper than average for these goods, were still expensive for the consumer public of the Voluntários da Pátria Street. In the area around them, blue jeans with an unknown brand can be found for BRL 19.99; while a fake brand can cost BRL 49.90 in the *camelódromo*. When consumers had the money, they didn't have the proper size.

In fact, when consumers go to a cheap shopping area only recently regulated by the state, most of them are looking for low prices. As *camelódromo* still carries the reputation of selling fake goods, its consumers also look for replicas whose price is slightly higher by virtue of the symbolic value of the brand they are copying. When consumers from low-income classes want to buy an expensive product, they look for the distinction that comes from a large shop, such as a department store, in a place that dignifies them as consumers and as citizens. *Camelódromo* offer no such distinction. As observed in other contexts, for consumers from low income classes, they are merely a confirmation of their own social condition of poverty (see Leitão 2004, Pinheiro-Machado, forthcoming). In these cases, the purchase can be staggered through payments over several instalments, even when there are high interest rates attached. As Maria concludes: 'people to prefer buy pants at Ughini [a neighbouring department store] in eight instalments of BRL 50, paying a total of BRL 400, than buying here the stuff for BRL 150 in cash.'

The stylist contracted by *camelódromo* congratulated Maria for her acquisition of new branded jeans. It seemed to speak to a positive desire to upgrade her business. As a professional she helped Maria to arrange the display, making these branded goods very evident. In fact, consumers were clearly interested in these jeans. They stopped in front of the shop, looked carefully at the goods, asked their price, and concluded: *too expensive!* Unsuccessfully Mirian explained to her customers that the jeans were authentic brands but the price of BRL 150 prevented any further negotiation. There was always an expression of contempt on the clients' face when they realized how high the price was – they saw this as reprehensible, and seemed set on making Maria and Mirian feel guilty their over ambition. As Maria lamented: 'it is not worth trying to take a step up.' And Mirian added: 'people do not know what quality is, they do not understand that our product lasts many years. They are not aware that the other jeans sold around lose their shape in the first washing.'

In order to understand the consumers' response to the Voluntários da Pátria market, I invited same teenagers to participate in this research. They were three girls who live in the biggest *favela* of Porto Alegre, and they belong to low income families. They usually buy clothes in the cheap shops of that urban area. The girls said that their financial capacity for jeans pants was at most BRL 30.

Calculating an average price in the local area, I asked to them which jeans they would choose for up to BRL 60. We walked along the whole street, from the *camelódromo* to the factories. I suspected they would search for the best quality and/or for the most beautiful jeans that they could find within that price range. However, they decided to look for the best value in relating looks to price. So instead of buying 'high quality jeans' (in the estimation of the traders) they opted instead for buying two pairs at BRL 30 each.

During our walk, they tried out the jeans of Maria's shop in *camelódromo*, but the cost at BRL 150 was something far beyond both their socioeconomic realities and their consumption habits. Priscilla, seventeen years old, explained to me:

> It is better buying every month a pair of jeans for BRL 30, and always having new items, rather than buying these expensive jeans [she was referring to Maria's good], and then feel obligated to wear the same thing for months. At school all people will see is that I am wearing the same clothes.

This explains part of the clients' reaction in the face of Maria's enterprise, and the reasons for her failure. In quite the opposite situation, other sellers of *camelódromo* had no problems trading denim. Joana (thirty-five years old) left the street market, where she sold cotton trousers, and now sell only blue jeans to teenagers and young people. She offers a price between BRL 29.90 and 59.90. This last price is for a fake of a famous brand called *Carmin*. The sales have been excellent and she has no regrets. The same thing happened to Susana (forty-two years old) who also decided to launch into denim. She admits she only trades in fakes.

Both these traders' success, demonstrates the consumers' vision of the *camelódromo's* skill in trading denim, since they remain a site marked by the ability to sell cheap and/or fake goods. Maria's attempt to sell expensive denim failed against her neighbour's fakes, since the context from which she sells cannot legitimate her commodities. According to Maria's neighbours:

> She [Maria] wanted to be better than the rest of us, and now she is paying for it. She is in debt, and her jeans are 'run aground'.

> Everything in Maria's shop is still fake stuff. She does not have the wherewithal to buy and sell *Osmoze* pants. Besides, there is no seller of *Osmoze* denim in São Paulo, so her stuff is fake stuff; she thinks she is able to cheat both me and my clients.

> She brought her daughter to work with her in order to make many changes. She invested more than she could actually afford. Now you can see the result.

Such gossip acts as an invisible and ruthless power that regulates that market within an internal symbolic system that prevents any such radical change. Changes are viewed with fear and distrust. Gossip is a form of discourse that informs about a group's identity, as well as its social history (Gluckman cited in Fonseca, 2000). It reflects an underlying moral code that generates a spontaneous discourse or denigration and denunciation and thereby achieves a high level of control. It is able to patrol the group boundaries, and to level, to lower or to upgrade individuals within certain parameters, at the expense of personal reputations and honour (Fonseca 2000). In this way, the narratives found regarding denim in this specific context are pedagogic: they inform people of their proper vocation in the sale of cheap products or fake goods. They remind people that whoever tries to venture beyond this universe will be punished – as Maria was.

Fake or not Fake? That Is the Question

A pair of jeans, a religious relic or a work of art would seem to have different kinds of authority, defined in particular fields of authenticity within each of which one is able to distinguish what is considered *real* and what *false* (by religious groups, connoisseurs, market, state). In the capitalist global market, authentic brands are distinctive symbols attached to commodities that possess intellectual property rights (IPR). The owners of the brand have social legitimacy that is sustained by market and political principles.

Through the Agreement on Trade-Related Aspects of Intellectual Property Rights (TRIPS), signed in 1994 by the World Trade Organization, companies acquired the right to go to court in a specific country to fight falsifications and to call upon the state police for assistance. In this context, imitations aggregate negative value, classified as criminal productions. As in the field of art, brand owners have the authority to reproduce authentic first samples. 'Intellectual Property Rights laws determine which copies are authorized, legitimate, and authentic, and which copies are unauthorized, illegitimate, and inauthentic - and therefore illegal' (Coombe, cited in Vann 2006). The social recognition of this legitimacy, however, is not automatic. As Vann (2006) points out in her ethnography in Vietnam, people have different notions about what is meant by fake goods, false, replica, adulteration, etc.

As already evident consumers of Voluntários da Pátria attribute different roles to traders. Old and formal shops acquire more reputation than the new *camelódromo*, because they are places where citizen feel part of a legitimate world – something important in an unequal society like Brazil. Despite the fact that trademarks define what is fake or not fake, in popular perception, these classifications will be re-elaborated. As Appadurai points out (1999) commodities in motion have floating regimes of value, getting and losing authenticity as they circulate in the world. To many consumers, real branded denim in the *camelódromo* will not be authenticated, while a fake one in a formal shop will be.

As we have noticed before, consumers of the *camelódromo* do not believe in the authenticity of the jeans sold by Maria. The ex-street vendors retain the label of fake goods, and their position in commerce is relegated to such an image. Indeed the fake and the informal have an intimate relation in Brazil. As Noronha (2002) suggests, the informal market is easily generalized to other social attribution, such as illegitimate, illegal, unfair. In this manner, we can understand why fake jeans sold for BRL 29.90 in shops are considered more legal, fair, and legitimate than in the *camelódromo*.

In a formal denim shop, I have found blue jeans in a display labelled *Oslen* – a direct reference to *Osklen*, a famous Brazilian brand. When I asked to the owner about that product, he said that the jeans were not replicas of *Osklen*, since *Oslen* is a legitimate trademark. As I have shown through more detailed analysis in other papers (Pinheiro-Machado, 2008), commodities that sport a brand like *Oslen* are ambiguous, because they cannot be immediately characterized as a fake product.[6] Does a change in the letter of a famous brand that it is imitating create a new brand? The new form may be accepted or it can provoke severe conflicts. Local, national, and international struggles will determine if *Oslen* pants are or not an illegal imitation of the *Osklen* brand.[7]

However, this ambiguity is implicitly solved according to the place where the commodity is being sold. As has been noted, it may be the context that can confer more or less legitimacy to the goods. The degree to which there is popular acceptance of the authenticity of a product will be influenced by many factors, beyond its material and intellectual properties. One of these is the traditions associated with the place where the product is being sold. In that context, *Oslen* jean will be certainly considered 'more legal' in an established shop than in a *camelódromo*. However, as

Oslen, it will still be generalized as a sort of shoddy imitation in comparison with shopping malls where *Osklen* (the spelling of the proper brand) is sold. Different power positions define these implicit classifications, where the aura of a commodity is more a belief, a social construction, an alchemy (Bourdieu, 1975, 1980; Eco, 1984) than intrinsic element of real objects (Benjamin 1980).

Conclusion

A critical point in the Denim Manifesto is the overwhelming emphasis upon homogenization and to some degree therefore also equalization. This is entirely reasonable when taking the Global Denim Project as a whole, but it is an essential requirement of the project that we find a new way to balance local and global research. This means we need to ensure that an emphasis upon homogenisation at the global level does not mask or reduce our acknowledgment of the presence of new forms of difference at each local level, which has been the aim of this chapter.

In the case study presented here cheap jeans appear as a quite specific, almost specialized product. The jeans I found in the field require far more care and attention in their purchase, they take much longer to select and therefore the shops need to carry much more stock. They are the very substance of what is seen as special and extraordinary, which is precisely why the street market vendors always considered that they should not actually stock jeans at all before they were artificially 'promoted' to the higher status of a formal economic position.

The other key point here is that jeans play a remarkable role in complementing the official transformations of these economic positions. After all when the state forced the vendors to change their place of sale to the fixed site around the bus station, they never said to them they also needed to change their position relative to the sale of denim. And yet what this paper suggests is that they couldn't help but make this further shift in the content of what they sold. Not because of any material quality of the jeans but because they sensed the centrality of jeans to social and status differentiation. Which meant that they were in a sense out of synch with their new situation unless they also stocked jeans. As this chapter shows, the process is dialectical, creating a contradiction in turn sensed by the consumers who cannot reconcile themselves to vendors selling authentic and, more to the point, expensive jeans.

The point, then, is to consider jeans as a mode of objectification. We start with a contradiction by which the state disrupts a symbolic continuum by putting vendors in an inappropriate position in terms of their spatial contrast with other kinds of vendors. But the nature and extent of this contradiction becomes both clearer and more elaborated when we see the consequences this has for the sale of jeans, because jeans themselves have such powerful emblematic positions in Brazilian society today.

Mostly we think of the anthropology of commerce as a study of how economic agents try to manipulate the symbolic qualities of commodities in order to profit at the expense of the consumers. But no one in this paper, either the consumers choosing between commodities, nor the vendors selling the commodities, seems to be able to act as economic agents, certainly not in the economists' version of rational calculation. All of them see, rather, the objects that are being manipulated in order to express certain contradictions that are worked through them rather than being worked out by them. If anything it is the jeans that act here as the powerful agency that impose themselves as products that have to be sold whether you want to sell them or not, and that confuse the buyers because of the contradictions they express.

At the start of this chapter it was argued that the main intention was to challenge the Manifesto argument by insisting on a focus on the more economic aspects of jeans retailing rather than the way they symbolized cultural forms such as homogeneity. But by the end of the chapter we found that what might be called the 'economic' is by no means an autonomous force that gives rise to symbolic manipulation. Rather it is itself subject to and constructed by these wider potentials in the commodity itself. By the end of the chapter we found that people cannot even 'see' these jeans in terms of an economic logic that would seem clear when the same jeans are sold for less by a cheap vendor than a more expensive looking shop. So, in conclusion, this chapter testifies to the ability of denim jeans as a commodity to control the economic relationship through which it takes on its particular significance to both those who sell and those who buy them.

Notes

1. Porto Alegre is a metropolitan region with around four million inhabitants.
2. Source: official websites of the cities.
3. In a completely different exercise I had previously used the the theory and methodology of global commodity chain in my doctoral thesis, during in which I followed a commodity chain that went from China to Brazil.
4. All informants' names have been changed or omitted.
5. Most of denim sold at Voluntários da Pátria market is from the city of Cianorte, a Brazilian Denim Centre. Many traders also bring their clothes from São Paulo.
6. Examples found in other moments of my research: Watches Cucci, Dolex and Coss instead of Gucci, Rolex and Boss.
7. According to rules that were established by TRIPs, companies can go to the court and ask for punishment of illegal copies in countries that belong to the World Trade Organization. But countries have different notions about intellectual property and different levels of tolerance. The national control, therefore, is not an automatic action. In short, depending on context Oslen can be or cannot be considered an imitation of Osklen.

References

Appadurai, A. (1999), 'Introduction: Commodities and the Politics of Value', in A. Appadurai (ed.), *The Social Life of Things, Commodities in Cultural Perspective*, Cambridge: Cambridge University Press.

Benjamim, W. (1980), 'A obra de arte na época de suas técnicas de reprodução', in Benjamin, W., *Os Pensadores*, São Paulo: Abril Cultural, pp. 4–28.

Bestor, N. (2000), 'How Sushi Went Global', *Foreign Policy*, 121: 54–63.

Bourdieu, P. (with Yvette Delsaut) (1975), 'Le couturier et sa griffe: contribution à une théorie de la magie', *Actes de la Recherche en Sciences Sociales*, 1: 7–36.

Bourdieu, P. (1980), 'The Production of Belief: Contribution to an Economy of Symbolic Goods', *Media, Culture and Society*, 2: 261–93.

Eco, H. (1984), *Viagem na irracionalidade Cotidiana*, Rio de Janeiro, Nova Fronteira.

Elias, N. (2000), *Os Estabelecidos e os Outsiders*, Rio de Janeiro: Jorge Zahar.

Fonseca, C. (2000), *Família, Fofoca e Honra. Etnografia de Relações de Gênero e Violência em Grupos Populares*. Porto Alegre: Ed. Universidade/UFRGS.

Foster, R. (2006), 'Tracking Globalization: Commodities and Value in Motion', in C. Tilley, W. Keane, S. Kuechler, M. Rowlands, P. Spyer (eds), *The Sage Handbook of Material Culture*, London: Sage, pp. 285–302.

Franco, S. (1998), *Porto Alegre*, Porto Alegre: Editora da Universidade.

Freidberg, S. (2004), *French Beans and Food Scares: Culture and Commerce in an Anxious Age*, New York: Oxford University Press.

Geertz, C. (1979), 'Suq: The Bazaar Economy in Sefrou', in C. Geertz, H. Geertz and L. Rosen (eds), *Meaning and Order in Moroccan Society*, Cambridge: Cambridge University Press.

Hughes, A. (2001), 'Global Commodity Networks, Ethical Trade and Governability', *Transactions of the Institute of British Geographers*, New Series, 26(4): 390–406.

Leitão, D. (2004), LEITÃO. *Roupa pronta é roupa boa: reflexão sobre gosto e hábitos de consumo de produtoras e consumidoras de uma cooperativa de costuras*. Paper presented at 24th Reunião Brasileira de Antropologia, Olinda, Brazil.

Leitão, D. (2006), Brasilidade à moda da casa, doctoral thesis presented at Federal University of Rio Grande do Sul, Porto Alegre, Brasil.

Miller, D. (2006), 'Consumption', in C. Tilley, W. Keane, S. Kuechler, M. Rowlands, P. Spyer (eds), *Handbook of Material Culture*, London: Sage.

Miller, D. and Woodward, S. (2007), 'Denim Manifesto'. *Social Anthropology/ Anthropologie Sociale,* 15(3): 335–51.

Mizrahi, M. (2007), 'Indumentária funk: a confrontação da alteridade colocando em diálogo o local e o cosmopolita', *Horizontes Antropológicos,* 13(28): 231–62.

Noronha, E.G. (2003), 'Informal, ilegal, injusto: percepções do mercado de trabalho no Brasil', *Brazilian Review of Social Sciences*, 18(53): 111–29.

Pinheiro-Machado, R. (2008), 'China-Paraguai-Brasil: uma rota para pensar a economia informal', *Brazilian Review of Social Sciences,* 23(67): 117–33.

Vann, E. (2006), 'Limits of Authenticity in Vietnamese Consumer Markets', *American Anthropologist*, 108(2): 286–96.

Zieger, C. (2007), *Favored Flowers,* Durham, NC: Duke University Press.

Index